# Practice Theory and International Relations

Are social practices actions or institutional frameworks of interaction structured by common rules? How do social practices such as signing a cheque differ from international practices such as signing a peace treaty? Traversing the fields of international relations (IR) and philosophy, this book defends an institutionalist conception of practices as part of a general practice theory indebted to Oakeshott, Wittgenstein and Hegel. The proposed practice theory has two core aspects: practice internalism and normative descriptivism. In developing a philosophical analysis of social practices that has a special relevance for international relations, Silviya Lechner and Mervyn Frost depart from Pierre Bourdieu's sociology of practice that dominates the current 'practice turn' in IR. The authors show that the contemporary global realm is constituted by two distinct macro practices – the practice of sovereign states and that of global rights.

SILVIYA LECHNER holds a PhD in International Relations from the University of Aberystwyth. Currently she is a visiting researcher at King's College London, Department of War Studies, where she was previously a lecturer. She specialises in IR theory and philosophy, especially social and political philosophy and philosophy of action. Her articles have appeared in the *Journal of International Political Theory*, the *Review of International Studies*, *International Studies Review*, *Oxford Research Encyclopedia of International Studies*, the *Hague Journal of Diplomacy* and the *American Journal of Bioethics*.

MERVYN FROST, MA (Stellenbosch), BPhil. (Oxford), DPhil. (Stellenbosch), is Professor of International Relations in the Department of War Studies, King's College London. From 2007 to 2013, he was Head of Department. His monographs include *Towards a Normative Theory of International Relations* (Cambridge University Press, 1986), *Ethics in International Relations* (Cambridge University Press, 1996), *Constituting*

*Human Rights: Global Civil Society and the Society of Democratic States* (2002) and *Global Ethics: Anarchy, Freedom and International Relations* (2008). He edited a four-volume reference book of articles entitled *International Ethics* (2011). He was President of the South African Political Studies Association and Chair of the Ethics Section of the International Studies Association.

# Practice Theory and International Relations

EDITORS

Evelyn Goh
Christian Reus-Smit
Nicholas J. Wheeler

*Cambridge Studies in International Relations* is a joint initiative of Cambridge University Press and the British International Studies Association (BISA). The series aims to publish the best new scholarship in international studies, irrespective of subject matter, methodological approach or theoretical perspective. The series seeks to bring the latest theoretical work in International Relations to bear on the most important problems and issues in global politics.

# CAMBRIDGE STUDIES IN INTERNATIONAL RELATIONS

*Series list continues after index*

# Practice Theory and International Relations

SILVIYA LECHNER
*King's College London*

MERVYN FROST
*King's College London*

CAMBRIDGE
UNIVERSITY PRESS

# CAMBRIDGE
## UNIVERSITY PRESS

University Printing House, Cambridge CB2 8BS, United Kingdom

One Liberty Plaza, 20th Floor, New York, NY 10006, USA

477 Williamstown Road, Port Melbourne, VIC 3207, Australia

314–321, 3rd Floor, Plot 3, Splendor Forum, Jasola District Centre,
New Delhi – 110025, India

79 Anson Road, #06–04/06, Singapore 079906

Cambridge University Press is part of the University of Cambridge.

It furthers the University's mission by disseminating knowledge in the pursuit of
education, learning, and research at the highest international levels of excellence.

www.cambridge.org
Information on this title: www.cambridge.org/9781108471107
DOI: 10.1017/9781108645775

First published 2018

Printed and bound in Great Britain by Clays Ltd, Elcograf S.p.A.

*A catalogue record for this publication is available from the British Library.*

*Library of Congress Cataloging-in-Publication Data*
Names: Lechner, Silviya, 1974– author. | Frost, Mervyn, author.
Title: Practice theory and international relations / Silviya Lechner, Mervyn Frost, authors.
Description: Cambridge, United Kingdom ; New York, NY : Cambridge University Press,
2018. | Series: Cambridge studies in international relations ; 148 |
Includes bibliographical references and index.
Identifiers: LCCN 2018013117| ISBN 9781108471107 (hardback) |
ISBN 9781108457163 (paperback)
Subjects: LCSH: International relations–Philosophy. | BISAC: POLITICAL
SCIENCE / International Relations / General.
Classification: LCC JZ1305 .L436 2018 | DDC 327.101–dc23
LC record available at https://lccn.loc.gov/2018013117

ISBN 978-1-108-47110-7 Hardback

# Contents

# Acknowledgements

We must confess that this book took an embarrassingly long time to complete. But perhaps speed is not the primary virtue in philosophy. If anything, the quest for coherence inside a world of ideas is. This quest for coherence is ongoing, and we hope that we shall entice the reader to follow us on this journey.

Mervyn thanks his co-author, Silviya Lechner, for her friendship, for the intense labour she put into this monograph and for her limitless enthusiasm. He thanks his partner, Lola Frost, for a lifetime of exhilarating conversations about Hegel, art, ethics, politics, power and many other things. These discussions have been foundational to all that he has written.

Silviya is happy to have been accompanied by Mervyn Frost, a friend and fellow traveller, on the difficult journey in the philosophical exploration of practices. Above all, 'Thank you for being there!' goes to her spouse, Martin Lechner, and little Max. It is in the domain of the personal that a philosopher's mind – torn as it is by the neurotic impulse to fight all that is incoherent, ambiguous and incomplete – finds solace.

Both Silviya and Mervyn wish to acknowledge the invaluable support of the editors of the Cambridge Studies in International Relations series, Nick Wheeler, Christian Reus-Smit and Evelyn Goh; of John Haslam, who guided this project through its various stages with acumen and patience; of Thomas Haynes, for his kind assistance during the entire publication process; and of the two anonymous reviewers whose insightful comments helped improve the final argument.

In putting together the argument in the book, the initial drafts of Chapters 1, 2, 3 and 6 were written by Lechner, those for Chapters 4 and 5 were written by Frost and the Introduction was a joint endeavour. It was from these beginnings that the final whole was crafted.

# Introduction
## Mapping Out the Problem of Practices

This book aims to provide a general analysis of social practices in order to advance our understanding of contemporary practices in international relations. Recently, the discipline of International Relations (IR) has experienced a 'turn' to practice, associated with Emanuel Adler and Vincent Pouliot and inspired by social theorists such as Theodore Schatzki and especially French sociologist Pierre Bourdieu.[1] A central premise underlying such sociological investigations is that practices represent doing or actions, including patterned actions carried out by a multitude of agents. In what follows, we do not elaborate on this sociological approach to practices but develop an independent account, a philosophical one, that is fundamentally critical of it. While our account owes much to Herbert L. A. Hart and John Rawls, it is above all indebted to Georg W. F. Hegel, the Hegelian philosopher Michael Oakeshott and the later Ludwig Wittgenstein.[2]

---

[1] Pierre Bourdieu, *Outline of a Theory of Practice*, trans. Richard Nice (Cambridge: Cambridge University Press, 1977 [1972]); Pierre Bourdieu, *The Logic of Practice*, trans. Richard Nice (Stanford: Stanford University Press, 1990 [1980]); Pierre Bourdieu, *Practical Reason: On the Theory of Action* (Stanford: Stanford University Press, 1998 [1994]); Theodore R. Schatzki, *Social Practices: A Wittgensteinian Approach to Human Activity and the Social* (Cambridge: Cambridge University Press, 1996); Theodore R. Schatzki, Karin Knorr-Cetina and Eike von Savigny (eds.), *The Practice Turn in Contemporary Theory* (London: Routledge, 2001). We examine the practice turn in IR in Chapter 2. Its most prominent proponents are Emanuel Adler and Vincent Pouliot – Emanuel Adler and Vincent Pouliot (eds.), *International Practices* (Cambridge: Cambridge University Press, 2011). See also Peter Jackson, 'Pierre Bourdieu, the "Cultural Turn" and the Practice of International History', *Review of International Studies* 34 (1) 2008: 155–181; and Chris Brown, 'The "Practice Turn", Phronesis and Classical Realism: Towards a Phronetic International Political Theory', *Millennium: Journal of International Studies* 40 (3) 2012: 439–456.

[2] The core texts include G. W. F. Hegel, *Hegel's Philosophy of Right*, trans. T. M. Knox (Oxford: Oxford University Press, 1967 [1821]); Ludwig Wittgenstein, *Philosophical Investigations*, 3rd ed., trans. G. E. M. Anscombe (Oxford: Blackwell, 1968 [1953]); John Rawls, 'Two Concepts of Rules', *Philosophical*

Although each of these three thinkers considered individually has been discussed within IR, in this study we have reworked and integrated their ideas into a coherent conceptual position for making sense of practices which we call *practice theory*.[3] The theory is expounded in Part I, and Part II extends it to the sphere of international practices, hence the book's title, *Practice Theory and International Relations*.

## A Philosophical Account of Practices

In contradistinction to a sociology of practices, we set out to develop a philosophy of practices. The benefits of a philosophical enquiry include conceptual precision, systematicity and open-endedness: conclusions reached are always open to further re-examination. To be sure, there are hazards as well. The greatest one is that the jargon employed by professional philosophers restricts the conversation to other professionals. Many would feel that this charge applies to Hegel, Oakeshott and particularly to Wittgenstein, given his riddle-like writing style. In venturing to translate Hegel's, Oakeshott's and Wittgenstein's insights about social practices to illuminate the puzzle of international practices, we recognise the need to use a vocabulary accessible to the non-specialist. However, in promising to craft arguments in plain English, we do not promise that the journey will be easy. A practice is a complex analytical object with multiple components which defy a neat

*Review* 64 (1) 1955: 3–32; H. L. A. Hart, *The Concept of Law* (Oxford: Clarendon Press, 1961); Michael Oakeshott, *On Human Conduct* (Oxford: Clarendon Press, 1975).

3  For a Hegelian perspective of international relations, see Chris Brown, 'Hegel and International Ethics', *Ethics & International Affairs* 5 (1) 1991: 73–86; and Mervyn Frost, *Ethics in International Relations: A Constitutive Theory* (Cambridge: Cambridge University Press, 1996). An Oakeshottian reading of international relations is provided in Terry Nardin, *Law, Morality, and the Relations of States* (Princeton, NJ: Princeton University Press, 1983). Wittgensteinian readings include Karin M. Fierke, 'Links across the Abyss: Language and Logic in International Relations', *International Studies Quarterly* 46 (3) 2002: 331–354; and Karin M. Fierke, 'Wittgenstein and International Relations Theory', in Cerwyn Moore and Chris Farrands (eds.), *International Relations Theory and Philosophy* (New York: Routledge, 2010), pp. 83–94. Wittgenstein's notion of 'grammar' is explored in Véronique Pin-Fat, *Universality, Ethics and International Relations* (London: Routledge, 2009), while 'meaning in use' is examined in Antje Wiener, 'Enacting Meaning-in-Use: Qualitative Research on Norms and International Relations', *Review of International Studies* 35 (1) 2009: 175–193.

summary. Clarifying the multidimensional relations between such components in their various aspects requires conceptual synthesis or theory. Inevitably, our exposition contains some repetition. This stems from the fact that the character of a practice cannot be ascertained by enumerating a list of essential features that are defining of it across all contexts; rather, practices have a 'core' of settled meanings and a 'penumbra' (Hart's terms), so it is important to know which contexts belong to the core and which to the penumbra.[4] Part I begins with a simplified account of practices (Chapter 1), is followed by an analysis of what we take to be a defective way of understanding practices (Chapter 2) and culminates in a fully fledged theoretical synthesis or practice theory (Chapter 3).

Let us define some key terminology. It is quite common to think that the term 'practice' refers to *action* (a doing that has an originator or 'agent') and that 'practices' represent different types of action.[5] In our view, this is a grave misconception – we argue that *a* practice (*practices*, in the plural) is not a type of action but an institution which constitutes a meaningful framework for interaction. This institution comprises rules of action as well as usages and understandings requisite for following the rules.[6] Henceforth, the emphasis is on rules of action and not on rules of reasoning, despite the fact that conduct may be and often is predicated on reasoning. The practice theory put forward in this book is a theory of institutions and norms, not of action per se.

The term 'theory' in *practice theory* indicates that we search for conceptual synthesis over and above a taxonomy of practices. Like Oakeshott, we do not distinguish theory from philosophy. For

---

[4] H. L. A. Hart, 'Positivism and the Separation of Law and Morals,' *Harvard Law Review* 71 (4) 1958: 593–629, p. 607.

[5] The idea that action is a doing that has an identifiable originator or 'agent' is a standard assumption in the philosophy of action. See, for example, Roger Scruton, *Kant* (Oxford: Oxford University Press, 1982), p. 59.

[6] Although we use the term 'institutions' as interchangeable with 'practices' in the sense defined by Oakeshott and Wittgenstein (a *practice* is an intersubjectively grounded, rule-governed domain of activity), there are also important distinctions. In Part I, we modify their views of practices. On 'practices', see Oakeshott, *On Human Conduct*, pp. 58–68; and Wittgenstein, *Philosophical Investigations*, §§7, 202. On 'institutions', see Wittgenstein, *Philosophical Investigations*, §§198–199, 337, 380, 540. Thus by 'institution', we mean a *human* institution and not an abstract procedure for choice aggregation of predefined individual preferences, as in social choice theory.

Oakeshott, philosophy is an activity of 'theorising' directed at the understanding of a not-yet-understood identity. And even though the theorist seeks to arrive at theoretical conclusions – or 'theorems' – by making conceptual distinctions, explicating hidden assumptions and establishing coherence inside a world of ideas, what matters is the activity itself.[7] Wittgenstein likewise says: 'Philosophy aims at the logical clarification of thoughts. Philosophy is not a body of doctrine, but an activity.'[8] Theorising or philosophising in this sense cannot be confined to any single academic discipline.

Our brand of practice theory is interdisciplinary: it traverses the fields of IR, moral, social and political philosophy – the conventional purviews for investigating practices – and in pondering the character of language, rules and meaningful conduct, it engages the philosophy of action.[9] At present, discussions of practices in moral and political philosophy are somewhat strenuously tied to the tradition of 'public reason', descendant from the social contract theories of Thomas Hobbes and Immanuel Kant, which separate private morality from public or political morality and appeal to impartial procedures for allocation of value that must be justified to all rational participants in the political process.[10] John Rawls's doctrine of political liberalism illustrates this tendency.[11] Rawls argues that given the fact of reasonable pluralism in modern societies expressed in citizens' disagreement about the good, a procedure of 'reasonable overlapping consensus' can

---

[7] Michael Oakeshott, *Experience and Its Modes* (Cambridge: Cambridge University Press, 1933), p. 82; and Michael Oakeshott, 'On the Theoretical Understanding of Human Conduct', in Oakeshott, *On Human Conduct*, pp. 1–107, esp. pp. 1–18.

[8] Ludwig Wittgenstein, *Tractatus Logico-Philosophicus*, trans. D. F. Pears and B. F. McGuinness (London: Routledge, 1961), 4.112. The *Tractatus* was originally published in German in 1921 as *Logisch-Philosophische Abhandlung*, and its text is numbered by consecutive paragraphs.

[9] Joseph Raz locates practices in the context of philosophy of action, an approach that shares affinities with ours. See Joseph Raz, *The Practice of Value* (Oxford: Oxford University Press, 2003).

[10] Thomas Hobbes, *Leviathan*, ed. C. B. Macpherson (London: Penguin, 1968 [1651]); Immanuel Kant, *The Metaphysics of Morals*, ed. Mary Gregor (Cambridge: Cambridge University Press, 1996 [1797]); Gerald F. Gauss, 'Hobbesian-Inspired Liberalism: Public Reason out of Individual Reason', in Gerald Gauss, *Contemporary Theories of Liberalism* (London: Sage, 2003), pp. 56–82.

[11] John Rawls, *Political Liberalism*, pbk. ed. (New York: Columbia University Press, 1996).

generate a liberal political constitution acceptable to all citizens.[12] Such views treat social practices as a limiting case for what at bottom are weightier considerations in theorising moral and political life, such as criteria of reasonableness or rules of impartiality.[13] We redirect the discussion away, though not against, this liberal public-reason tradition by elevating practices into a central concern and by reinstating the role of value in a comprehensive, ethical sense that extends beyond the remit of political value. Our argument is grounded in Hegel's view that the identity (ethical status) of self-conscious actors is constituted within social practices. Since, for Hegel, social practices, including the comprehensive practice of the state, are constitutive of identity, they themselves become a source of fundamental value.[14]

The ensuing enquiry does not commence by postulating some set of abstract properties by virtue of which practices can be said to exist. We ask, given that practices exist (in some non-abstract sense yet to be clarified), what is the procedure that an observer must use for *understanding them properly*? Espousing Hegel's assumption of the primacy of self-consciousness, we hold that whatever basic features a practice may have, it must be understood by a self-conscious agent – this leads to the problem of the mode of understanding or interpretation that is appropriate for making sense of practices that one does not yet understand. Typical here is the distinction between practice participants who must gain an understanding of their own practice in order to reproduce

[12] John Rawls develops the idea of reasonable overlapping consensus in *Political Liberalism*, pp. 15, 39 and Lecture IV, §3. Rawls's idea (stripped from the predicate 'reasonable') is the inspiration behind Charles R. Beitz's account of the global practice of rights in *The Idea of Human Rights* (Oxford: Oxford University Press, 2009), esp. pp. 74–95. Rawls's conception of public reason is largely based on Kant's notion of practical reason (*Political Liberalism*, Lecture III) and Thomas M. Scanlon's contemporary idea of justification in terms of reasons that must be acceptable to everyone. On public reason, see *Political Liberalism*, Lecture VI, §§4, 7, 8 and Rawls's reference to principles of justice 'justifiable to all citizens' (p. 224). Rawls refers (p. xlvi) to T. M. Scanlon, 'Practices and Promises', *Philosophy and Public Affairs* 19 (3) 1990: 199–226. The latter is refined in T. M. Scanlon, *What We Owe to Each Other* (Cambridge, MA: Harvard University Press, 1998), ch. 7, pp. 295–327.

[13] This is notable in Scanlon's argument in 'Practices and Promises', which is that the moral obligation of promising is grounded *independently* from the social practice of promising. His position is criticised in Niko Kolodny and R. Jay Wallace, 'Promises and Practices Revisited', *Philosophy & Public Affairs* 31 (2) 2003: 119–154.

[14] This is the core argument Hegel develops in his *Philosophy of Right*; see note 2.

it and a third party represented by the figure of the scholar (scientist, analyst) who observes, and in this sense attempts to understand, what practice participants understand themselves to be doing. Practices, that is, are not like chairs or stones; they are literally made of understandings. For this reason, the analysis of practices demands hermeneutic philosophy: the 'science of interpretation'. There are different variants of hermeneutics. Friedrich Schleiermacher, for instance, associates the procedure for interpreting texts with the discovery of original authorial intention.[15] Martin Heidegger, joined by Hans-Georg Gadamer, favours phenomenological hermeneutic, where the phenomenology (lived experiences) of the subject is to be understood by an ultimate appeal to the 'primordial' structures of 'Being'.[16] Such forms of hermeneutic enquiry point to foundations and ontology, whereas we are committed to a non-foundational Hegelian hermeneutic, as an epistemological project. As expressed by Hegel in *The Phenomenology of Spirit* (1807), the object of philosophical interpretation comprises the intersubjective understandings of agents, sublimated into social rules, practices and institutions. And if these institutions are to be understood properly, as concrete social forms, the philosopher must describe them in concrete terms, by transcending categories that are abstract and invariant.[17]

In this book, we seek to attain a fuller, more coherent understanding of the concrete practices that comprise the realm of international relations today. To this end, the general philosophical analysis of social practices will be brought to bear on the specific problem of international and global practices. As the intention is to contribute to both

[15] Friedrich Schleiermacher, *Hermeneutics and Criticism*, trans. and ed. Andrew Bowie (Cambridge: Cambridge University Press, 1998 [1838]). The aim of hermeneutics, according to Schleiermacher, is 'understanding the writer *better* than he understands himself' (p. 228; emphasis added).

[16] Martin Heidegger, *Being and Time*, trans. John Macquarrie and Edward Robinson (San Francisco: Harper and Row, 1962); Hans-Georg Gadamer, *Philosophical Hermeneutics*, trans. and ed. David E. Linge (Berkeley: University of California Press, 1977).

[17] G. W. F. Hegel, *Hegel's Phenomenology of Spirit*, trans. A. V. Miller (Oxford: Oxford University Press, 1977 [1807]). In describing the journey of consciousness in *The Phenomenology*, from immediate sense perception all the way to the development of self-consciousness and its expression in public cultural forms ('Spirit'), Hegel remarks that 'consciousness is spirit as *concrete knowing*'. G. W. F. Hegel, *Hegel's Science of Logic*, trans. A.V. Miller (Atlantic Highlands, NJ: Humanities Press International, 1989), p. 28.

philosophy and IR theory, we construct a philosophically informed practice theory that has relevance for international relations without deriving it from the disciplinary debates within IR. The twentieth-century IR discipline is commonly portrayed as organised around three consecutive 'great debates' – realism versus idealism (1930s and 1940s), history versus science (1960s) and (from the late 1980s onwards) positivism versus post-positivism (post-structuralism, critical theory and constructivism).[18] To these theoretical distinctions are added methodological ones, drawn from the arsenal of social theory: 'power versus norms', 'material factors versus ideas' and 'agents versus structures'. Exponents of the practice turn in IR, whose conception of practices we reject, have employed two vocabularies: (1) Bourdieu's sociology of practice and (2) constructivist IR theory.

The notion of practice has been foreshadowed in the writings of some early IR constructivists. In his 1987 article on the agent-structure debate, Alexander Wendt claimed that practices constitute the missing nexus between agents and structures.[19] Social structures, Wendt writes, do not exist independently from the activities they govern: they are not reified things that stand apart from the agents.[20] Here, 'practices' are interactions that have a discursive dimension and reflect

[18] We follow Lapid's presentation of the third debate. Yosef Lapid, 'The Third Debate: On the Prospects of International Theory in a Post-Positivist Era', *International Studies Quarterly* 33 (3) 1989: 235–254. Some prefer an alternative categorisation of four debates, where the third debate is realism/pluralism/globalism and the fourth debate (Lapid's third debate) is positivism/post-positivism. This alternative account is found in part 2 ('Legacies') of Steve Smith, Ken Booth and Marysia Zalewski (eds.), *International Theory: Positivism and Beyond* (Cambridge: Cambridge University Press, 1996). For a recent assessment of the 'great debates' in IR, see Ole Wæver, 'Still a Discipline after All These Debates?', in Tim Dunne, Milja Kurki and Steve Smith (eds.), *International Relations Theories: Discipline and Diversity*, 2nd ed. (Oxford: Oxford University Press 2010), pp. 297–318; and Brian C. Schmidt, 'On the History and Historiography of International Relations', in Walter Carlsnaes, Thomas Risse and Beth A. Simmons (eds.), *Handbook of International Relations*, 2nd ed. (Los Angeles: Sage 2013), pp. 3–28.

[19] Alexander Wendt, 'The Agent-Structure Problem in International Relations Theory', *International Organization* 41 (3) 1987: 335–370, esp. 358–359.

[20] Wendt draws on Roy Bhaskar's argument in *The Possibility of Naturalism* (Brighton, UK: Harvester Press, 1979), pp. 48–49. However, while both Wendt and Bhaskar begin by recognising the meaningfulness of social structures, they ultimately explain their efficacy in the causal terms of scientific realist theory. We discuss the tension between scientific realism and practice theory in the concluding chapter.

agents' self-understandings. Invoking this early constructivist argument, leading figures in the recent 'turn' to practice, Adler and Pouliot, followed by Christian Bueger and Frank Gadinger, have contended that practices form an ontology that can bridge the material-ideational and agential-structural divides in IR.[21] One drawback of such talk of 'ontology' and 'agents/structures' is that without further qualification, it remains too abstract to be analytically helpful.[22]

A separate group of Wittgensteinian IR constructivists have linked the concept of practices to Wittgenstein's later philosophy in the aftermath of the linguistic turn.[23] In *World of Our Making*, the book which introduced constructivism to IR, Nicholas Onuf argues that people make society and society makes people via the mediation of linguistically grounded social conventions.[24] The book opens with Goethe's aphorism, 'In the beginning was the deed', quoted by Wittgenstein.[25] It captures the spirit of Wittgenstein's mature conception of language as a rule-governed social activity or practice that was responsible for

---

[21] Emanuel Adler and Vincent Pouliot, 'International Practices: Introduction and Framework', in Emanuel Adler and Vincent Pouliot (eds.), *International Practices* (New York: Cambridge University Press, 2011), pp. 1–35; Vincent Pouliot and Frédéric Mérand, 'Bourdieu's Concepts', in Rebecca Adler-Nissen (ed.), *Bourdieu in International Relations: Rethinking Key Concepts in IR* (London: Routledge, 2013), pp. 24–44, p. 30; Christian Bueger and Frank Gadinger, 'The Play of International Practice', *International Studies Quarterly* 59 (3) 2015: 449–460, p. 453.

[22] Our argument prioritises the category of understanding and, as such, is epistemological. Whenever possible, instead of *labelling* a given position 'ontological' or 'epistemological', we have striven to explicate the *argument(s)* it contains.

[23] See Michael Dummett, 'The Linguistic Turn', in Michael Dummet, *Origins of Analytical Philosophy*, reprint ed. (London: Bloomsbury, 2014 [1993]), pp. 5–14, p. 6. Dummett associates the linguistic turn with Frege and Frege's 'contextual principle', stating that a word has meaning only within the context of a sentence. Gottlob Frege, *Die Grundlagen der Arithmetik: Eine Logisch Mathematische Untersuchung über den Begriff der Zahl* (Breslau: Wilhelm Koebner, 1884), §62. See also Richard Rorty (ed.), *The Linguistic Turn: Essays in Philosophical Method* (Chicago: Chicago University Press, 1992). In Rorty's view, the linguistic turn in twentieth-century philosophy conveys the idea that philosophical problems can be solved or dissolved by turning to language.

[24] Nicholas Onuf, *World of Our Making: Rules and Rule in Social Theory and International Relations* (Columbia: University of South Carolina Press, 1989), pp. 35, 46.

[25] Ludwig Wittgenstein, 'Cause and Effect: Intuitive Awareness', trans. Peter Winch, *Philosophia* 6 (3) and (4) 1976: 409–425, p. 420, quoted in Onuf, *World of Our Making*, p. 36.

the demise of his former view of language as a structure mirrored in the propositions of logic. On Onuf's reading, Wittgenstein's philosophy of language created a space for a social theory of practices (conventions), but it never produced such a theory.[26] An adequate social theory must show how agents, by participating in social conventions, generate asymmetric relations of advantage and disadvantage which implicate issues of legitimacy and authority.[27] In spite of his groundbreaking insight that speaking a language is a social practice, therefore, Wittgenstein must be considered a false beginning for constructivist social theory – both in IR and outside it. IR constructivist Karin Fierke has objected to this reading: Wittgenstein's philosophy of language, through its concepts of 'language-games' and 'rule following', enables us to make sense of social reality, including that of international relations.[28] A language-game is a human institution ('a practice', in our terms) constituted by rules. In the activity of rule-following, rules provide reasons for action. Such reasons are not mechanical causes, nor are they private motives hidden in the head of the individual; the acts of giving reasons and responding to reasons are carried out in a public language.[29] What a Wittgensteinian perspective discloses is that the world of international relations is a social world, constituted by language – by claims and counterclaims that are intelligible even amongst adversaries.

Naturally, such Wittgenstein themes are appealing to us. Nonetheless, IR theorists and, to a degree, contemporary philosophers have tended to regard the category of a social practice as intuitively transparent.[30] As a result, this category has seldom been problematised. Our theory of practices maps out such a problematic of practices by treading in the footsteps of Wittgenstein, Oakeshott and Hegel. The theory is predicated on Hegel's hermeneutic and structured around three central philosophical puzzles that occupied Wittgenstein and Oakeshott: (1) *rule-following*, as inscribed within social practices;

---

[26] Onuf, *World of Our Making*, pp. 44, 49.
[27] Onuf, *World of Our Making*, pp. 21–22.
[28] Fierke, 'Wittgenstein and International Relations Theory', pp. 87–88. Fierke's view is indebted to Baker and Hacker's reading of Wittgenstein's rule-following argument. G. P. Baker and P. M. S. Hacker, *Wittgenstein: Rules, Grammar, and Necessity* (Oxford: Blackwell, 1985), esp. p. 160.
[29] Fierke, 'Wittgenstein and International Relations Theory', pp. 86–87, 93–94.
[30] See note 12 on public reason.

(2) *descriptivism*; and (3) *internalism*. While descriptivism, seen as the converse of prescriptivism, is a straightforward view, rule-following and internalism (and their connection) have been the subjects of controversy.[31] Commentators have disputed whether by 'following a rule' Wittgenstein meant that a single individual can use a given rule as a guide for conduct in utter isolation from others on repeated occasions, or, conversely, whether a prior community agreement is necessary to determine what counts as following a rule in each case.[32] Wittgenstein and Oakeshott were also interested in the nature of the relation between knowing how to follow a rule and a proposition that expresses the rule. For Oakeshott, in expressing the rule, the proposition removes certain aspects of know-how which one has learned in using the rule: such aspects of actual rule use cannot be stated in the rule itself.[33] Wittgenstein similarly doubted that a rule, once formulated, can determine its own application for all future instances – a rule of this sort would be an oddity; it would look like rails extending to infinity.[34] Thus he concluded that 'obeying a rule is *a practice*'.[35] Part of our undertaking is to elucidate such troublesome philosophical questions.

Turning to IR, our central thesis is that those currently debating the character of social practices are prone to conflate the category of action

[31] Prescription is a rule telling the agents what they ought to do. A now classic study of the language of prescriptions is R. M. Hare, *The Language of Morals* (Oxford: Clarendon Press, 1952).

[32] Instructive here is the debate between two groups of Wittgenstein interpreters. Baker and Hacker make a case for the so-called 'regularity view', which holds that a rule is meant to guide the actions of a solitary individual on a regular number of occasions: 'The concept of following a rule is here linked with the concept of regularity, not with the concept of a community of rule-followers.' Baker and Hacker, *Wittgenstein: Rules, Grammar, and Necessity*, p. 140. Malcolm defends a 'social practice view' (sometimes called the 'community view'), stipulating that rule-following presupposes a community of language users or language as a social practice. Norman Malcolm, *Nothing Is Hidden* (Oxford: Blackwell, 1986) and 'Wittgenstein on Language and Rules', *Philosophy* 64 (247) 1989: 5–28, esp. p. 16. In this book, we follow Malcolm's reading.

[33] Oakeshott, *On Human Conduct*, pp. 68, 90–91. See also Oakeshott's early works, 'The Tower of Babel' (1948), in Michael Oakeshott, *Rationalism in Politics and Other Essays*, new expanded ed. (Indianapolis: Liberty Fund, 1991 [1962]), pp. 465–487, esp. pp. 478–480; Oakeshott (1950), 'Rational Conduct', in Oakeshott, *Rationalism in Politics*, pp. 99–131, p. 128.

[34] Wittgenstein, *Philosophical Investigations*, §218.

[35] Wittgenstein, *Philosophical Investigations*, §202, emphasis added.

(and interaction) with that of a practice, social activity constituted by rules. We trace this conflation to Bourdieu's 'theory of practice'. Since the aim is to limit the discussion in an appropriate way, in Chapter 2 we focus exclusively on this 'theory of practice' and on the 'practice turn' in IR it has inspired.

The primary reason for our disagreement with practice-turn scholars revolves around the question of rule-following. The thrust of our position is that to be able to achieve a proper understanding of practices, it is crucial to begin analysis with the concept of rules and rule-following (coupled with an internalist stance) before tackling the question of action as meaningful doing. And yet, rules and rule-following have been left out from the discussions of practice turn scholars. Another infelicity is that IR students are introduced to the general logic of practices through secondary sources that summarise the viewpoints of famous social theorists such as Bourdieu and Schatzki – an exception is Pouliot's masterful re-examination of Bourdieu's oeuvre.[36] Such abridgements of social theory and philosophy would be appropriate for a mature discourse, but the IR discourse of practices is far from being settled. Consequently, we have to support our theoretical choices by arguing *why* we prefer Wittgenstein's over Bourdieu's view of practices. Unless the argument is detailed enough, it would be unclear what its point is. Does it serve to define a practice or to justify it? Does it explore a specific practice (e.g., deterrence) or social practices in general? Such important details are lost in synoptic presentations, which is why we return to the careful distinctions in the original texts of Wittgenstein, Oakeshott and Hegel. For all that, our endeavour is to rethink these distinctions from a fresh perspective and not to pursue exegesis.

Our enquiry into the logic of social practices aims for depth, not breath. It is animated by the following set of philosophically basic questions: What are the core features of a practice as an analytical object?[37] In what respects (if any) do international practices differ from other social practices? What differentiates action from practice-dependent action? What is the appropriate standpoint for understanding

---

[36] Pouliot presents his reading of Bourdieu's theory of practice in chapter 2 of Vincent Pouliot, *International Security in Practice: The Politics of NATO-Russia Diplomacy* (New York: Cambridge University Press, 2010).

[37] Contrast the question, 'What is time?' (which is philosophically basic) with 'What is the time now in San Francisco?' (which is contingent).

(international) practices as a third-party observer? Another set of
silences we explore concerns the relation between normative theory
and practice theory.[38] Is practice theory a reincarnation of normative
theory or is it an independent theory? How would the endorsement of
practice theory change the current disciplinary matrix of IR theorising?
Since no answers are available in the extant IR literature, we construct
our argument from the bottom up. We first outline a philosophical
template of the basic characteristics of social practices (Chapter 3) and
proceed to examine the core practices in contemporary international
relations (Chapters 4 and 5). As will be shown, international practices
exhibit peculiarities reflected, inter alia, in their macro-level, comprehensive scope: they are globally extended macro practices made up of
other practices. In short, we write from the conviction that a return
to the philosophy of practices can illuminate the central practices
of international affairs and change the way in which IR is studied and
taught.

But if the principal way in which our philosophical analysis departs
from the sociology of practices currently dominant in IR is by opening
the black box of practices and exploring their logic, another salient
difference pertains to the standpoint appropriate for understanding
practices. Practice-turn scholars adopt the externalist standpoint of
social science, whereas we defend the 'internal point of view', an
expression originally coined by Hart.[39] The internal point of view
(alternatively referred to as 'internalism' or 'practice internalism')
poses the problem of understanding (making sense of ) a social practice
from 'within'. In the paradigmatic case, it involves an attempt by a
third-party observer to understand a not-yet-understood social practice in the terms its own competent participants themselves understand
it. As a limiting case, internalism involves the shared, intersubjective
understanding of a group of actors who have learned to perform
actions within the framework of their common practice. Thus the
attempt by an actor, a novice, to *learn* to participate in a practice *ab
initio*, by following the rules of the practice, is never a purely subjective
endeavour. As defined here, internalism does not connote the idea of

---

[38] An exception to this silence is Chris Brown's normative analysis of practices
(see his 'The "Practice Turn"'), which links them to Aristotelian *phronesis*.

[39] Hart develops the argument for an 'internal point of view' as an attitude of rule
acceptance within a system of legal rules. Hart, *The Concept of Law*, pp. 55,
86–89, 99, 114, 197.

subjectivism versus objectivism or historical understanding versus scientific explanation. Paradigmatically, internalism constitutes an observational perspective whereby an account of a putative object (a social practice) is sought and which typically goes under the label of 'explanation' – on our premises, though, explanation just is understanding (by a third party). Before we continue with the provisional outline of internalism in this chapter, it is useful to sketch the basic components of a practice as an analytical object.

## What, Briefly, Are Practices?

It seems that we all have some intuitive understanding of what a practice is. But once we get to spelling out its defining features, the task turns out to be a daunting one. Examples of practices include signing a treaty, voting in an election, waging war across state borders, presenting a conference paper, reciting a poem to an audience, coffee drinking and participating in global literary festivals. Such a motley assortment of practices frustrates any attempt to produce a straightforward definition of a practice in terms of necessary and sufficient conditions. The trouble is that while different sufficient conditions determine different practices, no single necessary condition underpins all practices: this is what Wittgenstein implied by saying that practices ('language-games', in his terms) share loose family resemblances.[40] One way to resolve the difficulty is to view practices as analogues of *customs* or *traditions*, two concepts adumbrated by Alasdair MacIntyre and Michael Polanyi.[41] But this analogy is strained because the notion of a practice is less coarse grained than either a tradition or custom. It is symptomatic that in his mature *magnum opus, On Human Conduct* (1975), Oakeshott abandoned the category of

---

[40] Wittgenstein, *Philosophical Investigations*, §67.
[41] Alasdair MacIntyre, *After Virtue*, 3rd ed. (Notre Dame, IN: University of Notre Dame Press, 2007 [1981]); Alasdair MacIntyre, *Whose Justice? Which Rationality?* (Notre Dame, IN: University of Notre Dame Press, 1988); Michael Polanyi, *Personal Knowledge: Towards a Post-Critical Philosophy*, rev. ed. (Chicago: Chicago University Press, 1962), pp. 53–54; Michael Polanyi, *The Tacit Dimension* (Chicago: Chicago University Press, 2009 [1966]). MacIntyre thinks of traditions as rational forms of enquiry, whereas Polanyi emphasises their tacit, 'knowing-how' character. One notable difference is that MacIntyre examines traditions of morality, whereas Polanyi is interested in the traditions of scientific knowledge.

traditions in favour of practices: this is not a change in *façon de parler* but a switch of major philosophical significance.[42]

With these qualifications in mind, we may now define a practice, recognising that it is a complex analytical object with a fuzzy set of interrelated features. Its most perspicuous feature is that it constitutes a whole: it is a common framework of rules governing the interaction of a multitude of individuals. Not just any form of interaction will do, however. It must be regular and jointly intelligible to the majority of individuals taking part in the practice – its participants. Patterns of interaction are discernible because the participants follow standards of conduct (rules) in common. The standards are common in two distinct senses. First, they are intersubjectively shared within a group of individuals, indicating that the relevant unit is a social group (a 'we-think') and not an aggregation of separate individuals (an 'I-think'). The expression *social practice* is a pleonasm, for any practice deserving the name is a 'public' device. This trait distinguishes it from a rule a solitary individual might devise for private use. Compare a rule, say, the rule of getting up at 5:00 o'clock in the morning, followed regularly by John in solitude, with that same rule followed regularly by soldiers jointly participating in military training. Only where rule-following is a non-solitary activity may we suppose that a common practice is at work. A normative test is required to determine whether this supposition is warranted. A practice, as mentioned, is a framework of intersubjectively shared meanings. These are the meanings of common *norms* – rules which stipulate what counts as proper as opposed to mistaken conduct. A practice, then, is common to its participants in a second, normative sense going beyond the first, intersubjective sense. Now, and this is the normativity test described by Hart in his study of legal and moral practices,[43] whenever an individual member of a social group breaches a rule accepted within the group, this aberrant conduct provokes criticism, sarcastic remarks and, at the limit, outrage by the other members. What such symptoms show is that the rule in question is a norm – in Chapter 3, we broach the problem of normativity in its multiple guises (prescriptions, rules as norms, values). As this is only a 'first cut' of the argument, it is permissible to treat norms and rules as

[42] Oakeshott focusses on traditions in his earlier writings in *Rationalism in Politics*, as noted by Terry Nardin, *The Philosophy of Michael Oakeshott* (University Park: Pennsylvania State University Press, 2001), p. 76.
[43] Hart, *The Concept of Law*, esp. pp. 55–56, 82–88, 114.

interchangeable. For now, we may think of a norm as a rule which *guides* conduct in an appropriate way. Any mistake, any inappropriate conduct, stimulates an adverse reaction and obliquely discloses the presence of the norm. Having detected the norm in question through the normativity test (a detector of adverse reactions to norm violation), we have advanced towards establishing that a common practice binds the individuals observed. But we have not yet established it conclusively, for a practice has complexity: it contains not just a single norm but an entire system of norms, and much beside.

A practice is a *system* of rules and norms. It constitutes a meaningful whole insofar as each rule is a meaningful proposition intended to govern the conduct of a thinking and choosing agent.[44] Rules considered as propositions – 'Taxes are to be paid annually', 'The King may move to any adjoining square not threatened by the opponent's pieces', 'States should conduct their affairs peacefully' – demand interpretation and can be understood as well as misunderstood, both by the agents themselves and by third-party observers. While a practice typically structures the interactions of a large number of individuals, it does not have the character of a general law of behaviour which an observer can discern, from 'outside', by attending to the patterns of their physical interaction and by abstracting away the meanings they attach to the rules and norms defining their shared practice. Understood from a non-physicalist observational standpoint labelled the *internal point of view*, a practice is a meaningful social whole; the meanings of its basic norms and rules account for the observed pattern of conduct of its participants. Unless an observer already understands, to some degree at least, what these rules and norms mean, it would be impossible to tell what the participants under observation are doing. The pattern of conduct that characterises practices is not reducible to regularities of physical behaviour. The difference is not only that physical regularities create expectations about the future, whereas rules create obligations that are past-referring; what matters most is that by virtue of being

---

[44] This is not meant to be a definition of a rule. At a minimum, a rule is a proposition intended to govern conduct, which has (1) meaning and (2) a certain generality. The requirement for generality implies that rules cannot be exhausted by being used on a single occasion and that they exclude references to designated persons – this distinguishes rules from commands, warnings, and pieces of advice. These two features are discussed in Oakeshott, *On Human Conduct*, p. 121, and pp. 124–125.

*relations* between persons, rules as well as the obligations and rights
they entail exhibit normative 'stickiness' and durability that a pattern
of physical behaviour lacks. The components enumerated so far – rules
of action, norms of action, the activity of following rules (and norms),
the understanding of meaning, and the internal point of view – roughly
outline the analytical architecture of a practice. In what follows, we
shall refine these components and show how they cohere.

## The Central Themes of This Book

In this study, we pursue a twofold aim: (1) to elucidate the general logic
of social practices from a philosophical perspective and (2) to expound
and defend a practice theory which can illuminate practices in international relations. To these correspond two key theses, presented in
Part I and Part II of the text. The first holds that in attempting to make
sense of an unfamiliar practice, third-party observers are required to
approach it from the internal point of view, an engagement which,
when properly undertaken, yields descriptions of the relevant practice.
The second thesis holds that the contemporary realm of international
relations is constituted by two macro practices: the practice of sovereign states and the practice of global rights.

### *Internalism, Elucidation and Social Science*

In embracing practice internalism, we concur with Wittgenstein's
premise that the method of philosophy is one of *elucidation*. In
Wittgenstein's words, 'A philosophical work consists essentially of
elucidations. Philosophy does not result in "philosophical propositions", but rather in the clarification of propositions.'[45] We may think
of elucidation as clarification, although there is more to the idea.
Wittgenstein takes elucidation to be a descriptivist method to be distinguished from explanation, a method of reduction. For Wittgenstein,
to *explain* an identity is to express it in terms other than what it is (and
thus to reduce it to another identity), whereas to *describe* it is to show
what it is on its own terms. In this reductive sense, explanation presupposes a search for foundations, first principles, essences or anything
that underpins the identity under scrutiny. But as Wittgenstein insists,

---

[45] Wittgenstein, *Tractatus*, 4.112.

'Philosophy simply puts everything before us, and neither explains nor deduces anything.'[46] Its task is to describe, not to prescribe or explain. Oakeshott's position has a striking affinity with that of Wittgenstein: to elucidate is to define – or to describe – an identity. Any putative identity must be described *qua* an individual under concepts that are non-abstract and concrete.[47] This reflects Oakeshott's Hegelian precept that 'reality is a coherent world of ideas, that is of things', where 'a thing is simply what is individual'.[48] By arguing that an identity must be conceptualised in its concrete individuality rather than in some alleged abstract terms, Oakeshott, like Hegel, associates abstraction with an account which is one-sided, partial or incomplete. Elucidation, then, involves either a non-reductive description of an identity (Wittgenstein) or a description of an identity *qua* concrete individual (Oakeshott). This elucidatory method entails a critique of scientific method, centred as it is on reduction, invariance and abstraction.

Oakeshott directly and Wittgenstein indirectly, by repudiating the mirror-of-reality model of language, have suggested that science, including social science, is a defective standpoint for making sense of social practices.[49] A practice constitutes a special type of object which places special demands on the observational standpoint appropriate to its understanding. A proper understanding of practices by a third-party observer requires internalism – or so we argue. To substantiate the point, let us consider the procedure of observation employed in modern physics. A physicist who (let us assume) sets out to study the trajectories of atomic particles must define key concepts – 'atom', 'trajectory', 'velocity' – and fix the level and units of measurement. The object of investigation, the thing described as an atom, is passive – it cannot object to the theoretical description imposed by the physicist and declare it to be incorrect. The procedure of observation changes dramatically when the object of enquiry is a practice or action constituted within a practice (also called 'practice-dependent action' or 'participatory action'). In this case, the analyst's descriptions are not a

---

[46] Wittgenstein, *Philosophical Investigations*, §126.
[47] Oakeshott, *Experience and Its Modes*, pp. 45–63; Bhikhu Parekh, 'The Political Philosophy of Michael Oakeshott', *British Journal of Political Science* 9 (4) 1979: 481–506. Parekh writes that for Oakeshott, to elucidate is to define an individual under a 'concrete concept' in Hegel's terms (p. 483).
[48] Oakeshott, *Experience and Its Modes*, pp. 58, 63.
[49] Oakeshott, *On Human Conduct*, pp. 21–31, 55ff.

matter of unlimited theoretical choice. There are limits to what can count as a proper description of a practice because the self-understandings of its participants pre-exist attempts by third parties to interpret these self-understandings. The observer is called upon to study a social world which is *already* intelligible to its participants. The participants may object to the theorist's interpretation (if it were communicated to them) and may find it defective, incomplete or downright confused. To generalise, in studying social practices, the observer seeks to understand that which is already understood – an engagement in 'double hermeneutics' propounded by Oakeshott and Hegel, among others.[50] Whereas observation in the hard sciences has as its object physical entities or processes, the object observed in hermeneutics is human understanding.

The procedures of observation currently adopted in social science comply with the standards of the hard sciences.[51] In effect, the category of human conduct has been reduced to behaviour, and the attempt to understand conduct has been replaced by abstract, quantifiable calculi of patterns of behaviour. We put forward a different view of social science, one which relocates its observational procedures where they properly belong: in the domain of the hermeneutic sciences. On our view, social science is a hermeneutic mode of enquiry.

## Meaning and Understanding

One difficult point that might generate confusion is the relationship between two of the major analytical elements of a practice – meaningful conduct, and rules and norms. The first thing to note is that meaningful conduct and rules do not stand in any necessary conceptual

[50] On the problem of understanding understandings, see Oakeshott, *On Human Conduct*, pp. 13–15, 23–24; and Michael Oakeshott, 'Education: The Engagement and Its Frustration' (1972), in Michael Oakeshott, *The Voice of Liberal Learning* (Indianapolis: Liberty Fund, 2001), pp. 62–104, esp. pp. 66–67. For Hegel, the double hermeneutics follows directly from the premise running throughout *The Phenomenology* (see note 17) – namely, that understanding is, ultimately, the self-understanding of a finite, thinking and choosing agent. To the extent that Heidegger's phenomenological hermeneutic in *Being and Time* adopts the premise of self-understanding, it also points to a double hermeneutics.

[51] The current state of the art on the question of IR as a social science is discussed in Roundtable: International Relations as a Social Science, *Millennium: Journal of International Studies* 43 (1) 2014: 328–368.

relation – we can analyse one without the other. It is uncontroversial that the analysis of meaningful conduct can dispense with the categories of rules and norms: the problem of meaning is broader – or 'weaker', as philosophers would say – than that of rules. Max Weber famously defined meaningful conduct as 'orientated in its course'.[52] This definition makes no reference to rules or an entire framework of rules (a practice). The question here is, What is distinctive about rules? One answer is that rules are action constraints. When performing a rule-governed action, the agent is free to choose a goal to enact but no longer free to ignore the constraints, imposed by the rule, which specify how the chosen goals are to be attained. If we consider Immanuel Kant's moral theory, the master rule of morality, the Categorical Imperative, requires the agent to act in a specific way – by treating oneself and others not merely as a means but always also as an end.[53] Because rules constrain goal-directed conduct, a fundamental tension persists between goal-based (consequentialist) and rule-based (deontological) theories of action that cannot be ameliorated by some sort of 'all-things-considered' position.[54]

However, there is a special reason why, when it comes to *practices*, the notion of rules is first in the order of analysis, outshining even the category of meaning. It is that the identity of a practice as a whole and, by extension, the identity of its participants, is defined by a class of *constitutive rules*. On John Searle's well-known definition, a constitutive rule is one that creates a new type of activity.[55] While throughout this project we shall mine Searle's insights about the constitutive powers of rules, his perspective and ours differ. Searle sets out to produce a unified account, beginning with physical reality, consciousness, as a biological category and building up to the institutions of

---

[52] Max Weber, *Economy and Society: An Outline of Interpretive Sociology*, ed. G. Roth and C. Wittich (Berkley: University of California Press, 1978), p. 4.

[53] This is the second formulation of Kant's Categorical Imperative. Immanuel Kant, *Groundwork of the Metaphysics of Morals*, ed. Mary Gregor (Cambridge: Cambridge University Press, 1997 [1785]), 4:429.

[54] See, for example, Samuel Scheffler (ed.), *Consequentialism and Its Critics* (Oxford: Oxford University Press, 1988).

[55] This is Searle's first definition of a constitutive rule (a rule that creates a new type of activity). His second definition of this same kind of rule reads: 'X counts as Y in context C'. John R. Searle, *Speech Acts: An Essay in the Philosophy of Language* (Cambridge: Cambridge University Press, 1969), pp. 33–34, 35–36.

language and society (property, marriage, money).[56] Conversely, we present the realm of human understandings, language and practices as autonomous and independent from the bedrock of the physical world or biology. In line with our hermeneutic premises, a human being is what Oakeshott called a 'self-enacted reflective consciousness'.[57] This is not a biologically determined consciousness supervening over a material body; it is a unitary agent whose actions are intelligent responses to a situation as an understood situation.

But if a practice is constituted by rules, it is notable that a formal enumeration of these rules is not enough for its proper identification. The rules enable us to discern the boundaries of the practice, but they do not capture the know-how necessary for *using* the rules. Second, a practice is a *common framework of rules*, not a list of disparate rules which various agents might follow on separate occasions. Each individual participant in a practice, when following its rules, acts by taking into consideration the fact that the rest of its participants also follow the rules: for this reason, these rules qualify as *common* norms in the first place.

Aside from the category of constitutive rules, another major component of a practice as an analytical object is meaningful conduct. The concept of meaning belongs to the philosophy of language. In his early work *Tractatus Logico-Philosophicus* (1921), Wittgenstein distinguishes words from linguistic propositions (statements composed of words, which express thoughts) and stipulates that the meaning of a word is the object it stands for, whereas the meaning of a proposition is a possible fact represented by the proposition.[58] The *Tractatus*, a treatise on logic, metaphysics and language, is designed to show how linguistic propositions connect to reality. For Wittgenstein, 'the world is the

---

[56] Searle writes, 'A socially constructed reality presupposes reality independent of all social constructions.' *The Social Construction of Reality* (New York: Free Press, 1995), p. 190. On the topic of consciousness, he remarks, 'Consciousness is an ordinary biological phenomenon comparable with growth, digestion or the secretion of bile.' 'Consciousness as a Biological Problem', in John R. Searle, *The Mystery of Consciousness* (New York: New York Review of Books, 1997), pp. 1–18, p. 6.

[57] Oakeshott, *On Human Conduct*, p. 37.

[58] At 3.12 of the *Tractatus*, Wittgenstein writes, 'I call the sign with which we express a thought a propositional sign' (see 3.2 in note 61). At 3.203, he states, 'A name means an object. The object is its meaning.'

totality of facts, not of things.'[59] An atomic fact designates an existing combination of objects, metaphysical simples.[60] Thought is a 'logical picture of facts' – that is to say, a combination of logical simples.[61] In claiming that the world is the totality of facts, Wittgenstein is anticipating a further, crucial possibility – that of *representing* this totality via a pictorial relation of 'logical form'.[62] Because there is an isomorphism in logical form between thought and reality, and between thought and language, language can represent reality. The conclusion is that the logical form of reality is mirrored in the structure of propositions or language.[63] This general theory of representation is the basis of what has become known as Wittgenstein's picture theory of meaning.[64] Wittgenstein did not explain satisfactorily what these simple logical objects, constituents of thought, are, and the picture theory of meaning faced intractable difficulties. Years later, it struck him that when it comes to ordinary language, people learn what a word or proposition means by actually using it within a language-game. This would lead him to jettison the philosophy of abstract propositional language for ordinary language philosophy under the motto 'Every sentence in our language is in order as it is.'[65] What ordinary language gives us access to is not the metaphysical reality of ontologically basic

[59] Wittgenstein, *Tractatus*, 1.1. 'Reality' is a broader category than 'world'. It includes the world ('The totality of existing states of affairs is the world' [2.04]) plus possible but not yet existing states of affairs.

[60] An atomic fact is a state of affairs (*Sachverhalt*). Ogden translates *Sachverhalten* as 'atomic facts' and Pears and McGuinness as 'states of affairs' – Ludwig Wittgenstein, *Tractatus Logico-Philosophicus*, trans. C. K. Ogden (London: Routledge 1990 [1922]), 2. We have used the Pears and McGuinness's translation, as it is more likely to be available to the reader). Wittgenstein, *Tractatus*, 2: 'What is the case – a fact – is the existence of states of affairs'; and 2.01: 'A state of affairs (a state of things) is a combination of objects (things).' On objects as simples, see 2.02: 'Objects are simple', and 2.021, 2.027.

[61] Wittgenstein, *Tractatus*, 3: 'A logical picture of facts is a thought'; and 3.2: 'In a proposition a thought can be expressed in such a way that elements of the propositional sign correspond to the objects of the thought.'

[62] This emphasis on representation in 'logical space' is evident in Wittgenstein, *Tractatus* 1.13: 'The facts in logical space are the world.' On logical form, see 2.18, 2.022, 2.12: 'A picture is a model of reality'; and 4.01: 'A proposition is a picture of reality.'

[63] Wittgenstein's Tractarian world does not comprise the whole of reality (see note 59).

[64] Anthony Kenny, *Wittgenstein* (London: Penguin, 1973), p. 54.

[65] Wittgenstein, *Philosophical Investigations*, §98. Wittgenstein criticises his own earlier theory of propositional knowledge and truth at §§ 97, 136.

objects but social reality composed of a multiplicity of practices or language-games. In the *Tractatus*, language is a logical system of symbols that serves to express the thoughts of a solitary thinker; in the *Philosophical Investigations* (1953), language is public or shared – it is a social practice reproduced by the participants in diverse language-games. This watershed change in the conception of language is reflected in the doctrine of 'meaning in use' prominent in the *Investigations*, a doctrine that Oakeshott would develop independently in *On Human Conduct*. Its gist is that novices in a (linguistic) practice learn how to use an expression properly – or how to play a language-game – from other, more experienced players.

The upshot is that if meaning consists in use, the defining (constitutive) rules of a practice are not rules written in books collecting dust on shelves: they are rules that the participants are using to navigate their lives. A practice, as Wittgenstein quipped, is a 'form of life'.[66] It should be clear that when, as theorists, we set out to disaggregate the components of a practice for the purposes of analysis, these components are to be seen not as atomic units but as 'parts' of a complex, dynamic social whole. Note that concepts like 'learning', 'understanding' and 'making a mistake' are terms of art. Understanding hinges on the possibility of learning, and one comes to learn by making and correcting mistakes. Mistakes help us distinguish normatively guided action or action governed by rules from what we call 'simple action' – we return to the crucial notion of making a mistake in Chapters 1 and 3.

The category of understanding differs in principle from knowledge. The idea of knowledge as justified true belief goes back to Plato.[67] On the Platonist view, to know something is to establish (justifiably) that it is true. In contrast to knowledge, understanding does not presuppose truth (true propositions). We can *understand* the proposition 'The population of Rome is smaller than the population of Birmingham' without *knowing its truth* or without knowing whether the (empirical) fact, asserted in this proposition, is true.[68] For the Platonist, truth is an

---

[66] Wittgenstein, *Philosophical Investigations*, §241.

[67] Plato, *Theaetetus*, trans. M. J. Levett, ed. Bernard Williams (Indianapolis: Hackett, 1992), 201C, 202C. Cf. Edmund L. Gettier, 'Is Justified True Belief Knowledge?', *Analysis* 23 (6) 1963: 121–123.

[68] The example is Ryle's. Gilbert Ryle, 'Are There Propositions?', in Gilbert Ryle, *Collected Papers*, Vol. II (1929–1968) (London: Hutchinson, 1971), pp. 12–38,

element within an objective worldview in which a subject, reasoning in perfect solitude, seeks knowledge of an objective reality. Finding the truth does not depend on intersubjective communication with others. A categorically different worldview, an intersubjective one, is postulated by Oakeshott and Wittgenstein who assume that a community of subjects share between themselves an understanding of what they are saying and doing within the bonds of a common social practice. Because occasionally such understanding can lapse into misunderstanding, the endeavour of a third-party observer to make sense of the practice is not trivial or pointless. A social practice consists of intersubjectively shared understandings – no deeper, objective reality is lurking behind it. To be able properly to make sense of such shared understandings, the social scientist must reason not in Platonic solitude but from *within* the intersubjective contexts that constitute these understandings or from within the relevant social practices.

## Appropriateness and Differentiation of Practices

Finally, and to reiterate one important consideration, there is an almost endless variety of social practices. Wittgenstein denounced the quest for foundations by emphasising that the differences between any two practices are far more perspicuous than the similarities.[69] Recall our list of practices mentioned earlier: waging war, coffee drinking, writing a conference paper, attending global literary festivals. A way of introducing coherence to this bewildering variety was hinted at by Oakeshott in a different context. The danger of modernity, Oakeshott wrote, is that it has turned the individual into a mass subject – a de-individuated member of a social group, class or cast – who, as such, is not a distinctive individual: a person with a life and death of one's own.[70] Extending Oakeshott's argument for the morality of individuality to the analysis of practices allows us to compare diverse practices to individuals with distinctive personal identities and to set them apart

---

p. 20. This chapter is a reprint of Ryle's article published in *The Proceedings of the Aristotelian Society* 1930, 30: 91–126. Even the early Wittgenstein recognised that one can *understand* a proposition without knowing whether it is true, *Tractatus*, 4.024.

[69] Wittgenstein, *Philosophical Investigations*, §§66, 67, 130.

[70] Oakeshott, *On Human Conduct*, p. 238. Oakeshott's term for the mass subject denuded from individuality is the 'individual manqué' (pp. 276–277).

from 'mass' objects with uniform identity such as numbers, chicken eggs or pebbles. Contrast the practice of buying and selling goods with the practice of conducting diplomacy – one is local, the other international; one is done for profit, the other for keeping the peace between hostile states; one may involve private persons or officials, the other involves officials only. The two hardly have any properties in common, yet we have no trouble recognising each as a distinctive domain of meaningful rules and usages that surround the rules.

We contend that the procedures of observation in the social sciences should take seriously the distinctiveness of practices. Social scientists must identify descriptions of actions, descriptions of key norms (stipulating correct performances) which are appropriate to a given practice, understood as a concrete practice. Our internalist message is that as observers (scholars, social scientists), we are searching not just for any set of descriptions but for appropriate ones. An appropriate description is distinctive, and to be distinctive, it should be expressed in a non-abstract (concrete) language. Consider the abstract terminology of 'inequality' and 'equality' that political philosophers often use. What does it mean to say that a given practice is a manifestation of inequality? Is it intelligible as a practice of symbolic exchange, of trade, or of exploitation? It is difficult to give a precise answer, since it is unclear in what *concrete* sense (symbolic, economic, political, or moral) the concept of inequality is intended. Now consider a practice described properly, in concrete terms, as a practice of diplomacy and not in some abstract terms, as a 'method of conflict resolution' or 'bargaining'. Assume that the social scientist seeks to establish whether it is true that an action described as 'signing an international treaty' is being performed. In this case, it would be an error to posit an invariant criterion (truth as an absolute notion) and then apply it, *across* practices, to ascertain whether, for instance, what is true of conduct in diplomacy is also true of conduct in the practice of buying and selling and so on. Instead, the proper procedure for establishing the truth of the action description 'signing an international treaty' is to consult the constitutive rules of the practice of diplomacy as a concrete system of rules. A reference to *these constitutive rules in particular* is requisite because the action description could not be made in their absence.[71]

---

[71] Searle states that for any action constituted by rules, the action *description* is given by the corresponding constitutive rule. *Speech Acts*, p. 36. We hold that

The procedure has an air of tautology about it – it is circular, even though its circularity is not vacuous as we shall see. Truth here is a criterion *internal* to the domain of a concrete practice – we may term it 'relevance'. As Oakeshott claims, considerations relevant to understanding one practice would most likely be irrelevant to understanding another – a practice is like a language 'having a vocabulary and syntax of its own'.[72] One notable corollary is that the internalist criterion of truth-as-relevance (or 'relevance', for short) has an independent authority and must be differentiated from the externalist criterion of truth-as-correspondence, which is satisfied whenever a proposition ('The cat is on the mat') corresponds to a state of affairs in the external world (the cat is sitting on the mat).

This completes the outline of Part I concerned with the general logic of practices. Part II is devoted to two concrete practices that constitute the contemporary sphere of international relations.

## International and Global Practices

In Part II (Chapters 4 and 5), we develop a neo-Hegelian analysis of the practice of society of states and the practice of global rights (global civil society). These contemporary practices originate in early modernity, when the sovereign state was emerging to become the main unit of political and juridical association on the European continent. Yet our analysis is not historical; we are interested in the philosophy of the present. Accordingly, our central thesis is that the practice of society of states and the practice of global rights constitute the basic contours of the international realm today. Whatever else might be going on in international relations at present, it is inscribed in the macro context of these two practices.

Practices that encompass other practices within themselves – such as the state, the society of states and global civil society – are referred to as 'macro practices'. By assigning priority to the category of macro practices, our account breaks with Michel Foucault's social theory of micro foundations, which is gaining increasing prominence in European and

---

the description must be *relevant*, pointing to the domain of a concrete practice *as a whole*, since different practices, as systems of rules, presuppose distinctive criteria for establishing the truth of descriptions made within them.

[72] Oakeshott, *On Human Conduct*, p. 62.

British IR.[73] Foucault studies the social world from the standpoint of micro practices, understood as transmitters of power relations operating in institutional settings below the state such as hospitals, mental asylums, prisons and educational institutions.[74] A comparison with realism in IR theory might help clarify Foucault's view of power. Realists ask to what uses power, and specifically military and economic power, can be put in the relations of states. In his social theory, Foucault asks, conversely, how power itself is constituted within non-state institutions by route of micro practices operating on the everyday level. His argument is that power is an ubiquitous determinant of social relations but that it does not have a common source or even common form. Rather than having a clear-cut hierarchy of social relations whose summit is sovereign power, diverse forms of social power are dissipated across various micro contexts. Mention should also be made of Foucault's no less popular concept of governmentality.[75] It consists of micro techniques of management and is deliberately contrasted with the traditional concept of government and the state, the macro structure of modern political life. In redirecting our attention away from the state and what he sees as its repressive, juridical power, Foucault urges a return to micro foundations: 'We need to cut off the king's head. In political theory this still needs to be done.'[76] Responding to Foucault's

---

[73] An insightful account of Foucault's view of power and political discourse that has relevance for IR is Jenny Edkins, *Poststructuralism and International Relations: Bringing the Political Back In* (London: Lynne Rienner, 1999), pp. 41–64. See also Andrew W. Neal, 'Michel Foucault', in Jenny Edkins and Nick Vaughan-Williams (eds.), *Critical Theorists and International Relations* (London: Routledge, 2009), pp. 161–170.

[74] Michel Foucault, 'Lecture from 14 January 1976', in Michel Foucault, *Society Must Be Defended: Lectures at the Collège de France, 1975–1976*, trans. David Macey, ed. Mauro Bertani and Alessandro Fontana (New York: Picador, 2003), pp. 23–42, esp. pp. 28–31. See also Michel Foucault, *Madness and Civilization: A History of Insanity in the Age of Reason*, trans. Richard Howard (New York: Vintage Books, 1988 [1961]); and Michel Foucault, *Discipline and Punish: The Birth of the Prison*, trans. Alan Sheridan (New York: Vintage Books, 1995 [1975]).

[75] Michel Foucault, 'Governmentality', in Michel Foucault, *The Essential Works of Michel Foucault, 1954–1984*, ed. Paul Rabinow (London: Penguin, 2002), pp. 201–222.

[76] Michel Foucault, 'Truth and Power', in Michel Foucault, *Power/Knowledge: Selected Interviews and Other Writings 1972–1977*, trans. Colin Gordon, Leo Marshall, John Mepham and Kate Soper, ed. Colin Gordon (New York: Vintage Books, 1980), pp. 109–133, p. 121.

challenge, Michael Walzer has argued that even though the state is not to be viewed as sacrosanct, it does provide a comprehensive macro framework within which the common good of the citizens can be determined and appraised – an activity Walzer dubs 'politics'.[77] In Foucault's universe of micro foundations, there is no place for politics.

We endorse Walzer's diagnosis with a twist: we place ethics before politics and view comprehensive macro frameworks such as the society of states and the global practice of rights as *fora* for deliberating matters of ethics and politics. On our Hegelian premises, 'ethics' is not coextensive with the realm of moral conduct alone but comprises all statuses that have non-instrumental value for their holders. For Hegel, social practices constitute the identity of actors in the form of valued ethical statuses such as family members, citizens of states and, as we claim, as holders of global rights or as citizens of states which themselves participate in the international practice of the society of states. A basic value that animates our contemporary international and global practices is that of equal freedom or 'anarchy' in the terminology of IR theory (a theme of Chapter 4).[78]

The major implication of the theoretical perspective defended in this book is that it gives a fresh answer to the question of what the primary object of IR theorising should be. Instead of researching problems such as power relations between states, discourses of power, global governance or structural inequalities between poor and affluent nations, IR theorists should study the macro practices that are global in scope, for these are the meaningful social wholes in which our understandings of these problems are constituted.

## The Plan of This Book

In Chapter 1, we present our first major thesis: practice internalism. It rejects externalism or the view that an *invariant* realm of knowledge,

---

[77] Michael Walzer, 'The Politics of Michel Foucault', in David Couzens Hoy (ed.), *Foucault: A Critical Reader* (London: Basil Blackwell, 1986), pp. 51–68.

[78] That the realm of international relations is anarchical is a cardinal postulate of IR theory. Classic statements are Helen Milner, 'The Assumption of Anarchy in International Relations Theory: A Critique', *Review of International Studies* 17 (1) 1991: 67–85; and Brian C. Schmidt, *The Political Discourse of Anarchy: A Disciplinary History of International Relations* (Albany: SUNY Press, 1998); cf. Jack Donnelly, 'The Discourse of Anarchy in IR', *International Theory* 7 (3) 2015: 393–425.

overarching all practices, must be postulated to make sense of any particular practice. Against this quest for abstract, invariant forms of knowledge, we make a case for understanding. According to practice internalism, understanding epitomises knowledge internal to the institutional context of a particular practice: such knowledge *varies* across practices. Internalism requires of us, as social scientists studying practices, to think from the vantage point of practice participants. There is still a difference between *theorising*, whose aim is understanding as such, and *acting*, where one seeks understanding in order to act. As Oakeshott puts it, the theorist's 'business is to make theorems, not to perform actions: but he is concerned with theorems about conduct'.[79] In other words, even though social scientists may not be players directly engaged in a practice, they count as its *participants* insofar as they are able to make sense of the core rules and usages comprising it as a meaningful whole. In this chapter, we clarify the key notion of making a mistake and the relation between explanation and understanding. We conclude by differentiating the elementary types of practices: instrumental ('purposive') from non-instrumental practices, and within the latter class, authoritative from constitutive practices.

Chapter 2 is a critique of the practice turn in IR and its intellectual pedigree: Bourdieu's theory of practice. Having examined the conceptual kernel of this theory – the triad of *habitus*, field and capital – we conclude that it amounts to an externalist view. We also show that the account of practices offered by practice-turn scholars in IR is beset by inconsistencies traceable to Bourdieu's argument, which fails to differentiate actions from institutions (practices). The discussion reveals the limits of externalism and points to the need for a proper – internalist and institutionalist – account of social practices. But while internalism, as presented in Chapter 2, poses the question of how practices are to be understood from an observer's perspective, it does not tell us how a practice is understood from an agent's perspective, a puzzle taken up in Chapter 3. There, we synthesise the previously analysed components of a practice into a basic philosophical template or *practice theory*, whose aim is to elucidate the general logic of social practices. We claim that a practice has five elementary analytical components: the internal point

---

[79] Oakeshott, *On Human Conduct*, pp. 33, 34–35, 106. As stated at the outset of this Introduction, Oakeshott's 'theorems' are the conclusions of theoretical enquiry or 'theorising'.

of view, rule-following, constitutive rules, the understanding of meaning, and norms – the first two (internalism and rule-following) making up its core. The challenge is not only to identify the relevant components of a practice but to adduce reasons for their order of priority. It is significant that we treat as primary internalism and rule-following and not, as is conventional in hermeneutics, the concept of meaning.

Chapter 3 completes the conceptual analysis of practices. Chapters 4 and 5 move to questions of normativity. In this segment of the discussion, we advance our second central thesis regarding the constitutive role of two macro practices beyond the domestic state: the practice of sovereign states and the practice of global rights.

Chapter 4 presents a neo-Hegelian reading of these two practices as grounded in the 'anarchical' value of equal freedom. This value, we contend, constitutes the ethical statuses of states and of individual rights-holders as self-conscious actors who value their freedom. This type of freedom can only be maintained within social forms which are horizontal or 'anarchical' in the sense of involving relations between formal equals. Although the practice of global rights and the practice of free states are both marked by formal equality, only the latter practice presupposes, in addition, the absence of a global state. The notable implication is that the currently existing anarchical society of sovereign states (as an institutional alternative to a global state) is an indispensable international practice that cannot be rendered otiose by any global practice. On our account, both the international and the global have importance.

Chapter 5 explores the question of how practices undergo change. The two core practices canvassed in Chapter 4 are subject to dialectical change in Hegel's sense of the term, tied to the notion of internal contradiction. Crudely put, there are deeply troubling aspects within the practice of the society of states and, correlatively, within the global practice of rights. These tensions are generated and subsequently overcome by route of a dialectical relationship within and *between* these two core practices – new tensions are bound to reappear once old ones have been resolved. Thus the problem of delinquent states who turn against their own citizens is overcome by the emergence of norms of humanitarian intervention, whose recognition becomes a precondition for participation in the mature society of free states. Similarly, the free participation of rights-holders in the global free market leads to the proliferation of global private actors with disproportionate amounts of resources who are not subject to public oversight and democratic control, a problem that is partially overcome by the concerted effort of the society of free states.

The conclusion develops the theme of macro practices. It also points to the potential of our practice theory to change the disciplinary practice of teaching and learning IR. The recommended theory cannot settle everyday questions about what we should be doing in international relations by providing 'solutions' or scripts for action. Rather, it is a macro account: it identifies those comprehensive social wholes, the society of states and the practice of global rights, which constitute the ramifications of our most cherished ethical and political concerns as participants in international and global affairs. If we wish to paint an image of international relations, it would not be a physical field of forces of action and repulsion, or an impersonal market mechanism, but a normative realm that has become global. This normative realm is structured by common rules and populated by participants who, most of the time, follow the rules but sometimes also misunderstand or deliberately break them.

Finally, we agree with Wittgenstein and Oakeshott that the proper task of the theorist *qua* theorist is to elucidate the practices under investigation by providing coherent and accurate descriptions. Once again, we should be mindful of the distinction between two levels of activity: *theorising* (which consists in the observation of another activity) and *acting* (which consists in performances).[80] The practice theory outlined in this book is descriptivist (at the level of third-party observation) even though its object is normative (at the level of action), since the practices observed by third parties, at the same time, present normative domains of interaction for the actors directly engaged in them. What follows is an exercise in normative descriptivism.

[80] See note 79.

# A Philosophical Analysis of Social Practices

# 1 Practice Theory
## A Preliminary View

The introductory chapter provided a provisional sketch of the key components of a practice. In the present chapter, we continue to tackle the basic philosophical problem of social practices by raising the following questions: What is the distinction between action without further qualification and action constituted within the framework of a social practice? In what ways does externalism differ from internalism, and why does internalism present the appropriate standpoint for making sense of practices? What principal kinds of practices are there? The arguments supplied here in response to these questions will be further refined in Chapter 3.

## Practice Internalism

In this book, we aim to show that a large class of actions, and particularly interactions, can only be properly understood in the context of the social practices within which they take place. Essentially, our position replaces the ambiguous category of social action with what we deem is a more coherent notion of action inscribed within practices. Thus action does not count as social because a multitude of agents perform it regularly (call this the regularity view) or because agents interact or transact with one another (call this the transactional view). Rather, it counts as social by virtue of being constituted as meaningful *within* the internal domain of a practice. Hence practices are *social* practices by default. Although this sort of argument has often been made, it has all too often been forgotten again. Here we reinstate it as a radically internalist standpoint which makes no concessions to any external point of view. The proviso as before is that 'internalism' (internal point of view) and 'externalism' (external point of view) stand for practice internalism and, correspondingly, for practice externalism. We develop our internalist argument by building on the insights of G. W. F. Hegel,

Ludwig Wittgenstein, and Michael Oakeshott.[1] Despite differences
otherwise, all three philosophers repudiate externalism, the idea that
understanding begins with abstract, invariant knowledge.

The term 'internalism' in this discussion has two distinct but related
meanings. First, it designates an agent perspective. In this sense, it
captures the common understanding which participants in a common
practice share and which enables them to make sense and interact
within their own practice – this theme will be elaborated in Chapter 3,
where we offer a full-fledged philosophical account of practices. In the
present chapter, internalism is explored as an *observational* perspective. Like its externalist rival, this observational standpoint supposes a
relation between a practice (an object) and an observer (a subject) who
attempts to understand the practice. Henceforth, 'observation' stands
for the observational activity of a third-party observer, not an actor
who is already engaged in the practice. For the moment, we may think
of a practice as a common framework of rules imposing conditions for
interaction which, when accepted and enacted by a number of individuals, turn these individuals into a social group. Internalism requires the
observer, in interpreting a practice, to use the categories which its own
participants use in making sense of their practice. That is, the language
of observation must match the language of action (the language used
by the practice participants). Externalism allows the observer to use
categories of analysis drawn from outside the practice so that the
language of observation can differ in principle from the language of
action (at the limit, the language of observation would be a different
*order* of language).

Because internalism – like externalism – is a procedure of coming to
know an object via a procedure of observation, it presupposes a
doctrine of knowledge. Hegel, Oakeshott and the later Wittgenstein
prioritise human understanding over abstract knowledge and see
human understanding as growing out of the context of *concrete* social
practices.[2] Conversely, the external point of view assumes that the

---

[1] G. W. F. Hegel, *Hegel's Philosophy of Right*, trans. T. M. Knox (Oxford: Oxford
University Press, 1967 [1821]); Ludwig Wittgenstein, *Philosophical
Investigations*, 3rd ed., trans. G. E. M. Anscombe (Oxford: Blackwell, 1968
[1953]); Michael Oakeshott, *On Human Conduct* (Oxford: Clarendon Press,
1975).

[2] Hegel discusses the state as a concrete universal (fusing universal with particular
interests) in *The Philosophy of Right*, §§258, 260, 261. His more general

conditions of knowledge are invariant with respect to the observer or the procedure of observation used. It might be tempting to think of Immanuel Kant's epistemology of invariant categories of 'pure reason' as the archetypal example of externalism. But these categories articulate only the *a priori* conditions of the possibility of knowledge; knowledge of actual objects is a product of the faculty of 'understanding' as con-joined with 'sensible intuition'.[3] This capacity for sensibility is a form of receptivity enabling us to experience reality in a particular way. Hence for Kant, what is known depends on the specific traits of the observer and on the cognitive procedure the observer relies on in coming to know. It seems that the precursor of the externalist idiom of invariance is Plato's theory of Forms – or what, closer to our time, Thomas Nagel has described as a 'view from nowhere'.[4]

Internalism places the category of understanding in the spotlight. And as Hegel reminds us, complete understanding is always an under-standing of an identity as something concrete.[5] Contrast the meaning of an abstract proposition 'All Xs are Ys' with the meaning of a concrete utterance, an epigram by Stefan Zweig or the meaning of an abstract action, $\phi$-*ing*, with that of some concrete action – delivering a speech in Parliament, launching a nuclear missile, or donating to Oxfam. Moreover, unlike knowledge, understanding presupposes a meaningful context. While the term 'context' has a wide range, we take it to be isomorphic with the domain of an entire practice so that the meaning of

---

epistemological discussion of the transition from universal to particular and their unity in the individual *qua* concrete universal is found in G. W. F. Hegel, *Hegel's Science of Logic*, trans. A. V. Miller (Atlantic Highlands, NJ: Humanities Press International, 1989), Vol. II, ch. 1 ('The Notion'), pp. 600–622. In *Philosophical Investigations* §§105, 107, 116, Wittgenstein retracts his earlier quest for *the* ultimate order of knowledge about language, construed as an ideal language of logic and mathematics, in favour of ordinary language in its various, concrete manifestations. Hegel's idea of concrete universal is central to Michael Oakeshott's argument about the character of human understanding in *On Human Conduct*, esp. pp. 92–107.

[3] On the role of sensible intuition, see Immanuel Kant, *Critique of Pure Reason*, unified ed., trans. Werner S. Pluhar (Indianapolis: Hackett, 1996 [1781/1787]). 'A' refers to the first edition of 1781 and 'B' to the second edition of 1787. See 'Preface to the Second Edition' (1787), B xxvi, A51/B75, A79/B104.

[4] Plato, *The Republic of Plato*, trans. Francis MacDonald Cornford (Oxford: Oxford University Press, 1945), bk. 6; Thomas Nagel, *The View from Nowhere* (Oxford: Oxford University Press, 1989).

[5] See note 2.

an action (or an utterance) is determined by the meaning of the practice hosting it.

Apart from practices, as observers we may seek to understand actions nested within practices – we label these 'practice-dependent actions' or 'participatory actions'. Here we should pause to note the ambiguity of the term 'action' and distinguish it from a practice. In a broad sense, 'action' designates the realm of doing as opposed to the realm of theorising. This is Aristotle's contrast between *praxis* and *theoria* (contemplation).[6] We refer to it by expressions such as 'action as such', 'action in general' or 'action without further qualification' to disclose its generic character. In a narrow sense, 'action' designates a performance carried out on a particular occasion – for example, Anna watered the flowers or John is playing chess (Aristotle, quite unhelpfully, used the same term, *praxis*, also for action in the narrow sense of dateable performance).[7] The standard premise in the philosophy of action is that a performance brings about a change in a state of the world or in one's understanding and that an agent is the originator of the performance.[8] If we imagine that the general sphere of action (action without further qualification) has been differentiated into various bounded domains of action and interaction, the result will be the notion of practices. Each practice is a common domain of interaction constituted by *rules*. Insofar as these constitutive rules are non-abstract

---

[6] On action (*praxis* in the broad sense) versus *theoria* (contemplation), see Aristotle, *Ethica Nicomachea* (*Nicomachean Ethics*), in *The Works of Aristotle*, Vol. IX, trans. and ed. W. D. Ross (Oxford: Clarendon Press, 1925), NE 1178b20 – the *Nicomachean Ethics* is abbreviated as NE and references are to numbered passages. On the difference between theoretical and practical knowledge, see Aristotle, *Metaphysica* (*Metaphysics*), in *The Works of Aristotle*, Vol. VIII, 2nd ed., ed. W. D. Ross (Oxford: Clarendon Press, 1928), bk. a, 993b 20.

[7] See our discussion in Mervyn Frost and Silviya Lechner, 'Two Conceptions of International Practice: Aristotelian *Praxis* or Wittgensteinian *Language-Games* ', *Review of International Studies* 42 (2) 2016: 334–350.

[8] This standard premise in the metaphysics of action emphasises the problem of change over time. In this sense, all actions are events (an event is a change in a state of affairs that has temporal duration) but not all events are actions, since unlike an event, an action *is brought about* by an agent and does not merely *happen* to the agent. Contrast 'Bob hit the ball' (action) with 'Bob was hit by the ball' (event). Classic works exploring metaphysical questions about actions, events and causes are Judith Jarvis Thompson, *Acts and Other Events* (Ithaca: Cornell University Press, 1977); and Donald Davidson, *Essays on Actions and Events*, 2nd ed. (Oxford: Oxford University Press, 2001).

and intelligible to ordinary human beings, it is a living human institution. Thus instead of one, we have two parallel notions of performance – performance as such (whose counterpart is action as such) and a practice-dependent performance (whose counterpart is a practice).

In any attempt to make sense of performances of either sort, it is crucial to learn how to distinguish between 'getting it right' and 'making a mistake'. It is the notion of *mistake* that is central here. Learning how to deliver an ultimatum involves learning what would count as having failed to deliver it. Because performances are of two basic kinds – either performances as such or practice-dependent performances – there are two modalities of making a mistake. Let us begin by considering performances as such. The first step is to define action as such, which we equate to *meaningful action* in line with our hermeneutic premises, bracketing metaphysical questions of what differentiates actions from events or causal chains.[9] The second step is to elucidate performances and the mistakes they entail. Here we lean on Oakeshott's analysis of intelligent conduct in *On Human Conduct* (1975).

For Oakeshott, conduct is an 'exhibition of intelligence' or, as we may say, it is meaningful action.[10] The category of 'intelligence' constitutes a fundamental 'order of inquiry' that subsumes within itself the entire world, as an understood or interpreted world. It includes the realm of reflection (thought), intelligent conduct (meaningful action) as well as artefacts (books, poems, tools, theories and institutions like the state).[11] A categorically different 'order of inquiry' represents the world as understood in terms of non-intelligent processes – organisms or physical events that exclude reflection, action and learning. Oakeshott says, 'A falling apple does not need to have learned a "law" of gravitation in order to fall.'[12] But 'to recognize a "going-on" as "conduct" is to acknowledge it to be something that has had to be learned.'[13] Everything which has had to be learned by a thinking and choosing human being potentially has meaning. To be actualised, meaning must be

---

[9] See note 8.
[10] The first part of Oakeshott's essay 'On the Theoretical Understanding of Human Conduct', in *On Human Conduct*, pp. 1–107, is devoted to the problem of intelligent (or meaningful) conduct; see pp. 12–54. On conduct as 'exhibition of intelligence', see pp. 13–17, 20–23, 25, 32, 37, 92. On 'intelligence in doing', see p. 39.
[11] Oakeshott, *On Human Conduct*, p. 32.
[12] Oakeshott, *On Human Conduct*, p. 13.
[13] Oakeshott, *On Human Conduct*, p. 32.

understood, interpreted or *recognised* by an actor who is 'reflective consciousness'.[14] The idea here is that any provisional 'going on' is not just recognised (assigned to a basic order of inquiry) but *recognised as* (identified in concrete terms).[15] Thus something can be recognised as an utterance (an exhibit of intelligence), and it can be recognised more concretely as a poetic utterance. In this sense, meaning cannot be what analytic philosophers call 'reference', an abstract logical operation that assigns objects or referents to words.

Oakeshott's view of meaningful action has two components: action and meaning. It qualifies as *action* because 'in acting an agent imagines, wishes for and seeks to achieve a satisfaction; that is, a condition in which the specific unacceptability of his current situation is remedied or abated'.[16] It is *meaningful* in virtue of being an actor's intelligent response to a situation, as an already understood situation. Now we turn from meaningful action to meaningful performances. A performance, Oakeshott writes, 'is a choice to do or to say *this* rather than *that* in relation to imagined and wished-for outcomes'.[17] Action has a formal aspect (it is a type of action) as well as a substantive one (it is a contingent response, substantively determined).[18] A performance represents this contingent aspect: it is a *choice* to act in a certain way carried out on a particular occasion.[19] (So it is permissible to use 'action' in the place of 'performance' with this qualification in mind.) When we seek to understand conduct among human beings, the action observed must be recognised as a response that seeks to elicit a further response from an audience.[20] To qualify as meaningful, both the performance and the response it is supposed to call forth must be

---

[14] On 'reflective consciousness' or 'reflective intelligence', see Oakeshott, *On Human Conduct*, pp. 13–14, 23, 32–33, esp. pp. 36–37, 40, 45, 47, 50, 53, 89, 93, 97.

[15] Oakeshott, *On Human Conduct*, p. 13–14

[16] Oakeshott, *On Human Conduct*, p. 39. In describing the agent, Oakeshott uses the pronoun 'his'.

[17] Oakeshott, *On Human Conduct*, p. 23.

[18] On action as substantively determined and contingent, see Oakeshott, *On Human Conduct*, pp. 36–41, 45, 92–107.

[19] Oakeshott, *On Human Conduct*, pp. 40, 42–45.

[20] Oakeshott's meaningful performance in front of an audience corresponds to Aristotle's *praxis* in the narrow sense or 'doing', to be distinguished from *poiesis* or 'making', even though Oakeshott sees both as compatible. Oakeshott, *On Human Conduct*, pp. 35–36. On the *praxis-poiesis* distinction, see Aristotle, *NE*, 1094a.

*intelligent* or non-mechanical. Since Oakeshott does not spell out the difference between mechanism and intelligence in detail, we may extend his analysis as follows. A machine exemplifies artificial intelligence in that it produces a specific response, or output, to a given input. The mechanism functions correctly if no mistakes are made; mistakes here represent deviations from an established input-output pattern. The obverse holds for *human* intelligence: the observed performance might happen to deviate from the audience's expectation: Alan was expected to do this (recite a poem), but instead, he did that (played trumpet). The *very possibility* that a response to a situation might be deviant within a range – and in this sense, be mistaken – is a mark of human intelligence. The mistake does not render what the actor is doing unintelligible but, paradoxically, makes it intelligible to an observer – as long as it falls within a range and outside the domain of utter unintelligibility. Here the baseline for understanding a specific performance is the broad realm of intelligent conduct.

So far, Oakeshott has supplied an account of meaningful action and of meaningful performances, noting how such performances might misfire. But he has not yet taken up the puzzle of practices and of what we termed 'practice-dependent action'.[21] Notice that this puzzle is not exhausted by the broad (or 'weaker', in philosophical jargon) problem of interpreting meaningful action. Its explication requires additional, more restrictive (or 'stronger') premises linked to another problem – *rule-governed* action. As a first approximation, a practice may be defined as a common institutional framework composed of rules. Rules, to use Oakeshott's definition, are meaningful propositions which specify a particular way, procedure or manner of performing an action.[22] Thus if we can say of an action that it has been performed *in the wrong way* (though not necessarily in the moral sense of wrong), then the action counts as a rule-governed action. For example, the current sentence is written in the right way, as determined by the rules of English grammar. These can be tacitly used – for in writing the sentence correctly, no explicit mention is being made of the rules themselves. What is important is that a rule determines not a type of action but *a way* of performing an action (of whatever type). Compare two distinct types of action – driving

[21] Oakeshott tackles the question of practices in the second part of 'On the Theoretical Understanding of Human Conduct', in Oakeshott, *On Human Conduct*, 55ff.

[22] Oakeshott, *On Human Conduct*, pp. 55–57, 113, 121.

as opposed to running to a nearby hospital – as alternative meaningful responses to a situation of medical emergency. For each, we may ask the corresponding, but altogether different, question of whether the action was done by following rules – to wit, whether in driving to the hospital, the driver followed the rules of the road. Such rules do not instruct the agent what to do (to drive or not to drive) but rather stipulate how to do it (in what manner one is supposed to be driving – say, on the left side of the road).[23] It is easy to see that the question of what represents an appropriate *way of performing* an action (driving on the left) involves a set of more restrictive premises than the question of whether a certain *type of action* (driving as such) is an appropriate response to a situation.

Once we move from the broad concept of action as such to the more restrictive notion of practice-dependent action, the attendant notion of performative mistake changes accordingly. In the former case, the making of a mistake is a contingent possibility (it might happen) and covers a vast range of performances which, in being mistaken, are still recognisable as meaningful. In the latter case, the mistake serves as a *strict* criterion of identity – it identifies the mistaken performance as governed by a specific rule. A practice, as mentioned, is a framework of rules. Since within the practice, doing something in *this way* counts as wrong and doing something in *that way* counts as right, the mistake points, strictly, to the background existence of a concrete rule (norm) that governs the action. On this normative view of mistakes, articulated by the Wittgensteinian philosopher Peter Winch, a mistake is the tell sign of rule-dependent action, a point we shall return to on multiple occasions.[24]

Internalism, it follows, has two distinct forms. *Meaning internalism* supposes that an action (or an utterance) has concrete, contextual meaning. Actions and utterances are interpreted *via* a hermeneutic procedure where the object of interpretation is treated as a 'text' that

---

[23] Some philosophers refer to the 'how' aspect of rules as their *adverbial* aspect. See J. L. Austin, 'A Plea for Excuses', *Proceedings of the Aristotelian Society* 57 1956–1957: 1–30, pp. 13, 16. Curiously, for Austin, this adverbial feature covers only a limited class of actions (p. 16), whereas for Oakeshott, it is central to rule-dependent and practice-dependent action. See Oakeshott, *On Human Conduct*, pp. 55–57.

[24] Peter Winch, *The Idea of a Social Science and Its Relation to Philosophy* (London: Routledge, 1958), p. 32.

must be read in its proper context.[25] But a practice, as presented here, is a finer-grained notion than meaningful context, and the procedure of understanding practices is more intricate than a contextualised reading of texts, even though the components of language and meaning are immensely important in elucidating the logic of practices, as we shall see later on. For now, we may define 'practices' *as distinctive domains of intelligent action and interaction, structured by common rules* (a complete explication is given in Chapter 3). On this preliminary definition, a practice comprises a whole – a constellation of rules of conduct that are followed in common by a social group. To this category belong rituals and ceremonies, social institutions such as the family, juridical and political institutions such as the state and inter- national society, which is a society made of states. In the light of these considerations, the proper label for our position is 'practice internalism' (henceforth, 'internalism'), as it shows that the object to be understood is not meaningful action *per se* but a practice or human institution.

## Internalism, Externalism and Social Science

In this section, we shall introduce the two rival elementary standpoints for understanding practices – externalism and internalism – and eluci- date their relation to social science. It is assumed that the object to be understood is either a practice as a whole or an action falling within its domain (practice-dependent action).

What observational standpoint is appropriate for describing a practice *as a whole?* We follow Winch, who denied that social science can provide such a standpoint.[26] By 'social science', Winch meant a systematic body of knowledge which seeks to explain human activity, of whatever kind, by invoking invariant (externalist) criteria such as rationality or impartiality. But different practices, as bounded domains of human activity, have distinctive internal logics, which cannot be illuminated by such prefabricated criteria. On this basis, Winch urged a return of social science to philosophy, as a critical activity which does not posit a degree of uniformity across practices but investigates their distinctiveness. Effectively, Winch was suggesting that social science is not an absolute standpoint for making sense of reality; it is a *practice*

---

[25] On hermeneutics, see the text accompanying notes 34 and 35.
[26] Winch, *The Idea of a Social Science.*

with its own internal criteria, which therefore it would be inappropriate to employ in the study of non-scientific practices. The intention of Winch's plea for rendering social science more philosophical was to adduce support for Wittgenstein's view that the proper task of philosophy is to describe and not to prescribe or explain.[27] That is, as social scientists, we are supposed to be crafting descriptions of practices from 'the inside' by taking into account their internal logics.[28] Winch's commitment to descriptivism is important because it is connected to internalism: it singles out practices as a special object of observation and the proper – characteristically internalist – procedure for grasping their identity.[29] Internalism holds that in observing a practice, the social scientist must not rely on a technical language that deviates from the one used inside the practice observed (the sin of the proverbial social scientist as portrayed by Winch) because doing so would open a gulf between two orders of language: description (by the actors themselves) and explanation (by the social scientists observing what the actors are doing or saying ). The internalist procedure of observation rejects the categorical distinction between explanation and description by imposing the requirement that the language through which observers investigate (i.e., 'explain') a practice is, at bottom, the same as the language of self-description its participants use in making sense of their own practice.

This sketch suffices to convey the idea of an observer who proceeds to study social practices from 'within'. More complicated is the question of how particular actions located within practices are to be properly observed. Examples of such actions from the sphere of international relations include declaring a war, signing a peace treaty, issuing an ultimatum and voting on a resolution in the United Nations. The understanding of such actions may be sought as a prerequisite for

[27] See our argument about descriptivism in the Introduction under 'Internalism, Elucidation and Social Science'.

[28] Wittgenstein's descriptivism has been rearticulated by Winch in *The Idea of a Social Science*. On Winch's critique of social science, see Phil Hutchinson, Rupert Read and Wes Sharrock, *There Is No Such Thing as a Social Science: In Defence of Peter Winch* (Aldershot: Ashgate, 2008); and John G. Gunnell, 'Can Social Science Be Just?', *Philosophy of the Social Sciences* 39 (4) 2009: 595–621.

[29] We discuss Winch's radical internalism in Mervyn Frost and Silviya Lechner, 'Understanding International Practices from the Internal Point of View', *Journal of International Political Theory* 12 (3) 2016: 299–319.

action or for its own sake. Either way, the difficulty is that the object we are seeking to understand is not 'given' or immediately intelligible.

We propose to get to internalism by route of descriptivism. Our descriptivist thesis holds that actions from the general class of rule-governed action and its sister concept, practice-dependent action, are only available under a description. The reason is that actions from this class are not identifiable by their physical properties alone; even when a partial physical identification is possible, it is insufficient to determine whether the agent is acting by following rules or not. Consider one typical subclass of rule-governed action. It is exemplified by Alan, who is crossing the street while following the rule 'Stop when the traffic light turns red; go when the traffic light turns green.' If this action is performed on a regular basis, an observer may discern what Alan is doing ('Crossing the street at a green light') by correlating Alan's bodily movements with the occurrence of green light and without knowing the rule involved. Nonetheless, a simple observation of this sort cannot settle the issue of whether, in crossing the street, Alan is *following* a certain rule or whether his action accidentally *complies* with the rule: in both cases, his physical movements are identical. To distinguish rule compliance from rule-following, it is necessary to have a description of the rule from the start.

Let us consider another major subclass of rule-governed action. Imagine that the question posed by an observer, 'What is the agent doing?', receives the answer 'Scoring a goal'. In this case, the action description cannot be generated unless one knows the rules of football. Absent such knowledge, the observer could at most say, 'A person is kicking a ball over a beam'. Contrariwise, the action we just described as 'crossing the street' is intelligible without an appeal to a rule. The thrust of our argument in this book is that games like football or practices like diplomacy are domains of rule-governed activity inside which the performance of actions depends logically on a set of basic rules. In the Introduction, such basic rules were labelled 'constitutive rules' (John Searle's expression), a topic revisited in Chapter 3.[30] As noted, with respect to an action constituted by rules, its putative description is rendered true not by states of affairs in the external

---

[30] See notes 55 and 71 on Searle in the Introduction. On constitutive rules, see John R. Searle, *Speech Acts: An Essay in the Philosophy of Language* (Cambridge: Cambridge University Press, 1969), pp. 33–36. On action description that requires constitutive rules, see p. 36.

world but by the constitutive rules of a practice. At work is an internalist criterion of truth, truth-as-relevance, which has purchase inside
the domain of a given practice but not outside it; what is true or
relevant within the game of football is not true or relevant within the
practice of diplomacy. That this internalist criterion is tied to a practice,
as a specific practice, is what sets it apart from the externalist criterion of
truth, truth-as-correspondence, which is invariant. Stated differently, if
we look for *relevant* action descriptions, then the practice which encloses
this sort of descriptions cannot be construed in some abstract, formalised terms. Indeed, it must be recognisable as a *concrete* practice that is
substantively and not merely formally distinctive from other practices.

Our internalist position suggests that in attempting to understand a
practice-dependent action that is not yet understood, all observers,
including social scientists, are in principle no differently situated to a
novice learning how to carry out the action for the first time. If, for
instance, we are trying to make sense of the meaning of an action that
may provisionally be described as 'A person putting a slip of paper in
that box' – a manoeuvre that we shall later come to recognise as
'Voting in a referendum' – we are in the position of those who are
learning how to vote *ab initio*. We shall have to learn the complex set of
rules which determines what voting in a referendum means, how it is
done correctly, and how to distinguish it from other actions that involve
putting slips of paper into boxes (as in inserting a five-pound note into a
collection box for charity). The idea is that this *concrete* practice, voting
in a referendum, has its own set of substantively distinctive criteria and
therefore its own relevant set of descriptions. Such criteria are anchored
to a practice *qua* a concrete domain of rule-following activity and
cannot be legitimately extrapolated to the analysis of other practices.

In contradistinction, externalism is a standpoint that gravitates
towards invariance, reduction and abstraction. It is represented by
the invariant method of orthodox social science, which involves an
abstract observational procedure positing in advance of analysis what
is to count as an adequate 'fit' between a given description (the hypothesis employed by the investigator) and the actions being described (the
object of investigation).[31] Although such an abstract method enables
generalisation across a large number of cases, it comes at a high price,

---

[31]  See Richard Rorty, *Philosophy and the Mirror of Nature* (Oxford: Basil
Blackwell, 1980).

since it assumes away the distinctiveness of the diverse provinces of human activity comprising our practical life. Internalism acknowledges the distinctiveness of practices. Recall Wittgenstein's remark that practices exhibit a bewildering variety, which is why finding the foundational criterion that underpins them all is a chimera.[32] Yet, apart from the notion of 'family resemblance', he did not specify how we should go about differentiating the identity of a concrete practice amidst other practices. We propose such a procedure: it requires limiting the comparison to two concrete practices at a time. Comparing two intelligible, concrete identities yields an intelligible result that also means something concrete. We can always tell how voting differs from chess playing or how chess playing differs from playing football. But if we became overambitious and tried to determine in what respects a large number (and at the limit, all possible) practices differ, then the permutations measuring their differences would grow exponentially, and we would not be able to describe them in a finite number of steps.[33] Alternatively, an object can be assumed to have a set of bedrock metaphysical properties which determine its identity. But if Wittgenstein's anti-foundationalist argument is correct, this is precisely what we cannot do. No hidden bedrock property (or set of properties) is common to practices such as voting, chess playing, and boxing; the more practices we add to the list, the more elusive this bedrock property gets. It seems that the best avenue for advancing our understanding is to seek to establish how practices *differ* (in substantive terms) and not what intrinsic properties they share.

The upshot is that externalism exerts a pull towards foundations and reduction to metaphysically basic properties, while internalism is committed to an observational procedure of differentiation between concrete practices. It is a central internalist thesis that different social practices have different *internal criteria* for establishing the truth (truth-as-relevance) of descriptions made within them. When we say that criteria of relevance differ across practices, the term 'different' is

---

[32] As Wittgenstein remarks in well-known passages in *the Philosophical Investigations* (§§65, 66), no invariant set of properties is common to all practices – at most, *some* practices share loose 'family resemblances' (§67).

[33] Nardin develops this point in his discussion of sovereignty. If two sovereign authorities contest whose authority is higher, a concrete answer can be found. If the question pertains to a larger number of authorities, it has no answer in a finite system of rules. Terry Nardin, 'The Diffusion of Sovereignty', *History of European Ideas* 41 (1) 2015: 89–102, esp. 92.

used in a strong sense, to mean *distinct* and *distinctive*. For example, the criteria for determining the rightness of a decision by a judge in the International Court of Justice are distinct and distinctive compared to those that determine the right outcome in an international TV game show such as the Eurovision Song Contest, to those used by universal churches to determine who qualifies for sainthood. In each case, observers need to identify the concrete social practice within which the relevant descriptions are made, and this demands learning how the specialised vocabularies are *used* by its participants. This, in rough terms, is the position we put forward under the rubric of internalism.

Our brand of internalism entails a critique of social science which resonates with the hermeneutic approach, also known as the *Verstehen* approach. In its modern version, its origins are attributed to nineteenth-century German philosophers Wilhelm Dilthey and Johann Gustav Droysen, who were interested in the historical world and the modes of understanding appropriate to it.[34] For Dilthey, an interpreter seeks to understand the 'lived experience' (*Erlebnis*) of actors by *reliving* it (*nacherleben*). Dilthey contrasts *Verstehen*, 'understanding', concerned with interpreting meaningful mental objects from 'the inside', by reliving the experiences that constitute them, with *Erklären*, 'explanation' from 'the outside', concerned with causal laws that govern physical events (that are not themselves meaningful).[35] Causal laws disclose nature as an atemporal structure, lived experiences unfold in history. Thus 'understanding' represents the method of the 'sciences of the mind' (*Geisteswissenschaften*) – human sciences as we would call them nowadays – whereas 'explanation' is the method of the natural sciences. Dilthey's view of the human sciences as capturing the historicity of experience resembles Wilhelm Windelband's distinction between ideographic

---

[34] Johann G. Droysen, *Grundriss Der Historik* (*Outline of the Principles of History*), trans. E. Benjamin Andrews as *Droysen's Principles of History* (Boston: Ginn, 1893 [1858]); and Wilhelm Dilthey, *Introduction to the Human Sciences, Selected Works*, Vol. I, ed. Rudolf A. Makkreel and Frithjof Rodi (Princeton: Princeton University Press, 1989). See also Anthony O'Hear, *Verstehen and Humane Understanding* (New York: Cambridge University Press, 1996).

[35] Dilthey, *Introduction to the Human Sciences*, 57ff. Dilthey includes in the category of the human sciences the social sciences (anthropology, sociology, psychology and economics). The question of whether the 'reliving of experiences' amounts to empathy or is, instead, non-psychological is an intricate one, considering that for Dilthey, 'experience' is manifest in forms transcending the individual mind such as artefacts, actions and texts.

sciences (history) and nomothetic sciences (physics).[36] It is important to emphasise that our defence of the *Verstehen* approach is not driven by a wish to reinvent the virtues of ideography or the reliving of experiences; its rationale is to acknowledge the pre-interpreted character of social practices. We urge social scientists to interpret practices from the internal point of view because each practice, as a meaningful social whole, pre-exists any such interpretive effort. In Winch's apt expression, 'Our practice is *prior to* any interpretation.'[37] Granted that the meaning of this social whole has *already* been understood by its own participants, this stock of understandings imposes a limit on the range of subsequent interpretations by an observer – not every interpretation is equally good (the problem of understanding pre-existing understandings is known as double hermeneutics). Therefore, the ground of our criticism of the contemporary social sciences such as economics, sociology and political science is not that they side with 'explanation' *contra* 'understanding' but that they are prone to be externalist standpoints. The internalist stance permeating the present project is directed not against explanation as such – since on our premises proper explaining just is understanding – but against the *externalist method of explanation* that so often characterises science as a mode of enquiry.

The proposed view about the role of social science in the understanding of practices from 'the inside' would be familiar to anthropologists who seek to make sense of the conventions and rituals of foreign tribes.[38] Simply observing the physical movements of tribe members will not reveal the meaning of what they are doing or, indeed, whether they are doing anything at all. The internal point of view implies that observation commences with a modicum of *prior* understanding, not with blank ignorance.

---

[36] Resemblance only, since for Windelband, understanding does not presuppose empathy or psychologism. Wilhelm Windelband, 'Rectorial Address, Strasbourg, 1894' ('Windelband on History and Natural Science'), *History and Theory* 19 (2) 1980: 169–185, p. 175. See translator's note by Guy Oakes in Wilhelm Windelband and Guy Oakes, 'History and Natural Science', *History and Theory* 19 (2) 1980: 165–168.

[37] Peter Winch, 'Facts and Superfacts', in Peter Winch, *Trying to Make Sense* (Oxford: Basil Blackwell, 1987), pp. 54–63, p. 57, emphasis added. This argument is applied to IR by John G. Gunnell in 'Can Social Science Be Just?', pp. 599–601 and 'Social Scientific Inquiry and Meta-Theoretical Fantasy: The Case of International Relations', *Review of International Relations* 37 (4) 2011: 1447–1469, esp. pp. 1467–1468.

[38] See, for example, Harold Garfinkel, *Studies in Ethnomethodology* (Malden, MA: Polity Press, 1967).

The process of understanding cannot get off the ground unless we, as observers, already understand – provisionally and perhaps defectively – the meaning of the action observed. Understanding is a concept which allows for degrees, so the contrast here is not between no understanding and understanding but between confused understanding and proper understanding. For example, if we were fully ignorant of the conventions of international diplomacy, attending to the physical behaviour of certain people exchanging pieces of papers would not reveal to us what they are doing – namely, diplomats presenting their diplomatic credentials to a foreign government. Analogously, observing the bodily movements of foreign warriors would not reveal the meaning of their war dance to those ignorant of the meaning of the background military culture.

An internalist understanding that adopts the point of view of the participants in a practice under observation cannot be acquired by identifying invariant relationships between variables, measuring specified 'bits' of behaviour. Imagine that a political scientist has established a correlation between two variables – 'visiting places of worship' and 'preparing for battle' – that is invoked to explain the behaviour of a tribe of warriors. Although this correlation may match the internal (meaning-ful) relationship between an act of worship and fighting, as understood by the warriors themselves, this match would be accidental. The culprit here is the externalist method of scientific observation. Its externalism is revealed in its invariance: the type of relationship holding between the *relata* does not change when their identity changes; it is a purely quantitative relationship. Compare this with a qualitative relationship – 'man' and 'child' (a relationship of parenthood). If the *relata* change to 'man' and 'wife', a qualitatively new relationship (between spouses) will result. Returning to the relationship posited by the political scientist, we may note that it remains invariant (it is a quantitative relationship of correlation) regardless of whether the variable 'preparing for battle' is correlated to the variable 'visiting places of worship' or to a completely different variable, say, 'experiencing a drought'. From the standpoint of the warriors themselves, however, the scientific hypothesis linking the preparation for battle to the occurrence of drought remains external – indeed, incomprehensible – since for them, such preparation makes sense solely in relation to the notion of visiting places of worship.

In sum, the major defect of externalism is that it outstrips the bound-aries of what is intelligible to the agents under study. An internalist understanding by a third-party observer who attempts to make sense of human conduct inscribed in a practice would not be one-to-one identical with the understanding of those observed: the 'theorems' that fascinate the theorist are not the 'pragmata' guiding the actor towards a wished-for goal.[39] Unlike an externalist observation, internalism minimises the distance between observers and actors. When observing a practice, a third-party observer committed to internalism is required to learn what the actors who are new to the practice must themselves learn in order to become *bone fide* participants – the art of appropriate performances. Mastering this art presupposes that the seasoned partici- pants will teach the novices what to do and that the novices will learn to distinguish correct from mistaken performances.

The message of practice internalism, then, is that even though as social scientists we adopt the role of third-party observers, we are not positioned outside the practice observed; we are inside it, under- standing (if not necessarily acting) like participants, judging whether certain actions have been successfully completed or whether mistakes have been made. In the following section, we shall clarify further the character of practice-dependent action by distinguishing it from the category of simple action.

## Simple Action and Practice-Dependent Action

### Simple Action

Certain actions such as walking, strolling, marching and skipping can be categorised as instances of *simple action* or action whose successful performance does not require observance of the conditions specified in any social practice. Simple action represents one possible sub-category of action and should not to be confused with the generic category of action as such (or action without further qualification) discussed in the first section. A key intuition is that simple actions can be properly described as physically determined bodily movements.[40] But the

---

[39] See Oakeshott, *On Human Conduct*, pp. 33–34, 40.

[40] In this account of simple actions, we are not implying an altogether different distinction between *basic* and *complex* actions. Basic actions cannot be reduced to the performance of yet more basic actions, whereas complex actions can only be done through the performance of basic actions. For example, opening a door involves the basic actions of gripping the handle, turning the knob, pulling it towards one and so on. See Jane R. Martin, 'Basic Actions and Simple Actions', *American Philosophical Quarterly* 9 (1) 1972: 59–69, p. 59.

difficulty is that the category of simple action is disjunctive.[41] Apart from the already mentioned notion of action which stands outside social practices (it can be labelled 'simple physical action'), it also includes the opposite notion of simple action nested within social practices (or 'simple social action'). Unlike the former, the latter category invokes a non-physicalist description that assumes the context of social practices as its starting point. This change in the relevant description – from physicalist to non-physicalist or social – changes the identity of the action concerned. Once we enter the world of social practices, it is no longer the case that we perform a given action, for example, marching, simply by virtue of the physical capacities at our disposal. Rather, we have been *taught* that doing this – in this particular way – counts as 'marching'. We know how to march because we have learned to distinguish the description 'marching' from 'walking' and 'running', 'smiling' and 'frowning', 'standing' and 'sitting', 'singing' and 'shouting'. As Oakeshott pointed out, a practice is a social engagement of teaching and learning: it is a human accomplishment, not a natural or physical process.[42] As such, it can only be mastered through effort and it can be mastered well or ill. The general consideration is that outside of a social context, we would have no way of acquiring the understanding requisite to establish that such-and-such way of acting counts as marching and not, say, as walking, particularly when both actions involve the same physical movements. But even though actions of this sort have a social dimension, they still qualify as simple because it is possible to learn how to perform them – how to walk, kick a ball, ride a bike, fly a kite, fire a rifle and swim – within the relevant practice, without having to learn any complex social facts about the practice as a whole. This set of actions exemplify *simple social actions*.

Many technical actions, although they might be complex to perform, fall into this category. Examples include setting up satellite communications links, measuring the width of a hole in the ozone layer and gauging the size of fish stocks in a sea. Here is an example taken from international history of a simple action that went wrong. In the run-up to the Boer War (1896–1902), Cecil Rhodes concocted a plan to foster

---

[41] In logic, a disjunction has the form 'X *or* Y'. It is true if X is true, *or* if Y is true, *or* if both X and Y are true. This last option indicates that X and Y, though distinct, are not mutually exclusive and can be brought together into a disjunctive category.

[42] Oakeshott, *On Human Conduct*, pp. 57–59, 91, 112, 120.

a rebellion in the Transvaal Republic, aiming to gain control for Britain of the gold mining boom that was taking place there. Rhodes set about instigating an uprising of miners in Johannesburg, against the government of the Republic. Part of the plan called for the cutting of the telegraph line which linked the Boer government in Pretoria with the outside world. Instead of cutting the telegraph wire, the rebels cut a fencing wire. They had made a mistake which had significant consequences. Identifying such a failed simple action is straightforward. No detailed knowledge of the historical background of the conflict, the local culture or international practices in which the actor is operating is required of a person learning how to cut a telegraph wire or of anyone venturing to understand such a simple action. A variety of such simple technical actions are carried out in international relations every day. These might relate to creating and maintaining the components of international cyber networks such as the internet or carrying out tests of pollution levels in the upper atmosphere or in the oceans. What the engineers do with regard to these matters can be described without reference to any social practices. Someone learning to run tests on the salinity of the Mediterranean Sea does not need to know about the states surrounding it or the companies exploiting it. Similarly, the conduct of war involves any number of simple actions such as shooting, firing missiles, controlling drones or using radar early warning systems. Identifying mistakes made in executing these simple actions does not require knowledge of social practices, including international practices. It is important for our purposes to distinguish such simple social actions from practice-dependent actions which exemplify complex social actions.

## Practice-Dependent Action

There is a class of actions whose successful performance is conditional on following the rules of a social practice – what we refer to as 'practice-dependent actions' or 'participatory actions'. To understand such actions and learn how to perform them in the first place presupposes that we have an understanding of the rules and attendant usages of the social practice as a whole, including the actions and anticipated reactions of other participants in the practice. A condition for the successful completion of a participatory action, by a single participant, is the taking into account of the anticipated actions and reactions of other participants in the practice. This anticipation is not a matter of probability – namely, that others are *likely* to act or react as they have regularly done in the past – but is normatively determined: there are rules (or norms) specifying what actions count as proper within this specific practice, and mistaken actions that infringe on the norms provoke hostile reactions. A variety of participatory actions are housed within specific practices. Here are a few examples: scoring a goal, writing an academic essay, making a political speech, issuing verdict in a court case, signing a commercial contract, taking marriage vows, voting, writing a book, staging a demonstration (strike, sit-in), swearing an oath of allegiance to a state, declaring war, guarding a border and negotiating a cease fire. In all of these, executing the action involves a 'performative' – or colloquially, it involves 'the making of a move' – within the context of the relevant institution or practice.[43] As with all rule-governed actions, we only come to understand practice-dependent actions (participatory actions) *after* we have learned how to distinguish between getting it right and making mistakes.

Judging whether a practice-dependent action has been successfully executed or whether a mistake has been made is much more complicated than it would be with regard to a simple (social) action such as riding a bicycle. The reason is that to determine whether a participatory action has been correctly performed, we should consider a whole set of criteria internal to the relevant practice – amongst other things, whether the actor was a qualified participant in this concrete practice, whether what was done was one of the legitimate manoeuvres available to all bona fide participants, whether it was done in the appropriate circumstances and (sometimes) whether it was in accord with the underlying values built into the practice. Imagine that an observer has to describe a move made by a boxer participating in a boxing match. To accomplish this, the observer must ascertain whether the person who knocked down an opponent was a *bone-fide* participant in the match (and not someone who is pretending to be boxing), whether the

---

[43] A path-breaking work on performatives is J. L. Austin, *How to Do Things with Words*, 2nd ed., ed. J. O. Urmson and Marina Sbisà (Cambridge, MA: Harvard University Press, 1975 [1962]). Austin analyses *performative verbs* (such as 'to promise', 'to request', 'to name', 'to baptise', 'to warn') to show that for this class of verbs, saying something ('I promise') is not just making a report but performing an action (promising). A theory of *performative acts* or speech acts stipulating that speaking is a form of rule-governed activity was developed later by Searle in *Speech Acts*.

move made was appropriate to the game, whether it amounted to falling into a trap set by the player's adversary and whether it was made in the context of a suitable short-, medium- and long-term strategy. If the move fell short of any of these criteria, we would say that the player had made a mistake in doing what he or she did.

It is important to differentiate between two types of mistakes: 'constitutive' and strategic. A player must learn the constitutive rules of a given game – boxing, in this case – to be able to participate in it. Mistakes which violate the basic rules of the game amount to constitutive mistakes: the resultant moves are invalid. But in order to win a given match, each player also needs a strategy: a sequence of moves which culminate in a winning outcome and which are permitted by the rules. It is possible to make a strategic mistake by inadvertently picking a move that deviates from the chosen strategy. While understanding mistakes, in both the generic (constitutive) and the strategic sense, is a key aspect of understanding failed instances of practice-dependent action, in this study we focus on the more elementary problem of practices as social wholes and on the relation between simple action and practice-dependent action.

## Purposive Association and Practical Association

### Purposive Association

One final question we take up in this chapter concerns the basic types of social practices. We begin with Oakeshott's point that it is wrong to assume that all institutionalised human associations automatically qualify as practices. Agents may interact in terms of sporadic or even one-off transactions, or they can be related on a durable basis, within standing institutions or associations. Oakeshott goes on to distinguish 'enterprise association' from 'civil association' (whose model is the state as a system of law), where the latter represents the 'practical' or non-instrumental mode of association.[44] In *Law, Morality, and the*

---

[44] Oakeshott, *On Human Conduct*, pp. 114–119, 157–158, 315–317. The distinction between civil and enterprise association is a *modal* distinction. As such, this distinction is categorical (non-graded) as well as ideal (purged from empirical elements). Modality, construed as an epistemological category of understanding rather than as a metaphysical category of being, is central to Oakeshott's *Experience and Its Modes* (Cambridge: Cambridge University Press, 1933).

*Relations of States*, Terry Nardin has reworked Oakeshott's argument for the domestic state into an account of international relations by replacing the term 'enterprise' with 'purposive' association'.[45] Inside such associations, members are united by the pursuit of some common goal or purpose. In international relations, for example, Microsoft is an enterprise whose aim is to develop, produce and distribute computer software for profit; British Petroleum is a consortium set up to discover and exploit oil and gas on a global scale; the North Atlantic Treaty Organisation (NATO) is a defence organisation uniting the United States, Canada and a number of European states and Oxfam is an international charity directed towards relieving poverty. Individuals join this type of organisation with the aim of securing the purposes for which it was created. Their participation may depend on the mastering of specialised skills needed for the achievement of the goals of that enterprise. Understanding actions in highly specialised enterprise associations might require considerable technical knowledge about a complex range of actors, their roles and the standards of compliance expected of them within the organisation.

The defining trait of purposive association is already contained in its title. This kind of association is integrated around a shared, fixed purpose which might be the making of profit, the provision of development aid or the provision of security. The relationship between members and the association itself has a voluntary character. Once its purpose has been achieved, the association might go out of business, and some specialists might leave the association to work for another one with better prospects. Efficiency is the major preoccupation of all such associations. In general, this should be easy to measure, and such organisations regularly employ consultants to advise them on how to maximise their efficiency. The rationality inherent in such organisations is a means/ends rationality.[46] The core question when analysing actions undertaken within associations of this sort is always, Is the organisation optimally arranged to achieve its purposes? If the organisation is in competition with other organisations trying to achieve the same purpose, it may be important to maintain internal secrecy about

---

[45] Terry Nardin, *Law, Morality, and the Relations of States* (Princeton, NJ: Princeton University Press, 1983), pp. 4–5.

[46] On instrumental rationality, see Max Weber, *Economy and Society: An Outline of Interpretive Sociology*, ed. G. Roth and C. Wittich (Berkley: University of California Press, 1978).

the methods of operation within the enterprise. Understanding and describing what is being done by a single actor (or many) within this kind of association requires an understanding of the organisation as a whole. But the interpretation of individual actions in an enterprise association is straightforward and so, too, is the evaluation of its performance as a whole. What has to be determined is whether the individual actor or the organisation itself was successful in achieving its projected purposes.

Enterprise associations may develop rules and procedures which specify *how* the common goal of the association is to be best achieved. Thus actors engaged in enterprises have to follow the normal procedures which specify the conditions for performing the requisite participatory actions. For example, in all natural resources exploration companies, before commencing drilling, engineers must consider whether certain standards pertaining to health and safety have been implemented by the safety team and those in charge of storage. They need to know whether the sub-contractors installing the safety equipment have understood these standards. Over time, the common usage of such rules, standards and procedures may give rise to common practices. But although practices may emerge and become part of the functioning of an enterprise association, they do not constitute its ground. What grounds the association is the *common purpose* uniting its members. Hence the rules and procedures the members employ represent convenient instruments for achieving this purpose; if better instruments could be devised, the current ones would be discarded and the enterprise would continue to function – presumably even more efficiently than before. Enterprise associations in effect give us at most an instrumental conception of practices.

## Practical Association

The instrumental conception of practices treats practices as an auxiliary element of an enterprise association. A categorically distinct type of association can be postulated, whose fundament is composed of practices. It is reflected in what Nardin calls 'practical association', whose opposite category is 'purposive association'.[47] The former

---

[47] Nardin, *Law, Morality, and the Relations of States*, pp. 6–14, esp. pp. 8–10. Oakeshott includes an element of practices within enterprise associations

corresponds to our concept of a practice. Its distinguishing trait is that it is not directed towards achieving some external goal; instead, it specifies common conditions that its participants are required to observe in pursuing self-chosen goals. Participants in practical associations are not partners in an enterprise but individuals who subscribe to common *conditions*.[48] Because this subscription is limited to common conditions and does not imply a further commitment to common goals and purposes, it allows a wide range of actors with divergent projects and life plans to co-exist.[49] One good example is the speaking of a natural language such as English. The rules of English grammar do not dictate particular sentences or utterances to language users but enable them to speak or write properly, whatever utterances or sentences they may wish to articulate. Another example are the rules of the highway code: they do not prescribe where users of a highway system must go or what purposes they must pursue.[50] The highway code enables them to get along while using the road system to reach any destination of their choice.

A practical (civil) association has the character of an authoritative practice. Nardin, who theorises international law, describes it as an authoritative practice of the society of states that determines the basic conditions of state-to-state interactions. Here authority is understood as a source of final, overriding or 'exclusionary reasons' for acting in Joseph Raz's terms.[51] Reasons of this type block other, non-authoritative reasons. An authoritative practice constrains the inter-actions of its participants by setting *limits* on the proper means they

(*On Human Conduct*, p. 122). Nardin excises this element from enterprises. He draws a basic distinction between 'purposive associations' as goal-based and 'practical associations' as rule-based (*Law, Morality, and the Relations of States*, pp. 10–11). On the contrast between practical and purposive association, see also Terry Nardin, 'Globalization and the Public Realm', *Critical Review of International Social and Political Philosophy* 12 (2) 2009: 297–312, pp. 298–300.

[48] On rules as conditions of performing an action, see Oakeshott, *On Human Conduct*, pp. 55–56, 112–113, 120.

[49] Nardin, *Law, Morality, and the Relations of States*, p. 8.

[50] Nardin, *Law, Morality, and the Relations of States*, pp. 7–8.

[51] Nardin adopts his concept of authority from Joseph Raz's notion of 'exclusionary reasons' (*Law, Morality, and the Relations of States*, p. 11n7). The reference is to Joseph Raz, *Practical Reasons and Norms* (London: Hutchinson, 1975), p. 39. On authority, see note 58.

can use in attaining their goals.[52] But a state or, correlatively, a society of states is an authoritative practice with respect to *law*. Its character of a common legal authority is captured by the idea that 'citizens agree to disagree and accept the outcomes of authoritative [i.e., overriding] procedures for settling disputes'.[53] Because the baseline is marked by common procedures and not by common ends, an authoritative practice, as already noted, is non-instrumental. Last, but not least, authoritative practices exhibit normativity. The language of authority is, at the same time, the language of rights and thus of obligations correlated with rights. That the state holds final juridical authority (sovereignty) in the realm of law it creates means that it has a right to rule and that its citizens have an obligation to follow the law of the realm.[54] But a state which represents a non-instrumental, authoritative practice 'respects the rights of citizens to pursue their own purposes'.[55]

## Constitutive and Authoritative Practices

In the preceding sections, we sketched two kinds of associations: purposive and 'practical'. The defining feature of the first is that they are directed towards the achievement of specific goals (and hence include instrumental practices). The defining feature of the second is that they make a common life possible between actors who have diverse aims, aspirations and life plans (and hence embody non-instrumental practices). Purposive associations are voluntary associations – their participants are at liberty to contract in and out of these social arrangements without adverse implications. Their associational life would be similar to that portrayed by Alexis de Tocqueville in his *Democracy in America*.[56] De Tocqueville described American associational life as one where actors have created multiple associations for advancing their interests. In such practices, the fundamental 'atoms' of the edifice are individual men and women (or collective actors, like states) who, through contract, combine to form groups for a range of different purposes. As the bond between the individual and the association is an instrumental one, the actor's membership of the association is

---

[52] Nardin, *Law, Morality, and the Relations of States*, esp. pp. 233–234.
[53] Nardin, 'Globalization and the Public Realm', p. 299.
[54] Nardin, 'Globalization and the Public Realm', p. 299.
[55] Nardin, 'Globalization and the Public Realm', p. 300.
[56] Alexis de Tocqueville, *Democracy in America*, trans. Henry Reeve, ed. Isaac Kramnick (New York: Norton, 2007).

not constitutive of his, her or its (where 'it' refers to a collective actor such as a state) status or identity in any fundamental sense.

This is in sharp contrast to what might be termed constitutive practices. A practice is 'constitutive' where it determines, indeed constitutes, the identity of its participants. It is holist in that it is not just an aggregate of atomic units: the participating individuals. To elucidate the idea, we may compare people forming a crowd (atomism) with people coming together in a state as citizens (holism). This holist perspective of the state is adopted by Hegel, who claims that it is only within the state that individuals come to enjoy the status of a citizen (a theme of Chapter 4). Were the state to collapse, they would no longer be citizens. Constitution, on this Hegelian construal, presupposes self-consciousness: inside their shared practice, participants see themselves, and are seen by other participants, as bearers of an identity. This identity is of fundamental value to them. And since this valued identity is constituted within a practice as a social whole, this whole itself carries more than an instrumental value for its members. Thus constitutive practices and authoritative practices may be treated as synonymous categories, both representing *non-instrumental* practices.

Nonetheless, some subtle differences between authoritative and constitutive practices can be pointed out. The first is that the exponents of authoritative practices are primarily occupied with the regulative (constraining) aspect of rules internal to a practice, whereas theorists like us who stand closer to Hegel tend to focus on their constitutive (defining) aspect.[57] The second difference pertains to the distinction between law and ethics. The idiom of authority is borrowed from legal discourse. Its contemporary proponents – Oakeshott, Nardin, Hart and Raz – construe law as a basic social practice that comprises a system of authoritative rules for reducing uncertainty and settling disputes.[58]

---

[57] The distinction between constitutive and regulative rules is discussed in Chapter 3, under 'Constitutive and Regulative Rules'.

[58] On authority within a system of law (*lex*), see Oakeshott, *On Human Conduct*, pp. 154–159; and Michael Oakeshott, 'The Rule of Law', in Michael Oakeshott, *On History and Other Essays* (Indianapolis: Liberty Fund, 1983), pp. 129–178. The basis of Hart's position of law as an authoritative social practice comprising a system of primary and secondary rules is contained in chapters 5 (pp. 77–96) and 6 (pp. 97–120) of *The Concept of Law*. It is analysed by Joseph Raz in *The Concept of a Legal System: An Introduction to the Theory of Legal System*, 2nd ed. (Oxford: Clarendon Press, 1970). Raz is a (mild) critic of Hart's social practice view. Raz analyses the concept of authority in terms of authoritative

Even though normally such rules are coercively enforceable, they derive their authority from what Hart calls the 'internal point of view'.[59] For Hart, the criterion for the existence of a social practice is that the majority of societal members are prepared to accept its rules as authoritative. The voice of authority is internalist, whereas that of coercion is externalist. The rules of a legal system are taken to be authoritative for the citizens even in the absence of coercive constraint. A key question here is, What fixes the boundaries of a legal system, or what differentiates valid (authentic) rules which belong to the system from invalid ones which fall outside it? In response, Hart introduces the concept of secondary rules – and particularly 'rules of recognition' linked to the office of the courts – which determine the validity of primary rules such as rules of morality. But what determines which rules are to count as proper secondary rules? It will not do to refer to a higher order of rules, since this entails infinite regress. The answer Hart provides is 'social fact'; for Hart, the secondary rules in a legal system exist because a special class of officials (judges) accept these rules as a matter of social fact.[60] The social fact of acceptance, not validity, is what establishes the existence of secondary rules.

Hart depicts law as a complex, stratified social practice that incorporates both officials and ordinary citizens. One of its distinctive features absent from the cognate practice of morality is that it can resolve situations of uncertainty that accompany moral conflict. While moral grievances can be endlessly iterated between contending parties, the law can ensure closure by declaring one of the parties to be right in the legal sense of rightness. The consideration is that authoritative pronouncements of the courts are final (like Raz's 'exclusionary reasons') or that the judges, as office holders authorised to determine the content of valid law, are entitled to issue verdicts in individual court cases. It may be that the party whose conduct is pronounced right in a court of law might still be morally wrong. Nonetheless, in contrast to a moral judgement, a judicial verdict possesses finality: it closes the moral

reasons defined as 'exclusionary reasons' in *Practical Reasons and Norms*, ch. 1, pp. 15–48, esp. pp. 35–48. In *Law, Morality, and the Relations of States*, Nardin views Hart's and Raz's positions – authority as authentic rules and authority as exclusionary reasons – as compatible (p. 11).

[59] Hart, *The Concept of Law*, esp. pp. 86–89.

[60] On the rule of recognition, see Hart, *The Concept of Law*, pp. 92–96, and ch. 6, esp. pp. 97–108.

dispute and allows the contending parties to move on with their lives. On Hart's view, therefore, law differs in principle from morality, and legal officials enjoy a special status compared to ordinary citizens.

A central concern for philosophers such as Oakeshott, Nardin, Hart and Raz is to pinpoint the defining features of law as a system of rules and to clarify the character of law's authority. For them, law is the prototype of non-instrumental practices. In Chapters 4 and 5 (Part II) of this book, devoted to the basic constitutive practices in international relations, we locate non-instrumental practices in the domain of ethics. This implies a distinction between law, morality and ethics. On our Hegelian premises, 'ethics' designates social relations which encompass, but are not limited to, law and morality. The term 'morality' is usually taken to refer to the moral world. In this context, it is often said that we, men and women, are moral agents in virtue of being thinking and choosing beings: our participation in the moral world and our capacity for moral judgement is not conditional on holding statuses or offices within specialised social, political or juridical institutions. The peculiarity of Hegel's concept of ethics, *Sittlichkeit* (literally meaning 'mores', or 'customs') is that it is *institutional*.[61] Hegelian 'ethics' designates non-instrumentality and concretely non-instrumental statuses, roles and identities accorded within specific institutions. In *The Philosophy of Right*, Hegel discusses the three principal social institutions (practices in our terms) of modernity – the family, civil society and the state – that accord valued ethical statuses to their members.[62]

A third distinction between authoritative and constitutive practices should be noted. Constitutive practices understood in a Hegelian manner are constitutive of valued ethical statuses. A theory that regards law as a system of authoritative rules emphasises the category of rules. Our neo-Hegelian constitutive theory (whose objects are constitutive practices) combines a rule-based (deontological) with a value-based (axiological) perspective. According to it, participants in a common practice subscribe to the practice because they *value* the statuses it accords, on non-instrumental grounds. In Hegel's account, the family is not just an authoritative practice that enables people with diverse goals to coexist. Nor is it a social organisation we join for certain

---

[61] Contemporary philosophers use the term 'ethics' to refer to the philosophical study of the moral world. In this book, we employ the alternative term 'moral philosophy' and reserve the term 'ethics' for Hegel's *Sittlichkeit*.

[62] See note 1.

instrumental purposes. Within the family, one achieves that status of being a family member, a loved one, a status that is valued highly, over and above any possible instrumental value that might accrue from it.

One of Hegel's major insights is that practices have a dynamic or 'dialectical' facet. This is so because like any other province of human conduct, practices are not free of conflict. Often a group of participants within a practice will endeavour to reform its constitutive rules to bring about a desirable change. When this occurs, certain participants will advocate change while others will resist it. Oakeshott dubbed the activity involved in contesting the constitutive rules of a practice 'politics'.[63] This activity, taking place inside the domain of non-instrumental practices – be it authoritative or constitutive practices – is distinct from the conventional understanding of politics as a clash of interests between competing groups. Whenever the aim of political action, in this Oakeshottian sense, is to rewrite the rules of the game, what is at stake are not simply the actors' interests but their identities: here the losers in the political game cannot be compensated with 'side payments'. But political arguments for or against change would have to stop somewhere, and this point of arrest, we can say with Hegel, resides in the domain of value. In short, participants in a non-instrumental practice are engaged in political disputes whose normative dimensions concern the constitutive rules of the practice as well as its core values.

## Conclusion

Our neo-Hegelian argument, to be presented in Part II, is that many of the actions that interest students of international relations today take place within the purview of two major constitutive practices: global civil society (global practice of rights) and the society of sovereign states. But this neo-Hegelian constitutive theory is only one possible variant of the basic practice theory expounded in Chapter 3. Prior to this, in Chapter 2, we shall show that the current 'practice turn' in the study of International Relations lacks the resources for developing such a basic theory of practices.

---

[63] Oakeshott, *On Human Conduct*, pp. 158–165, esp. pp. 161–162. See also Mervyn Frost, *Global Ethics: Anarchy, Freedom and International Relations* (London: Routledge, 2009), p. 30.

# 2 | Bourdieu and the Practice Turn in International Relations

This chapter offers an assessment of the recent 'practice turn' in International Relations (IR).[1] This 'turn' came about spontaneously as an increasing number of IR scholars began to engage, with approval or criticism, the theses of Emanuel Adler and Vincent Pouliot, who have linked the notion of international practices to the 'theory of practice' of French sociologist Pierre Bourdieu.[2] The aim here is to evaluate the

---

[1] Unless otherwise specified, the expression 'practice turn' refers to the practice turn in the discipline of IR.

[2] It would not be an exaggeration to see Emanuel Adler and Vincent Pouliot as the leading proponents of the Bourdieu-inspired practice turn. Emanuel Adler and Vincent Pouliot, 'International Practices', *International Theory* 3 (1) 2011: 1–36; Emanuel Adler and Vincent Pouliot (eds.), *International Practices* (New York: Cambridge University Press, 2011); Vincent Pouliot, *International Security in Practice: The Politics of NATO-Russia Diplomacy* (New York: Cambridge University Press, 2010); Vincent Pouliot, 'The Logic of Practicality: A Theory of Practice of Security Communities', *International Organization* 62 (2) 2008: 257–288, revised as chapter 2 in *International Security in Practice*, pp. 11–51; Vincent Pouliot, '"Sobjectivism": Towards a Constructivist Methodology', *International Studies Quarterly* 51 (2) 2007: 359–384, revised as chapter 3 in *International Security in Practice*, pp. 52–91. For a roundtable on Pouliot's monograph, see H-Diplo/ISSF Roundtable: Review of Vincent Pouliot, *International Security in Practice*, 2 (5) 2011: 1–53, available at www.h-net.org/~diplo/ISSF. For an argument which traces the origins of practices in sociological theory beyond Bourdieu's 'theory of practice', see Christian Bueger and Frank Gadinger, *International Practice Theory: New Perspectives* (Basingstoke: Palgrave, 2014). Adler and Pouliot's as well as Bueger and Gadinger's conceptions of practices are criticised in Médéric Martin-Mazé, 'Returning Struggles to the Practice Turn: How Were Bourdieu and Boltanski Lost in (Some) Translations and What to Do about It?', *International Political Sociology* 11 (2) 2017: 203–220. An Aristotelian review of the practice turn is Chris Brown, 'The "Practice Turn", Phronesis and Classical Realism: Towards a Phronetic International Political Theory?' *Millennium: Journal of International Studies* 40 (3) 2012: 439–456. A critical evaluation of the practice turn indebted to Thomas Kuhn's sociology of science is Erik Ringmar, 'The Search for Dialogue as a Hindrance to Understanding: Practices as Inter-Paradigmatic Research Program', *International Theory* 6 (1) 2014: 1–27. Bourdieu's notion of practice is connected to international history in Peter Jackson, 'Pierre Bourdieu, the "Cultural Turn" and

extent to which this particular theory has advanced our understanding of social and international practices and not to overview Bourdieu's broader sociology or its possible contribution to the field of IR.[3] The thrust of our argument is that Bourdieu's approach represents a defective, 'externalist' standpoint for understanding practices and that the resultant view of practices adopted within the practice turn is strained. We offer reasons why these difficulties arise. To restore coherence, in Chapter 3, we develop practice theory, which is radically internalist.

Because Bourdieu's theory of practice is subject to conflicting interpretations, in the first part of our exposition, we provide a close reading of its conceptual kernel – the triad of capital, *habitus* and field. In the second part, we explore the practice turn. The discussion is informed by two basic philosophical problems that are central to the argument advanced in this book: (1) the opposition between the internal point of view and the external point of view as rival platforms for making sense of practices, and (2) the relation between social science and a practice as a putative object of scientific investigation.

## Bourdieu's Theory of Practice

### *Capital,* Habitus *and Field*

Bourdieu's oeuvre spans questions of culture, domination, lifestyle distinctions, the ethnography of the Algerian Kabyles and scholastic philosophy.[4] But a common theme runs through this variety of concerns.

the Practice of International History', *Review of International Studies* 34 (1) 2008: 155–181. A 'linguistic turn' view of practices in IR is offered by Iver B. Neumann, 'Returning Practice to the Linguistic Turn: The Case of Diplomacy', *Millennium: Journal of International Studies* 31 (3) 2002: 627–651. A sociological account of everyday practices of IR research is proposed by Oliver Kessler and Xavier Guillaume, 'Everyday Practices of International Relations: People in Organizations', *Journal of International Relations & Development* 15 (1) 2012: 110–120.

[3] For a research on Bourdieu in IR not limited to the problem of practices, see Didier Bigo and Mikael R. Madsen, 'Bourdieu and the International', special issue, *International Political Sociology* 5 (3) 2011: 219–347; Rebecca Adler-Nissen (ed.), *Bourdieu in International Relations: Rethinking Key Concepts in IR* (London: Routledge, 2013).

[4] Pierre Bourdieu, *Outline of a Theory of Practice*, trans. Richard Nice (Cambridge: Cambridge University Press, 1977 [1972]); Pierre Bourdieu, *The Logic of Practice*, trans. Richard Nice (Stanford: Stanford University Press, 1990 [1980]); Pierre Bourdieu, *Distinction: A Social Critique of the Judgement of*

As a social theorist, Bourdieu is asking, Why do different individuals in society tend *consistently* to act in a *similar* way? Despite that individuals exhibit disparate traits of body, mind and character, a recurrent pattern of similarity in their conduct is discernible, at the macro level of observation, when a sociologist observes what agents, construed as a society, do. Choices of lifestyle, marriage partners or political party platforms reveal such patterns of similarity, which Bourdieu calls *homology* ('diversity within homogeneity').[5] Reversing the argument of classical sociology propounded by, inter alia, Karl Marx, where the existence of classes and their interests is treated as a given, Bourdieu employs homology as a factor to explain the formation of classes and social groups.[6] Apart from Marx, intellectual influences on Bourdieu include Max Weber and Emile Durkheim in sociology and Marcel Mauss in ethnology.[7] These influences set the context for the investigations Bourdieu will undertake in *An Outline of a Theory of Practice, The Logic of Practice* and *Practical Reason* – the three works containing his 'theory of practice'.[8] As Bourdieu announces in the Preface to *Practical Reason*, his theory of practice is a philosophy of action. This philosophy is 'relational' or non-essentialist.[9] Its starting premise is that the agent's identity is dynamically dependent on social relations with other agents. The principal unit of analysis thus is not individual action or even social action but social *relations*, which Bourdieu proposes to measure in terms of similarity ('homology') and difference ('distinction').[10] In contemporary philosophy, the term 'action' usually implies that some agency has

    *Taste*, trans. Richard Nice (London: Routledge 2010 [1984]); Pierre Bourdieu, *Practical Reason: On the Theory of Action* (Stanford: Stanford University Press, 1998 [1994]); Pierre Bourdieu, *Pascalian Meditations* (Cambridge: Polity, 2000 [1997]).

[5] On homology, see Bourdieu, *Outline*, pp. 83, 86; Bourdieu, *The Logic of Practice*, pp. 55, 60–61.

[6] Bourdieu, *Outline*, p. 86; Bourdieu, *The Logic of Practice*, pp. 59–61; Bourdieu, *Practical Reason*, p. 33.

[7] For an account of such influences, see Pierre Bourdieu, *In Other Words: Essays towards a Reflexive Sociology*, trans. Matthew Adamson (Stanford: Stanford University Press, 1987), pp. 27, 106–107, 124–127; and David L. Swartz, *Culture and Power: The Sociology of Pierre Bourdieu* (Chicago: University of Chicago Press, 1997), pp. 38–48, 66–73.

[8] See note 4.

[9] Bourdieu, *Practical Reason*, p. vii. See also chapter 1, 'Social Space and Symbolic Space', esp. pp. 3–4.

[10] On the relation between homology and distinction, which is a source of symbolic capital, see Bourdieu, *The Logic of Practice*, pp. 135–138.

brought about a change in the external world, either as an altered state of affairs or as a product. It may further imply that the action is meaningful and that it is intended to evoke an intelligent response by an audience.[11] But Bourdieu excludes meaning from the definition of action, so action in his approach is not equivalent to a meaningful doing – an important point to which we return later on.

Three concepts – *habitus*, capital and field – are central to Bourdieu's theory of practice. *Habitus* and capital are introduced in his *Outline*, whereas field figures more prominently in *The Logic of Practice* and *Practical Reason*.[12] Before elaborating on the specific meaning of each concept, a brief overview of their analytical connection might be helpful. For Bourdieu, capital constitutes the primary social relation. Any specific distribution of capital (or capitals) among a group of social agents is a 'field', and *habitus* – loosely translatable as 'habitual action' – mediates the reproduction of capital inside fields. The *habitus* has both capital and field as its input and as its output. 'The coherence to be observed in all products of the application of the same *habitus*,' Bourdieu explains, 'has no other basis than the coherence which the generative principles constituting the habitus owe to the social structures (structures of relations between groups ... or between social classes) of which they are the product and which, as Durkheim and Mauss saw, they tend to reproduce.'[13] Capital and field exemplify macro social relations or social structures. They amount to objective relations in two senses. In a broad sense, 'objective' stands for that which is relational and non-arbitrary. A geometric analogy may clarify the idea. A point by itself is an arbitrary posit, but the *relation* between any two points, forming a line, is non-arbitrary or 'objective' in the required, relational sense. In a narrow sense, 'objective' is contrasted with 'subjective'. Unlike capital and field, which are objective social structures, the *habitus* contains an irreducible subjective dimension – it

---

[11] See our discussion of meaningful action in relation to Oakeshott's category of 'intelligent conduct' in Chapter 1, under 'Practice Internalism'.

[12] On the *habitus* and capital, see Bourdieu, *The Logic of Practice*, ch. 3 ('Structures, *Habitus*, Practices', pp. 52–65); Bourdieu, *Outline*, ch. 2 ('Structures and the Habitus', pp. 72–95). On field, see Bourdieu, *Outline*, p. 184; Bourdieu, *The Logic of Practice*, pp. 66–68; Bourdieu, *Practical Reason*, chs. 2 ('The New Capital', pp. 19–34) and 3 ('Rethinking the State: Genesis and Structure of the Bureaucratic Field', pp. 35–74).

[13] Bourdieu, *Outline*, p. 97. The same passage appears in Bourdieu, *The Logic of Practice*, p. 95.

is a disposition to think or act whose ultimate bearer is the individual subject located inside society. In effect, the *habitus* captures the micro dynamics of macro-level social relations (fields and capital) and serves to correct the hyper-objectivism of classical Marxism by injecting it with a subjective component. Hence Bourdieu's social theory may be described as a peculiar kind of subjectivist objectivism.[14]

Let us now consider the specifics of each category in the triad, beginning with capital. Bourdieu follows Marx in defining 'capital' as a social relation dependant on scarcity of resources. There is a notable difference, however. For Marx, capital is essentially a relation of economic production, whereas Bourdieu, perhaps under Mauss's influence, attaches basic significance to the category of symbolic capital, making the scarcity of *non-economic* resources a central determinant of human conduct.[15] One obstacle to deciphering Bourdieu's argument is his abstract vocabulary, peppered by topographic metaphors. One example is the notion of 'social space'. Bourdieu uses it to capture the aggregate distribution of capital in a given society at a time. Inside this space, each agent, or group of agents, occupies a social *position*, measurable as a relative difference from the positions of adjacent agents or groups. As Bourdieu remarks,

This idea of difference, or a gap, is the basis of the very notion of *space*, that is, a set of distinct and coexisting positions which are exterior to one another and which are defined in relation to one another through their *mutual exteriority* and their relations of proximity, vicinity, or distance, as well as through relations of order such as above, below and *between*.[16]

---

[14] Bourdieu points to his endorsement of a subjectivist objectivism or, as he calls it, 'subjectivism/objectivism'. See Bourdieu, *Outline*, pp. 3–4, 83–84; Bourdieu, *In Other Words*, pp. 126, 129; Bourdieu, *The Logic of Practice*, p. 52.

[15] Marcel Mauss, *The Gift: The Form and Reason for Exchange in Archaic Societies*, trans. W. D. Halls (London: Routledge, 2008 [1950]). In his study of gift exchange in archaic societies, Mauss contends that commodities of economic value acquire a parallel symbolic value, as integrated within a larger system of symbolic exchange regulating the transfer of women and violent acts. A symbol or sign is an object that stands in the place of (signifies, means) another object. Bourdieu transposes Mauss's doctrine into an analysis of the economy of symbolic goods – into a 'general theory of the economics of practice'. Bourdieu, *Outline*, p. 177.

[16] Bourdieu, *Practical Reason*, p. 6, original emphasis. On social space, see also Bourdieu, *In Other Words*, pp. 126–127, 129.

Any particular social position is a function of capital endowments. Because Bourdieu seeks to explain the similarity (homology) in the behaviour of agents, the explanatory category (e.g., capital) must exhibit difference. Bourdieu's key premise is that social life is a game, a contestation for gaining access to scarce resources representing qualitatively different forms of capital: economic, cultural, symbolic, political, financial and statist. These forms are mutually convertible, within limits. The limits are set by the fact that economic capital (wealth) is not fully translatable into cultural capital (educational credentials) and vice versa. Bourdieu brands these two forms of capital the basic 'principles of differentiation' in the most advanced capitalist societies today (Japan, the United States, France).[17] In his view, the struggle for social domination in the epoch of modernity takes place within powerful economic or educational institutions.

The second principal concept in Bourdieu's analysis, field, stands for an autonomous region of social space. Autonomy indicates that the field in question is internally homologous and externally differentiated from adjacent fields. Homology is explained by the fact that each field is made up of a specific blend of capitals. What matters, then, is not the intrinsic nature of capitals (no such nature is present) but their mutual relation and cohesion into a self-subsistent area inside social space. Examples of fields include law, politics, economics and even power, which is a separate field.[18] In this sense, it would be an overstatement to read Bourdieu exclusively as a theorist of power, as some IR theorists are inclined to do.[19] Bourdieu's concerns are at once broader, to provide a theory of social relations including power relations and, subtler, to shed light on the constitution of various fields, as mutually differentiated and distinctive domains of social relations. And since social relations must be reproduced over time, a further puzzle tackled by Bourdieu is legitimacy. Thus actors who interact within a common field engage in exchanges and contestations by deploying the types of capital that count as legitimate within that particular field. Symbolic capital, whose purpose is to legitimise all other forms of capital, is of momentous

[17] Bourdieu, *Practical Reason*, p. 6.
[18] On the field of power, see Bourdieu, *Practical Reason*, p. 34.
[19] See Vincent Pouliot and Frédéric Mérand, 'Bourdieu's Concepts', in Rebecca Adler-Nissen (ed.), *Bourdieu in International Relations*, pp. 24–44, p. 36. Cf. Rebecca Adler-Nissen, 'Introduction', in Adler-Nissen (ed.), *Bourdieu in International Relations*, pp. 1–23.

importance in social life.[20] Even the state, which commands 'meta capital', allowing it to redraw the boundaries of other fields in social space, is ultimately an arena of struggle over symbolic resources.

The last concept of the triad, *habitus*, designates a disposition to act. It has three different but closely related meanings. The first is subjectivist – it means habitual action performed by a single subject in the anticipation of the reaction(s) of other subjects.[21] Like any action, dispositional action is non-mechanical and reveals an element of spontaneity and improvisation. But because, at the same time, this type of action involves the *anticipation* of a response, it is a part of a background structure of social relations where the individual *regularly* interacts with others.[22] The *habitus* has two additional senses. Bourdieu notes that dispositional action has memory: it conserves traces of past occurrences.[23] These traces are conserved inside the individual's body, in a physical sense. Having learned to anticipate other people's reactions in a quasi-automatic manner, the body 'knows' how to react to them. In this second sense, *habitus* stands for embodied knowledge, a species of practical knowledge underpinning the unreflexive bodily disposition to act.[24] This embodied knowledge is not a mental act of knowing; it discloses the whole person and what the person tends to do. It may be used as an indicator of personal identity and social status by the social scientist. For instance, voice modulation, gestures and demeanour are arguably more reliable indicators of social status compared to a formalised, disembodied record of a person's views expressed in a questionnaire. In its third sense, the *habitus* is the embodied dispositional property of classes or

---

[20] In his *Outline*, Bourdieu is concerned primarily with symbolic capital (pp. 171–183). For a lucid discussion of symbolic power, symbolic violence, and symbolic capital, see David L. Swartz, *Symbolic Power, Politics and Intellectuals: The Political Sociology of Pierre Bourdieu* (Chicago: University of Chicago Press, 2013), esp. pp. 82–106.

[21] A *habitual* action involves *anticipatory* response. Bourdieu, *Outline*, p. 73; Bourdieu, *The Logic of Practice*, pp. 53–54, 60–62, 64, 66, 81.

[22] Bourdieu often refers to the habitus as a 'system of durable, transposable dispositions' to capture its background structural component. Bourdieu, *Outline*, pp. 72, 82, 85; Bourdieu, *The Logic of Practice*, pp. 53, 57.

[23] On *habitus* as a repository of the past, see Bourdieu, *Outline*, pp. 78–79, 81–83; and Bourdieu, *The Logic of Practice*, pp. 53–54, 56, 58, 60.

[24] On *habitus* as embodied, see Bourdieu, *Outline*, pp. 15, 81–82, 87–93; Bourdieu, *The Logic of Practice*, pp. 56–57, 68–79.

social groups.[25] In all three senses, the term prioritises overt action, as publicly observable bodily movements, at the expense of private mental processes.

So far, Bourdieu's theory of practice can be summarised thus: agents occupy positions inside social space, develop dispositions and engage in 'position taking' (choices). In Bourdieu's own words, 'the space of social positions is retranslated into a space of position-takings through the mediation of the space of dispositions (or *habitus*)'.[26] Subjects located inside a common field occupy homologous positions as holders of similar in kind and volume capital. But what ensures the continued reproduction of that field over time is the homology of their dispositions, their shared *habitus* as a social group.

This brings us to the central theme addressed in this book: practices. By 'practices', Bourdieu understands publicly observable actions, outcomes of habitual dispositions to act, which are responsible for the formation of social groups. Here the *habitus* is invoked to explain social *differentiation* – it identifies the distinctive social group to which a given individual belongs:

Habitus are generative principles of distinct and distinctive practices – what the worker eats, and especially the way he eats it, the sport he practices and the way he practices it, his political opinions and the way he expresses them are systematically different from the industrial owner's activities. *But habitus are also classificatory schemes*, principles of classification, principles of vision and division, different tastes. They make distinctions between what is good and what is bad, between what is right and what is wrong, between what is distinguished and what is vulgar, and so forth, but the distinctions are not identical. Thus, for instance, the same behavior or even the same good can appear distinguished to one person, pretentious to someone else, and cheap or showy to yet another.[27]

Recall that Bourdieu saw in the *habitus* the basic source of homology underpinning the dynamic construction of social groups or classes. It is only because certain individuals are disposed to conduct themselves in such-and-such a manner (disclosing their settled habits and tastes),

---

[25] On class *habitus*, see Bourdieu, *Outline*, pp. 77, 81, 85–86; Bourdieu, *The Logic of Practice*, pp. 55–60.

[26] Bourdieu, *Practical Reason*, p. 7.

[27] Bourdieu, *Practical Reason*, p. 8, emphasis added.

which is consistently similar and stable over time, that it is possible for us as observers to recognise them as, say, workers (a class), thereby differentiating them from industrial owners (another class). But judging from the passage just quoted, Bourdieu now invokes the *habitus* to explain *both* homology *and* differentiation, and it is hard to see how this dual task can be performed without resorting to language and meaning.

In the same passage quoted previously, Bourdieu refers to the *habitus* as 'classificatory schemes'. While the category of classificatory schemes may look like meaning, Bourdieu declares his intention to break with any meaning-centred analysis:

[My] approach is thus radically opposed ... to the interactionism which reduces the constructions of social science to 'constructs of the second degree, that is, constructs of the constructs made by the actors on the social scene', as Schutz does, or, like Garfinkel, to accounts of the accounts which agents produce and through which they produce the meaning of their world ... Only by constructing the *objective structures* (price curves, chances of access to higher education, laws of the matrimonial market, etc.) is one able to pose the question of the mechanisms through which the relationship is established between the structures and the practices or representations which accompany them, instead of treating these 'thought objects' as 'reasons' or 'motives' and making them the determining cause of the practices.[28]

Here Bourdieu is appealing to objective structures to explain the emergence of social practices. But it might be objected that this renders the subjectively tinted, mediating category of *habitus* redundant as an explanatory category, since purely objective structures – capital and field – suffice as *explanans*. Bourdieu may retort that the *habitus* is supposed to explain both the homology *and* the difference between social practices.[29] But this answer is not satisfactory, as Bourdieu still relies on an abstract notion of difference. The problem with abstract difference, whose equally abstract counterpart is homology, is that it does not allow us to pick out a concrete object, a concrete practice. What is needed is a notion of *concrete* difference, a distinction in

---

[28] Bourdieu, *Outline*, p. 21.
[29] In this sense, 'habitus are generative principles of *distinct* and *distinctive* practices'. See note 27.

Hegel's sense,[30] and making distinctions requires meaning and language. Compare a practice described in concrete language, as *gift-giving*, with a practice described in abstract language, as *economic exchange*.

With respect to meaning, Bourdieu faces a dilemma. Either meaning matters and must be made part of the *habitus* or it does not matter and must be factored out from the *habitus*. In the first case, certain people will be able to recognise each other as members of a distinctive social group because they share an understanding, expressed in concrete terms, of what their common *habitus* means. In the latter case, these people will not be able to recognise each other as members of a group in mutually intelligible terms, even though they may be recognisable as such by an external observer, in terms intelligible *to the observer*. The dilemma points to a deeper opposition between the internal point of view (of participants who understand the meaning of their own practice) and the external point of view (of an observer observing a practice from 'the outside'). In a sense, Bourdieu wants to have it both ways. Thus he describes the *habitus* as 'schemes of perception, thought and action,' a category of experience, but also as 'classificatory schemes', an observational category.[31] Perceptions and thoughts are lived experiences that have concrete contents or meaning. After some hesitation, Bourdieu opts for the second horn of the dilemma: he treats such lived experiences as reducible to abstract categories by approaching them from 'the outside', from the perspective of reflexive social science. This is an externalist solution, whose aim is to discount the internalism of meaning. The subjects under investigation, the argument runs, have thoughts and perceptions, but since their actions are not driven by a conscious awareness of the meaning of their own thoughts and perceptions, the aspect of meaning can be safely bracketed by the analyst. The subjects under examination are to be analysed as unreflexive beings. Note that Bourdieu's 'reflexive' agent, as one who deliberately

---

[30] This is what Hegel calls 'difference *qua* difference of content'. G. W. F. Hegel, *Hegel's Phenomenology of Spirit*, trans. A. V. Miller (Oxford: Oxford University Press, 1977), §154.

[31] Bourdieu refers to the *habitus* as 'schemes of perception, thought and action' in *Outline*, pp. 17–18, 83, 86, 90, 97, 164, esp. p. 83. See also Bourdieu, *The Logic of Practice*, pp. 53–55, 60–61, 95. The *habitus* is associated with 'classificatory schemes' in Bourdieu, *Outline*, pp. 164, 167–170; and Bourdieu, *The Logic of Practice*, pp. 94–95, 139–140.

distances oneself from a given object of investigation or from one's own process of thinking, is not identical to Oakeshott's 'reflective consciousness' (a thinking and choosing agent immersed in understandings and self-understandings).[32]

Effectively, the *habitus* becomes a sister concept to Marx's false consciousness: 'As an acquired system of generative schemes objectively adjusted to the particular conditions in which it is constituted, the *habitus* engenders all the thoughts, all the perceptions and all the actions, consistent with those conditions, and no others.'[33] It ensures the reproduction of *doxa* – ideas tacitly accepted as self-evident knowledge by societal members:

Schemes of thought and perception [habitus] can produce the objectivity that they do produce only by producing misrecognition of the limits of the cognition that they make possible, thereby founding immediate adherence, in the doxic mode, to the world of tradition experienced as a 'natural world' and taken for granted.[34]

Doxic knowledge, as a form of taken-for-granted, tacit knowledge, sustains the *habitus* operating within specific fields.[35] Even when explicit contestation arises within a field, making it into a 'field of opinion', it is still implicitly circumscribed by *doxa*, which is why the agents inevitably fall back on their unreflexive, embodied knowledge, or 'practical sense'.[36]

All these considerations indicate that, ultimately, Bourdieu favours the external point of view. The capital endowments of agents, their social positions within various fields and even the *habitus* as a group-level category represent objective relations amenable to social scientific investigation, including that provided by statistical methods.[37] For Bourdieu, the task of the social scientist is to unearth the true logic of such relations, which remains opaque to the social agents who remain

---

[32] On Oakeshott's view of the agent as 'reflective consciousness', see Chapter 1, note 14.

[33] Bourdieu, *Outline*, p. 95; Bourdieu, *The Logic of Practice*, p. 55–56.

[34] Bourdieu, *Outline*, p. 164, emphasis added.

[35] On the relation between *doxa*, field and *habitus*, see Bourdieu, *The Logic of Practice*, pp. 55–56, 66–67.

[36] Bourdieu uses the expression 'field of opinion' in *Outline*, p. 168. On practical sense, see Bourdieu, *The Logic of Practice*, pp. 68–69.

[37] On statistical methods, see Bourdieu, *Outline*, pp. 53, 77, 86; Bourdieu, *The Logic of Practice*, pp. 54, 60.

entrapped in their unreflexive, quasi-automatic mode of conduct. Social science must be reflexive: it must acquire distance from the unreflexive universe of the human relations it investigates.[38] The demand for reflexivity entails a demand for the external point of view.

## Bourdieu's Externalism and Social Science

We now turn to the basic theme of this chapter, which is that a particular point of view is requisite for making sense of social practices. Bourdieu claims that the proper perspective must be externalist. As may be recalled from Chapter 1, the contrast between externalism and internalism concerns the relation between the language of action and the language of observation employed by an observer who attempts to understand the action. In this discussion, the object of observation is not a simple action but practice-dependent action, or action conducted within practices. Internalism holds that an investigator who attempts to understand what participants in a practice say or do must use the terms of discourse which the participants themselves use in making sense of their own practice. Externalism denies this. It asserts that it is permissible to use any conceivable theoretical language as long as it is intelligible and consistent. The account supplied is thus an *imputation*, imposed from 'the outside'. Stated differently, externalists urge that in making sense of the practice of a social group, the analyst must move beyond the intersubjective standards accepted by that group and rely instead on standards of explanation that are invariant or objective. Bourdieu may not be a full-fledged objectivist, since the *habitus* contains a subjectivist moment, but he is nonetheless an externalist in this sense. By making reflexivity a condition of valid social science, he requires the investigator to use a language of observation that *differs in principle* from the language of action used within the social practice under investigation. In the present section, we adduce reasons to show why such externalism is untenable.

Bourdieu's ethnographic study of the Kabyle practice of gift exchange illustrates his externalist stance. When the Kabyle peasants give one another artefacts, accompanied by certain words and gestures, they understand their actions to constitute a practice recognisable as

---

[38] Hence Bourdieu's reference to reflexive sociology in the title of his book. See note 7.

the practice of gift exchange (temporally deferred exchange). Bourdieu introduces the figure of the ethnologist, an observer who ventures to explain their practice by adopting the procedures of reflexive social science. The gist of the ethnologist's explanation is that it eliminates the temporal element of deferral and exposes the 'gift' as a challenge to reciprocate.[39] So far, this is a valid distinction between the internal point of view (of the participants in a practice) and the external point of view (of an observer). But, Bourdieu goes on to say, the ethnologist alone can detect the material interest – the real, objective relation – concealed behind what may appear, not the least to the participants themselves, to be a disinterested practice of gift exchange: 'In short, contrary to naively idyllic representations of "pre-capitalist societies" (or of the "cultural" sphere of capitalist societies), practice never ceases to conform to economic calculation even when it gives every appearance of disinterestedness.'[40] Bourdieu's argument is externalist. It holds that by discounting the participants' own understanding of their practice, the social scientist is able to establish the correct, objective meaning of that very practice. But this will not do.

The difficulty is not confined to the Kabyle case. To explicate this more basic problem, imagine a scenario where an anthropologist seeks to explain a ritual dance a tribe performs to plead for rain. For the ritual performer, the action (dancing) is intrinsically related to an end (plea for rain addressed to the gods), where 'intrinsic' stands for 'internal to the bounds of a shared practice' (the rain ritual).[41] The duo of elements, dancing and rain pleading, constitute an *internal relation* in which neither element can be replaced without destroying the meaningful relation in question and floating the wider practice of which it is a part. Bourdieu insists that the social scientist should maintain analytical distance from such internal relations – this is what reflexivity demands. Because the premise of distance cancels out the premise of internal relations (holding between a practice and *its* ends), the anthropologist's explanation may well turn out to be that the

---

[39] Bourdieu, *Outline*, pp. 5–16, 191, 194–195.     [40] Bourdieu, *Outline*, p. 177.

[41] Kasher argues that internal ends define rule-based or 'deontological', practices. Naomi Kasher, 'Deontology and Kant', *Revue Internationale de Philosophie* 126 (4) 1978: 551–558. On internal ends relative to the internal domain of a practice, see our discussion in Mervyn Frost and Silviya Lechner, 'Two Conceptions of International Practice: Aristotelian *Praxis* or Wittgensteinian *Language-Games* ', *Review of International Studies* 42 (2) 2016: 334–350.

tribesmen dance to satisfy some *different end*, say, to solidify their morale. But an explanation of this kind would be 'external' and incomprehensible to the tribesmen, were they to be queried, since *for them*, to dance is to plead for rain: one element signifies or means the other. The point is not that the anthropologist and the dancers differ in what they take to be going on: a dance for the gods as opposed to an exercise in strengthening morale in hard times of drought; rather, this difference reveals the clash of two incompatible standpoints: external versus internal. The anthropologist is not explaining *the same* practice as the one understood by its participants, *pace* Bourdieu, but a completely different practice that has been conjured up *de novo*.

We shall offer an extended defence of this complex argument in Chapter 3. Here it suffices to set out its basic idea – namely, that a practice constitutes a more or less autonomous domain of internal relations or meanings intersubjectively shared by and within a social group. In performing the rain ritual, a tribesman follows the standards intersubjectively validated within his tribe. There is no place for either radical subjectivity here, be it embodied or not, or a Bourdieu-style methodology which seeks to objectify subjective dispositions. This argument can be extended to the sphere of international relations. The British citizen John Clark cannot, by issuing a unilateral statement 'I declare war on Iraq', succeed in declaring war on another state. Only the British prime minister can do this, within the accepted international practice of interstate relations which authorises heads of states to issue war declarations. This does not imply that participants in a practice are debarred from acting or judging as separate individuals, but that their subjective judgements and actions are validated by a *prior* practice, constituted by intersubjective standards. In our example, the prime minister's act of declaring a war is not only an act validated within the international practice of sovereign states. It is also a performative act. It counts as such an act in virtue of a prior practice, the practice of performatives, which makes it possible.[42] A practice, if you wish, comprises a common framework of conditions that certain individuals must accept to be its participants; the individual judgments and actions of its participants proceed from this common framework. The reverse

---

[42] On performatives, see J. L. Austin, *How to Do Things with Words*, 2nd ed., ed. J. O. Urmson and Marina Sbisà (Cambridge, MA: Harvard University Press, 1975 [1962]), sec. 1, 'Performatives and Constatives', pp. 1–11, esp. pp. 5–7 and pp. 40, 156 (Austin's example on declaring war).

relation does not hold: aggregating a number of judgements of separate individuals does not add up to a common practice in the absence of consolidating intersubjective standards.

The key idea here is that a practice is a system of internal relations or *meanings*. Meaning is necessarily concrete, particularised or 'substantive', in Michael Oakeshott's terms.[43] An action or utterance cannot mean something in general; to be intelligible, it must mean something in particular – pulling a cat by the tail, speaking to a Russian diplomat. A practice admits candidates into membership on the condition that they have learned to understand what its standards mean, and since these standards are meaningful linguistic propositions, they delimit the identity of a practice in an appropriate way. This is one consideration among many for why a practice can only be understood from the standpoint of its participants – from the internal point of view. Bourdieu's neo-Marxist alternative in which agents are constrained by social laws whose meaning they do *not* understand exemplifies the external point of view. The major shortcoming of externalism is that by not focussing on the meanings of actions as understood by participants in the practice, it leaves the identity of that practice undetermined, producing explanations that are haphazard if not downright wrong. This is our answer to the first question raised in this chapter, whether making sense of a practice requires the internal point of view, or conversely, the external one.

Now proceeding to the second question, we shall probe the bid made by reflexive social science to be the proper platform for making sense of practices. On Bourdieu's conception, ethnology (and analogously, sociology) is a social science that ideally must maintain reflexive distance from its object: the practices and *habitus* of the ordinary people it studies. 'Reflexivity' here means distancing oneself from, and critically attending to, an object by suspension of belief. Nonetheless, this act of distancing should not collapse into complete disconnect, since, as we saw, the Bourdieuan ethnologist purports to be deciphering the Kabyle practice of gift exchange itself and not some hypothesised object. Bourdieu, moreover, emphasised that the social scientist is able to understand this same practice better than its own participants understand it, by virtue of reflexivity. That this is a highly unpersuasive line

---

[43] Michael Oakeshott, *On Human Conduct* (Oxford: Clarendon Press, 1975), pp. 37, 39–40.

of reasoning can be shown by examining the relationship between reflexivity and the *habitus*.

Bourdieu regards the *habitus* of the social scientist as inherently reflexive – here 'reflexivity' designates not distance but a second-order operation of thinking about thinking (or thinking about acting). On Bourdieu's premises, the social scientist realises what ordinary people do not – namely, that their habitual, day-to-day actions are classificatory schemes in disguise; such schemes are modes of perception and self-perception that reproduce the divisions in society in an insidious way. The inconsistency here is that Bourdieu first defines the *habitus* as an unreflexive manner of thinking but then attributes a *reflexive habitus* to social scientists. But even if we set aside this infelicity, a further problem remains. Bourdieu assumes that different kinds of *habitus* accord different identities to agents – unreflexive ordinary people as opposed to reflexive social scientists. If so, the latter cannot claim to be engaged in an investigation of *the same practice* they share with the non-scientists. At most, the scientists could claim to be reflexively investigating *their own practice* of social science production. There is, then, not one common practice but two separate ones (one for the scientists and another one for the non-scientists). Bourdieu's argument for reflexivity (in both senses of reflexivity) demands the premise that the reflexive agents occupy a position inside a shared practice. But this is a premise of internalism, not externalism.

Bourdieu's stance discloses a core limitation of the external point of view. As a standpoint located outside all practices from which they can be impartially, scientifically or, indeed, reflexively evaluated, externalism cannot generate knowledge *of* any practice; it only generates knowledge *about* the practice. And since multiple external platforms from which statements about a practice can be made are available at any time, the resultant explanation of what participants in the practice do or have done would tend to exhibit analytical arbitrariness. Imagine the following example: A group of diplomats have performed an action they recognise as signing an international peace treaty. A social scientist comes along and makes the case that in spite of what the diplomats profess to have done, a reflexive examination shows that their action is best understood as reproducing the structure of empire. But this explanation may be questioned as arbitrary. How do we tell? At stake here is the question of the relevant *baseline* which serves to establish what counts as a typical successful performance within a social practice. Internalism has an answer to this question: the baseline is determined by the public standards, which constitute the practice as a common domain of rule-following activity. But these standards have determinate, concrete meaning only when they are seen from 'the inside': from the internal point of view of their own participants. By denying the relevance of such an internalist baseline, advocates of the external point of view like Bourdieu fail to specify what criteria, if any, enable us to sift proper from improper interpretations. Reflexivity, as a requirement of critical distance in an investigation, cannot overcome the problem of missing criteria and explanatory arbitrariness, even though it might be useful for other purposes. It may aid us, as observers, to register instances of confused action within practices by showing that a practice participant is confused about his or her own action, not realising that it violates the public criteria of the practice. The idea we wish to flesh out is that such a reflexive attempt by a social scientist to stipulate how a misfired performance is to be corrected would have to be made in a language intelligible to the agent(s) performing it – or from the internal point of view. A social scientific conclusion which prioritises the external point of view, because it is hardly intelligible to the actors themselves, cannot help them realise their mistakes (if such a realisation is a concern). More generally, as we suggested in Chapter 1, the principal reason why internalism constitutes the proper vantage point for the interpretation of practices is that any practice, as a public system of internally connected rules, meanings and usages, *pre-exists* any attempt by an individual agent to interpret it.

If we are to pinpoint the 'summative' defect of Bourdieu's externalism, it is that it has been designed to eliminate the concept of rules from social enquiry. Rules must vanish because they hinge on internalism and meaning, the arch nuisances for Bourdieu. As he admits, 'I can say that all of my thinking started from this point: how can behaviour be regulated without being the product of obedience to rules.'[44] A position which discards rules for regularities is not objectionable *per se*. But it is objectionable in light of Bourdieu's overarching task: to outline a theory of practice. It transpires that what Bourdieu has been analysing all along is not the problem of *practices* – rules, institutions and the like – but the categorically distinct problem of *practice*, the

---

[44] Bourdieu, *In Other Words*, p. 65; Bourdieu, *Outline*, pp. 19, 27, 29, 72, esp. 19. See Swartz, *Culture and Power*, p. 95.

sphere of action broadly construed (Aristotle's *praxis*) whose contrary is theory (Aristotle's contemplation).[45]

The basic distinction between *a* practice (with the definite article *a*) and practice (action) runs as a thread throughout this book. Here we offer a provisional definition of a practice to be refined in Chapter 3: *a practice is a system of rules, and a rule is a frame which constrains the manner in which an intended action is to be performed.* Writing a cheque, buying property, promising, voting in an election, dispatching diplomats and signing peace treaties are familiar practices. Bourdieu raises the following basic question for us: Can a theory which denies that practices are systems of rules purport to be *social* theory in any respectable sense of the term? We address this question by considering how Bourdieu's view of practice has been appropriated by scholars in the discipline of IR.

## The Practice Turn in International Relations

The 'practice turn' in IR is the most systematic attempt to date to translate Bourdieu's theory of practice into an approach to international practices. Led by IR scholars Adler and Pouliot, it has yielded a series of articles, an edited volume, *International Practices*, and Pouliot's monograph, *International Security in Practice: The Politics of NATO-Russian Diplomacy*.[46] We have selected entries for discussion that take up important conceptual aspects of practices, are relevant to international relations and have not been previously analysed. Thus we concentrate on Pouliot's monograph, briefly considering Adler and Pouliot's article 'International Practices' together with two chapters from *International Practices* – by Ole Sending and Iver Neumann, and by Patrick Morgan.[47]

---

[45] See reference to Aristotle's *praxis* in Chapter 1, note 6.      [46] See note 2.

[47] Ringmar ('The Search for Dialogue') offers a summary critique of some of the thirteen essays collected in the edited volume *International Practices*, including Adler and Pouliot's introductory essay in that volume, 'International Practices: Introduction and Framework', 3–35. The latter has been reworked as an article: Adler and Pouliot, 'International Practices' – see note 2. We have analysed Adler and Pouliot's article in Mervyn Frost and Silviya Lechner, 'Understanding International Practices from the Internal Point of View', *Journal of International Political Theory* 12 (3) 2016: 299–319, but here we focus on one specific argument (about competent action) which has not been previously examined. In addition to Pouliot's monograph, we also discuss two chapters from

## Bourdieu and International Practices

### The Practice of Diplomacy

In *International Security in Practice*, Pouliot sets himself the task of explaining the changing character of diplomatic practice in Russia-NATO security relations in the post–Cold War era. The point of departure is the concept of security community developed by Karl Deutsch in the 1950s. This type of community is one where there is a 'real assurance that the members of that community will not fight each other physically, but will settle their disputes in some other way'.[48] Pouliot has rebranded 'security community' into a practice of 'self-evident diplomacy'.[49] The term 'self-evidence' refers to Bourdieu's concept of tacit, taken-for-granted knowledge. Diplomacy is self-evident whenever a group of security officials accept it, unconsciously and habitually, as a matter-of-course mode of interaction. Even though self-evident diplomacy has not materialised in post–Cold War NATO-Russia relations, Pouliot argues, a second best, a *normalised* practice of diplomacy, has become entrenched.[50] During the period under examination (1992–2008), bilateral relations exhibited two 'honeymoons' (1992–1994, 2001–2002) followed by episodes of deterioration, as in NATO's bombing of Serbia in 1999 and Russia's military intervention in Georgia in 2008.

To explain the absence of a self-evident diplomacy, Pouliot employs Bourdieu's concept of *hysteresis*.[51] *Hysteresis* is a misalignment between *habitus* (a subjective disposition) and its corresponding field (objective relations) – between what the agent subjectively believes to be the case and how the world objectively stands. Such a misalignment between belief and reality might be costly to the agent. A person who

---

International Practices not covered in Ringmar's review – Patrick M. Morgan, 'The Practice of Deterrence' (ch. 6), in Adler and Pouliot (eds.), *International Practices*, pp. 139–173; and Ole Jacob Sending and Iver B. Neumann, 'Banking On Power: How Some Practices in an International Organization Anchor Others'(ch. 9), in Adler and Pouliot (eds.), *International Practices*, pp. 231–254.

48 Karl W. Deutsch et al., *Political Community and the North Atlantic Area: International Organization in the Light of Historical Experience* (Princeton, NJ: Princeton University Press, 1957), p. 5, quoted in Pouliot, *International Security*, p. 3n2.

49 Pouliot, *International Security*, pp. 40–43, 97, 232.

50 Pouliot, *International Security*, pp. 1–2, 97, 234.

51 Bourdieu, *The Logic of Practice*, p. 62; Pouliot, *International Security*, pp. 2, 174–193, and ch. 6 (pp. 194–230), esp. 232–237.

believes that humans can fly may jump off a precipice to find out otherwise. Such a misalignment besets Russia, Pouliot contends. Russia perceives itself as a great power – a tendency among Russian officials traceable to the awakening of nationalist sentiment in the epoch of Peter the Great.[52] But this is an illusion; in the post–Cold War world, Russia does not have, objectively speaking, the standing of a great power. The *hysteresis* of Russian conduct has been disclosed in its assertiveness in the Georgian conflict, its demands for carrying out negotiations with NATO within a dedicated institution, the NATO-Russia Council (NRC) rather than the 'mass' forum of the Partnership of Peace and its exaggerated reactions to the process of NATO dual expansion (geographic and functional) that began in 1994.[53] NATO too suffers from *hysteresis*. It is revealed in the illusory belief on the part of the Alliance that it speaks for the entire international community.[54]

Pouliot concludes that at present, NATO unilaterally defines the field (in the Bourdieuan sense of 'field') of post–Cold War international security.[55] Consequently, cultural/symbolic capital (rule of law and democracy promotion) has been appreciated, whereas material/institutional capital (military resources), the traditional strength of the Soviet Union and of post-Soviet Russia, has been depreciated.[56] Pouliot has managed to untangle the cryptic layers of Bourdieu's theory of practice and articulate an original perspective of international practices which elucidates the connection between various forms of capital, on the one side, and the struggles over symbolic capital that sets the parameters of fields such as international security and diplomacy, on the other. Yet difficulties lurk in the details.

One key theoretical question is, Which field or fields (in Bourdieu's sense) are central to an understanding of NATO-Russia relations? Pouliot regards the field of diplomacy as coextensive with that of international security. Diplomacy is the practice of international security officials, or what international security officials *do* in a diplomatic (non-violent) manner of dispute resolution.[57] The proposal is to

---

[52] Pouliot, *International Security*, pp. 2, 140–146, 177–178, 235.
[53] Pouliot, *International Security*, pp. 183–184, 191–192, 210, 231–232.
[54] Pouliot, *International Security*, pp. 141–142, 237.
[55] Pouliot, *International Security*, ch. 5, esp. pp. 150–161, 212.
[56] Pouliot, *International Security*, pp. 151–155.
[57] Pouliot, *International Security*, pp. 2, 43, 232.

analyse diplomatic practice, so construed, by extending Bourdieu's brand of objectivism into a novel methodology, 'sobjectivism' – a merger of subjectivism, intersubjectivism and objectivism.[58] More than seventy security officials working in Brussels, Washington, Ottawa, London and Moscow were interviewed for the book to register the subjective opinions of practitioners dealing with NATO-Russian relations and to detect intersubjective patterns of agreement. The findings were objectified via a historical analysis. When added together, these three analytical steps produce the sobjectivist methodology. One difficulty here is that the intersubjective and the objective are not additives but alternatives. The intersubjective standpoint asserts that given standards of thought and action count as valid because they are accepted between subjects (*inter*subjectively), while the objective standpoint holds that standards of thought and action – natural law, Marx's laws of economic development – are binding on individuals regardless of whether they accept them.

There is a further problem. The notion of intersubjective agreement by itself is too crude to capture the finer-grained idea of *intersubjective agreement within a social practice*. It is possible for a number of subjects to agree between themselves (intersubjectively) on a common proposition without thereby participating in a common practice. Pouliot deduces from fact that a multitude of security practitioners agree among themselves that something is the case – that the current (as of 2008) NATO-Russia relations are less confrontational than they were during the Cold War – that a common practice of normalised diplomacy binds them. But an intersubjective agreement within a common practice must issue from the shared rules and norms accepted by its participants. As a practice participant, each player is required to take into account the anticipated response of other players, not as a mere anticipation of a behavioural regularity, as implied by Bourdieu's *habitus*, but as a *criterion* of appropriate action in the normative sense. When challenged by an investigator, a bona fide practice participant would exhibit a sense of guilt or discomfort if it turns out that his or her action or evaluation infringes the internal standards of the practice concerned. This is so because unlike an outsider, a bona fide insider knows what is appropriate *to be done or said* within the domain of the relevant practice – this appropriateness discloses the normativity of

[58] Pouliot, *International Security*, pp. 6–7, and ch. 3, esp. pp. 59–65.

practice-dependent action.[59] Pouliot's security officials are individuals who happen to agree intersubjectively on a proposition, but their agreement has the character of a contingent fact. It is not normatively tied to any internal standards of conduct that these individuals accept in common, and therefore it does not testify to the presence of a common practice binding them.

### The Logic of Practicality

To support his view of diplomatic practice, Pouliot develops a 'logic of practicality'. It represents a two-pronged thesis. Its first prong concerns practicality, 'this inarticulate sense that allows agents to perform social activities'.[60] It asserts the primacy of tacit knowledge: 'While representational knowledge is conscious, verbalizable and intentional, practical knowledge is tacit, inarticulate and automatic.'[61] The term 'tacit' is ambiguous: it can mean unreflexive or unconscious. With respect to unreflexive action, Pouliot's insight is that the agents, in the course of acting, need not be thinking *that* they are acting. Having learned how to address an ambassador, a diplomat does not pause to think 'Now I am addressing an ambassador' each time this type of action is performed. The art of diplomacy demands various skills whose exercise over time would tend to become routine or unreflexive. Pouliot plausibly suggests that such diplomatic skills must be learned by doing.[62] But sometimes he equates tacit knowledge to *unconsciously* held knowledge.[63] This is a stretch, as a diplomat could not have learned to analyse, describe or judge in an unconscious manner, even though many diplomatic skills may subsequently be deployed in a tacit (unreflexive) manner. The tacit skills displayed in day-to-day diplomatic life are clearly based on background knowledge about diplomacy, which a diplomat could discuss and evaluate publicly if the occasion demanded it. That this underlying knowledge is usually tacit should not be read as implying that it is

---

[59] We continue our analysis of the normativity of practices in the final section of Chapter 3.

[60] Pouliot, *International Security*, p. 13, 27–31.

[61] Pouliot, *International Security*, p. 28.

[62] Pouliot, *International Security*, p. 12.

[63] Pouliot departs from Bourdieu by singling out 'non-representational' (tacit or unconscious) knowledge as the basis of practicality. Pouliot, *International Security*, p. 13n15. On 'tacit' as 'unconscious', see p. 12.

*unconscious* and could not be articulated by the actor when required to do so. The very notion 'tacit' indicates that the knowledge could be made public.

Pouliot further argues that the tacit skills of security practitioners, their diplomatic *habitus*, elucidates the continuity and transformation of diplomatic practice. What explains the change in recent Russia-NATO relations is the emergence of a new *habitus* of 'normalised diplomacy'. This hypothesis does not differentiate what is to be explained (*explanandum*) from that which explains it (*explanans*). It postulates that the collection of skilled actions amassed by certain security practitioners in the course of everyday experience – their diplomatic *habitus* or 'practical sense' of acting in a non-violent manner – explains the change in the practice of diplomacy. The reason these skilled actions cannot be an explanation for the change in the practice is that, per assumption, the practice itself just is the sum of the tacit-skill-displaying actions of the diplomats. The argument is circular in a vicious sense, so that contradictory bits of evidence count equally in its support. By Pouliot's lights, NATO and Russian officials changed their diplomatic *habitus* after the birth of post-Soviet Russia in 1992. Prior to 1992, a direct military confrontation was conceivable; afterwards, a practice of normalised diplomacy has taken the front seat. But it is equally plausible to argue the converse – that *during* the Cold War, diplomats across the Iron Curtain did not countenance an open military confrontation; hence the war never became hot.[64] The question remains: Has the practice of Cold War diplomacy changed?

Puzzles concerning how a practice changes its identity cannot be tackled by Pouliot's approach because this approach is indeterminate – it does not supply a set of relevant descriptions (identity criteria) that would fix the identity of the practice concerned. According to Pouliot, the practice of diplomacy consists in what security practitioners actually do. But how are we to determine whether what they are doing now amounts to a *change* in the overall practice of diplomacy? Or is it diplomacy as usual? It is unhelpful to be told in response that diplomacy is what diplomats actually do, for this begs the question.

---

[64] See Peter Jackson's criticism of Pouliot's distinction between Cold War and post–Cold War international security fields in H-Diplo/ISSF Roundtable, pp. 14–22, p. 20.

What we need are criteria of what constitutes a given practice as a determinate or concrete practice – diplomacy, in this case. Without such criteria, it is logically impossible to tell whether *it* has changed or not.

Now let us consider the second prong of Pouliot's practicality thesis. It reads, 'It is not only who we are that drives what we do; it is also what we do that determines who we are.'[65] The performance of a certain (non-violent) mode of action makes diplomats who they are, and correlatively, their being diplomats determines what they do. Pouliot enlists in the category of diplomats, representatives to international organisations, university professors, military personnel, journalists, heads of states, members of parliament and minsters.[66] It is not clear on what basis people have been assigned to this category. Once again, the problem of missing identity criteria resurfaces: How are we to determine who is to count as a diplomat and what type of action is to count as diplomacy? We contend that it is not the case that doing X qualifies as an action within the practice of diplomacy on the basis of self-testimony of agents. Nor should any conceivable action performed by a diplomat – say, lighting a cigarette, playing the piano or giving a speech – count as an act of diplomacy simply because the actor performing it bears the official role of diplomat. A given action qualifies as diplomatic conduct only if it coheres with the canons of the practice of diplomacy. To be able to determine who counts as a diplomat in the practice of diplomacy and what counts as diplomatic action within it, a set of relevant descriptions are requisite. Our descriptivist stance holds *that the elementary rules which define a social practice provide the relevant descriptions of actors and actions properly belonging to the domain of the practice.*[67] Thus the relevant descriptions of 'diplomat' and 'diplomatic conduct' demand recourse to the context of diplomacy as a social practice, where a practice is a domain of rule-governed activity jointly accepted and reproduced by a group of agents. This notion social practices is absent from Pouliot's discussion because he assumes that a practice is the totality of habitual actions.

---

[65] Pouliot, *International Security*, p. 5.
[66] Pouliot, *International Security*, pp. 98, 102–107, 112–115.
[67] See our earlier discussion of truth-as-relevance in the Introduction, under 'Appropriateness and Differentiation of Practices'; and Chapter 1, under 'Internalism, Externalism and Social Science'.

To think of a practice as a rule-governed activity is to envisage a determined set of rules, and to refer to it as a *social* practice is to suggest that certain agents follow these rules together, as a group. Construed in this way, the practice of diplomacy has elementary rules – known as constitutive rules – which determine its identity and enable us to identify its participants (diplomats) under the descriptions specified by these rules. Concretely, the constitutive rules of modern post-Renaissance diplomacy include the system of embassy, the exemption of diplomats from local jurisdiction, the non-violability of the diplomat's person, and sovereign states as the principal (if not sole) agents represented by diplomats in international affairs.[68] The wider practice of states, known as 'international society', may include, in addition to diplomacy, the practices of international law, war, or the balance of power. But however many different practices there may be, each practice binds its participants through its common requirements: rules.

The upshot is that within the domain of a practice, one does not merely act; one acts *as required* by the rules of the relevant practice. A practice-dependent action is a species of rule-governed action – its meaning can only be understood by reference to the practice as a system of rules. Familiar examples of rule-governed actions are the making of a move in a game of chess, conferring a degree in a university and delivering speeches at the United Nations (UN). Now we are in a position to identify the root of the difficulties with the practice conception espoused by practice turn scholars: it is one thing to say that somebody does X and quite another to say that one is *required* to do X within the bounds of a social practice. Recall that Bourdieu treated practices (institutions) as if they were identical with the realm of action broadly construed (Aristotle's *praxis*).[69] And we just showed that by adopting Bourdieu's scheme, practice-turn scholars collapse the idea of action performed under constraint (rule-governed action) within the category of action *simpliciter* (simple action).[70] In the next section, we argue that the analytical scope of action *simpliciter* is immensely broad and that accounts based on it suffer from indeterminacy and inchoateness.

---

[68] On the genesis of Renaissance diplomacy, see Garrett Mattingly, *Renaissance Diplomacy* (New York: Dover, 1988 [1955]).

[69] See note 45.      [70] On *action simpliciter*, see Chapter 1, under 'Simple Action'.

## International Practices and Simple Action

### Practice as Competent Action

In this part of the discussion, we explicate the distinction between simple action and rule-dependent action (and, by extension, practice-dependent action) while examining three contributions from the practice turn in IR. We begin with Adler and Pouliot's article 'International Practices', which supplies a useful synopsis of what its authors consider to be the five determining features of a practice.[71] A practice, Adler and Pouliot write, 'is a *performance* '; 'tends to be *patterned*, in that it generally exhibits regularities over time and space'; 'is more or less *competent* in a socially meaningful and recognizable way'; 'rests on *background knowledge*, which it embodies, enacts and reifies all at once' and 'weaves together the discursive and the material worlds'.[72] The feature that is crucial is that 'practices are competent performances.'[73] It deserves attention because it equates a practice (rule-governed action) with a form of action *simpliciter*: an equation we deem problematic.

The question here is not whether competence matters for action (it does) but whether it can serve as a defining criterion for a certain class of actions or as a source of relevant descriptions in our terms. Assume for a moment that competence roughly corresponds to skill, as suggested by Bourdieu, who Adler and Pouliot follow.[74] Skill is a graded notion, so that an action (say, bicycle riding or cooking) can be more or less skilful. Skills need not be restricted to motor skills (as in bicycle riding) but are associated more broadly with the degree of realisation of an end state or product. The skill, and the concomitant technique, has been more or less well mastered once a desirable outcome has been reached (proper balance of the bicycle, a savoury dish). However, a parallel notion defines competence in terms of an antecedent rule, not skill. We refer here to rule-following and, particularly, to following of constitutive rules within social practices. Consider the action we may describe as 'taking up of a seat in the UN Security Council'. Only an authorised representative of a UN member state, which now has a turn to sit on the Security Council according to the appropriate rules, can

---

[71] See note 2.    [72] Adler and Pouliot, 'International Practices', pp. 6–7.
[73] Adler and Pouliot, 'International Practices', p. 4.
[74] Adler and Pouliot, 'International Practices', p. 7.

properly take up a UN seat. Without satisfying all the complex requirements of the UN practice, no set of physical actions would qualify as
the practice-dependent action identifiable as 'taking up a UN Security
Council seat'. Success in performing this type of action does not
depend on going through certain physical motions directed at certain
outcomes (which can be realised with varying degrees of satisfaction);
it consists in meeting certain *conditions*. These conditions are not
physical or causal conditions for acting but logical conditions
expressed as rules. One's action is either competent, if it fulfils the
basic conditions of the practice in question as compressed in its constitutive rules, or it is not, if it fails to fulfil them.

There is, then, a principled difference between two types of competence. When competence is equivalent to a skill, a competent action, as
an action embellished by a skill, can be downgraded into a simple
action. For instance, 'excellent cooking' can become just 'cooking'
(simple action) without lapse into unintelligibility. When, however,
competence is defined by the antecedent rules of a practice (as in the
UN example), these rules set the logical condition for performing the
action.[75] Here the action cannot be downgraded or upgraded by
removing or adding rules to it at whim, since these rules, rather than
being an embellishment, represent a constitutive part of its identity.
Without these constitutive rules, the action does not *count as* an action
of the appropriate kind at all (it is not 'taking up a UN Security Council
seat' but something else). Therefore, the only avenue for us to become
competent participants in a practice is to first learn the rules that
constitute it, as a concrete practice.

If we attend to Adler and Pouliot's concept of 'competent performance', it is easy to see that it interprets competence as skill and not as
rules. In short, by 'practice', Adler and Pouliot do not mean a rule-
governed action but action *simpliciter*. This is revealed by their description of the practice of war: 'War for example is a socially meaningful
pattern of action which, in being performed *more or less competently*,
simultaneously embodies, reifies, and acts out background knowledge
and discourse in and on the material world.'[76] If we substituted 'fox
hunting' in the place of 'war', this would leave the meaning of the
preceding sentence unaffected. This substitution is permissible because

[75] Oakeshott, *On Human Conduct*, pp. 55, 58–61, 113, 120.
[76] Adler and Pouliot, 'International Practices', p. 8.

the sentence is a definition of simple action: it fits 'war' as well as any other meaningful doing. What renders this portrayal of war unsatisfactory is its abstract and indeterminate character: it does not indicate by virtue of what *concrete* features the skilfully competent action in question counts as war and not as fox hunting.[77] This can be corrected by understanding war in a different idiom, as a practice in the rule-dependent sense. So construed, war comprises the conduct of hostilities carried out by public authorities (states) bound by shared rules concerning the declaration and ending of war, non-combatant immunity, and prisoners of war. Moreover, because such rules are meaningful linguistic propositions, they must have concrete content: to understand what a rule says is to understand something concrete and determinate. By reintroducing the component of concrete meaning, the rule-governed conception of action offers us the first, crucial step for overcoming the indeterminacy which encumbers accounts of action *simpliciter*.

### Practices and International Organisations

We now turn to the arguments of IR scholars who have embraced Adler and Pouliot's view of practices as simple actions. In chapter 9 of *International Practices*, Sending and Neumann analyse organisational practices produced by the interactions between international organisations and states. The World Bank, as an organisation, they argue, exerts power over states by means of its expertise embodied in 'anchoring practices'.[78] The World Bank's Country Policy and Institutional Assessment practice anchors or 'makes possible' its Performance Based Allocation practice, where the latter governs the negotiations between the organisation and its member states over fund allocation to recipient states.[79] This anchoring practice aims to evaluate the fulfilment of target indicators (good governance, governmental corruption) by a candidate recipient state by assessing its annual performance in the realm of structural development. To support their hypothesis, Sending and Neumann adopt an approach centred on practices, described as moving away from the 'boundaries of things' and searching instead for the 'things of boundaries': 'Our things of

---

[77] We develop this critique of abstraction in detail in Frost and Lechner, 'Understanding International Practices from the Internal Point of View'.
[78] See note 47.
[79] Sending and Neumann, 'Banking on Power', pp. 232, 235–236.

boundaries are practices, which in and of themselves define where the inside of an [international organisation] stops and the outside begins.'[80] The claim is that it is possible to determine what an international organisation (or a state) is by looking at what it does or at its 'practices' (doings). This is a restatement of Pouliot's practicality thesis: who we are is determined by what we do.

In this case, the practicality thesis is invoked to expose the limitations of IR as a social science preoccupied with definitions. Against major IR theories such as rationalism, realism and constructivism, which try to settle matters *a priori* by stipulating how an identity – an international organisation in this case – is to be distinguished from its environment, Sending and Neumann

seek to bypass the problem of how to determine the boundary of [international organisations] and their environment by looking instead at the practices through which states and [international organisations] interact . . . the question of possible [international organisations'] authority and autonomy may then be analyzed as the *effects* of concrete practices rather than as emanating from *a priori* defined features of [international organisations] and/or states.[81]

The recommendation here is that IR students should study 'the *practices* through which states and international organisations *interact* '. But since 'practices' are seen as equivalent to 'interactions', this claim is a tautology: we are invited to explore the interactions through which states and international organisations interact. To escape such tautologies, it is necessary to define our key units – 'international organisations' as opposed to 'states' – prior to analysis. Any proper investigation demands clear definitions of key terms to avoid incoherence and equivocation in the subsequent analysis and should not to be confused with the altogether different, epistemological question of *a priori* knowledge.

Furthermore, the best type of definitions are not just idiosyncratic stipulations of singular concepts but definitions of concepts *within theories* that are intersubjectively accepted by a community of scholars. Within the present IR community, for example, realist theory takes international organisations to be epiphenomena of state interaction, rational choice theory takes them to be interest-driven institutions, and constructivist theory, to be institutional identities that can reconstitute state identities.[82] Regardless of which theory we think is more attractive on explanatory, normative or other grounds, a set of descriptions is required to tell us *what* to observe, and this implies that the object of observation must be defined in some way. When this object is a practice, the relevant descriptions would need to be logically coherent as well as concrete, enabling us to meaningfully distinguish one concrete practice from another – to wit, the practice of interstate war from the practice of structural reforms undertaken by the World Bank. Sending and Neumann's position is that theoretical definitions are redundant because observing what a given agency does (its 'practices', in their terms) is sufficient to fix its identity and differentiate it from its environment. But this claim is misconstrued. Practice, even if we accept for a moment that it stands for action *simpliciter*, is still the action of some specific agency in some specific context. We do not observe 'action' as such but 'humanitarian intervention', 'revolution' or 'election in Libya'. What we observe is always an object given under some description.

### International Practices of Deterrence

The last contribution to consider is the Cold War practice of deterrence explored by Morgan in chapter 6 of *International Practices*.[83] He advances three claims. First, that this practice developed in the aftermath of the Second World War, which transformed previously local conflicts into a global East-West confrontation whose protagonists sought not 'just physical expansion, but thorough ideological and cultural domination'.[84] Second, that deterrence is a complex practice that is at once military and political in character. Third, that even though the post-1945 practice of deterrence emerged under conditions of unprecedented ideological divide marked by the absence of a 'cooperative community' between the superpowers, it has contributed to the subsequent constitution of such a community. As Morgan concludes, 'There was a gradual rise in similarity in the superpowers' behaviour on deterrence ... their strategic postures came to be more

---

[82] For a discussion of the main lines of contention between realism, rational choice and constructivism in IR, especially in relation to interest and identity, see chapter 3 of Alexander Wendt, *Social Theory of International Politics* (Cambridge: Cambridge University Press, 1999), pp. 92–138.

[83] See note 47.    [84] Morgan, 'The Practice of Deterrence', p. 144.

alike . . . They became more aware of their interdependence in terms of security, and the implications of that.'[85]

For Morgan, what explains this convergence of Cold War deterrence practices is the quest for stability in the international system. As the context changed after the 1945 nuclear revolution, the need to ensure system stability could only be met by making corresponding adjustments in the deterrence practices of the USSR and the United States, leading to their gradual convergence. A community between the two superpowers, grounded on a convergent practice of deterrence, was created. While this implies that the actions of agents are subject to some sort of background constraint, its nature could be interpreted in two different ways. The first reading assumes that this constraint stems from the core norms constituting a social practice. Here, states intentionally follow rules as participants in a common social practice, international society, of which the practice of deterrence is a specific sub-practice. Within international society, member states engage in specific practices (such as deterrence) and pursue goals (international stability, international security) by intentionally taking each other's actions into consideration in a *normative sense*. In short, that states keep to the rules of the game called international society is not an unconscious, automatic action on their part. The second reading takes deterrence to be a more or less automatic response of agents whose actions are constrained differently – namely, by an international structure that operates as a physical field of forces or an impersonal market mechanism. On this second reading, the demand for international stability and international security in the international system is the *unintended* outcome of actions and reactions of actors who happened (but did not intend) to produce similar responses to their environment.

Morgan's argument seems to resonate with the second interpretation. He presents the convergence in superpower deterrence practices as the unintended outcome moulded by factors such as the similar organisational structure of the Soviet and the US military apparatuses and their political learning in the aftermath of the Cuban missile crisis.[86] The decisive factor for convergence is that

deterrence itself, in its fundamental objective, was a version of arms control. It was primarily for stabilizing conflicts at a point short of outright warfare,

---

[85] Morgan, 'The Practice of Deterrence', pp. 154, 158.
[86] Morgan, 'The Practice of Deterrence', pp. 156–157.

just as the activities usually labelled 'arms control' were mainly about stabilizing mutual deterrence.[87]

Deterrence, in other words, was a common response to the Cold War environment, where international stability had to be achieved through arms control. Drawing such a tight association between deterrence and arms control is a debatable proposition.[88] But even if we grant it, the question still remains: Was deterrence the unintended cumulative effect of structural factors or, conversely, a social practice that states pursued in the post-1945 world within the wider practice of international society? By portraying deterrence in terms of automated, unconscious consequences, reminiscent of Bourdieu's *habitus*, Morgan indicates that he departs from the practice-dependent perspective of actions that views actions as inscribed within contexts of shared meanings and shared rules. Once again, we have returned to the fundamental opposition between practice-dependent action and action *simpliciter*.

## Conclusion

The preceding assessment of the practice turn in IR identified three main problems. The most perspicuous one pertains to the concept of action. Bourdieu, as noted, reduced the notion of a practice (institution) to the realm of action broadly construed (*praxis*). Our critique showed that by embracing Bourdieu's premises, practice-turn scholars have divested themselves of the conceptual materials necessary to differentiate the idea of practice-dependent action (which presupposes the context of social practices for its successful performance) from action *simpliciter* (whose successful performance does not presuppose a social practice). The more general point is that making sense of performances often demands an understanding of the concrete, social context within which they are located. What this suggests is that the very 'stuff' of international relations – war, balances of

---

[87] Morgan, 'The Practice of Deterrence', p. 158.
[88] Thomas Schelling differentiates deterrence from defence – one is a strategy of prevention used to dissuade an opponent from inflicting harm, the other is a reprisal following harm infliction. Arms control can rely on both deterrence and defence or indeed on neither (it can be accomplished by treaties). See Thomas Schelling, *Arms and Influence* (New Haven: Yale University Press, 1966), pp. 35, 78–79.

power, diplomacy, international legal norms, treaty making and so on – comprises social practices.

The second no less significant but perhaps less obvious problem is theoretical scepticism. IR scholars from the practice turn whose positions we canvassed analysed international practices that vary in kind and scope: diplomacy, deterrence and practices within international organisations. Despite such variations, all these scholars remained sceptical about the role of theory in making sense of practices that are not yet understood. As they see matters, theorising should be replaced by empirical and/or historical studies tracing what international actors do on the ground. On this view, international practices designate the day-to-day interactions of international relations practitioners: diplomats, military officials and security experts. The hidden premise is that it is possible to establish the identity of actions through observations unmediated by theory. But if our descriptivist argument has cogency, this premise cannot be sustained because actions falling within the basic category of practice-dependent action are intelligible only a under a prior description and, hence, are 'theoretical' by default. It is important to acknowledge that theorising does not imply consensus over how a certain practice is to be understood, and indeed, different researchers might disagree over the concrete parameters of its domain; over its basic, constitutive rules and over who qualifies as a participant in it. Yet *some* criteria must be spelled out to fix the identity of the practice under investigation, and they cannot be formulated without some form of conceptual synthesis or theory.

At bottom, the infelicities exhibited in the writings of the recent practice turn have their source in the entrenched idea that practice is practice and theory is theory: like oil and water, they do not easily mix. But this assumes without argument that any investigation of practices must commence with the category of practice (*praxis*) construed as the converse of theory. In this book, our point of departure in investigating practices is different: we begin with the hermeneutic category of *understanding*, which transcends the theory-practice binary. In the next chapter, we develop our brand of practice theory directed at explicating the general logic of social practices and make the case that the proper understanding of practices demands the internal point of view. This is our take on the third, most difficult, problem posed by Bourdieu's 'theory of practice': the clash between externalism and internalism.

# 3 | *Practice Theory*
## *A Basic Philosophical Template*

Our diagnosis of the 'practice turn' in International Relations (IR) was that its proponents have unduly collapsed the distinction between action and social practice. To rectify this, in this chapter, we outline a basic (in the philosophical sense) template of practice theory. We call it basic because it aims to supply a coherent account of the general logic of social practices by asking what a practice, *as such*, is and what conditions enable its proper understanding by thinking and choosing human beings. The practice theory advanced here is indebted to Ludwig Wittgenstein and Michael Oakeshott, using the ideas of John Rawls and Herbert L. A. Hart as supplementary sources.[1] We have reworked their arguments into an independent position which presents a practice as a common domain of interaction with five analytical components: (1) the internal point of view (internalism), (2) rule-following, (3) constitutive rules, (4) the understanding of meaning and (5) norms.

Concretely, our central thesis is that the internal point of view and rule-following constitute the conceptual core of a practice. We begin by a sketching these two core elements, adding the rest – constitutive rules, the understanding of meaning, and norms – as we proceed. Since internalism was discussed previously, the problem of rule-following occupies the centre stage in the present chapter. Rule-following is a special type of rule-governed action, tied to a particular theory of meaning ('meaning in use', as articulated by Oakeshott and Wittgenstein) which presupposes a special, 'internal' relation between meaning and action. The opening section explicates the generic concept of rule-governed action by deploying an idealised model of a chess game, and the next takes up the theme of regulative and constitutive rules. As will become clear, the

---

[1] Ludwig Wittgenstein, *Philosophical Investigations*, 3rd ed., trans. G. E. M. Anscombe (Oxford: Blackwell, 1968 [1953]); John Rawls, 'Two Concepts of Rules', *Philosophical Review* 64 (1) 1955: 3–32; H. L. A. Hart, *The Concept of Law* (Oxford: Clarendon Press, 1961); Michael Oakeshott, *On Human Conduct* (Oxford: Clarendon Press, 1975).

chess model of rules cannot accommodate the concept of rule-following. We argue that rule-following, as predicated on the notion of 'meaning in use', represents an exclusive characteristic of practices. The significance of this point is that actual human practices differ in principle from games like chess. While the terms 'practices' and 'games' are used interchangeably at the outset, their differentia is examined in the section 'Games versus Practices'. But even though rule-following dominates the discussion, the internal point of view continues to lurk in the background. Thus in the section 'The Understanding of Meaning within a Practice', we revisit the epistemological aspect of internalism (the question of how agents are able to *understand* the common rules of a practice) and broach its normative aspect (the question of why agents *accept* the rules of a practice as action guiding) in the final pages.

## Rule-Following and the Internal Point of View

The overarching thesis of our practice theory has two parts. It holds that a practice is a distinctive, relatively autonomous domain of a *rule-following activity* and that a proper understanding of this domain of activity demands *the internal point of view*. It is important to reiterate that our approach is calibrated to one specific object of investigation – a practice – and that 'internalism' refers not to the understanding of meaningful action per se but to the understanding of social practices and of practice-dependent action. In earlier chapters, we defined 'internalism' as an observational standpoint that an investigator adopts in studying a social practice from 'the inside'. The reason the investigator's understanding qualifies as internal is that it captures the common understanding which *practice participants themselves have of their own practice*. The contrary, external point of view, we said, is typical of discourses committed to reduction and invariance, as exemplified by certain forms of scientific explanation.[2] In this chapter, the internal point of view is taken to represent a common epistemological perspective of understanding, undertaken not by observers but by the actors located *within* a common practice. In this basic epistemological sense, internalism presents intersubjective or 'public' understanding to

---

[2] See our argument in Chapter 1, under 'Internalism, Externalism and Social Science'; and Chapter 2, under 'Bourdieu's Externalism and Social Science'.

be contrasted with a purely subjective or 'private' standpoint. As a general concept, then, internalism designates the common intersubjective understanding – roughly, common knowledge – shared by a group of actors who have learned to perform actions within the framework of a common practice.[3]

Before we proceed, let us retrace the components of a social practice with which we are already familiar. In Chapters 1 and 2, we suggested that to do something in a practice is to perform an action under some description of it. The descriptions must be *relevant* (bound to the domain of a *concrete* practice), and they must be shared by the practice participants. Since the internal point of view is affixed to a given practice, the relevant descriptions are condensed in the rules defining the practice, where a rule is a meaningful linguistic proposition (statement) telling one *how* to do something. A special class of rules, constitutive rules, matter because they specify the conditions by virtue of which an action counts as an action of the appropriate kind. For example, we may learn that putting a certain document before a certain person under such-and-such conditions counts as the action 'presenting a passport to a border control official'. This rule-dependent action is at the same time, obliquely, a practice-dependent action. In performing the action under the specified conditions, the premise is that we also know the meaning of the wider social practice to which it belongs. That is, we know that the rule-dependent action described as 'presenting one's passport to a boarder official' is, obliquely, also a practice-dependent action – an element in the wider practice recognisable as a 'legal crossing of the border'.

However, to understand something is one thing; to act on this understanding is quite another. To support our main thesis about what constitutes the logical core of a practice, we shall have to explicate the connection between the internal point of view, as type of understanding, and rule-following, as type of activity (which itself demands internalist understanding). This connection is manifest on two planes. The first is that rule-following is a *meaningful* activity. As such, it presupposes understanding on part of the agent, where the category

---

[3] The term 'common knowledge' usually designates knowledge of the sort 'A knows that B knows that $p$', where $p$ is a proposition and A and B two agents – the classic statement is David Lewis, *Convention: A Philosophical Study* (Oxford: Blackwell, 2002 [1969]), pp. 52–57. By 'common knowledge', we mean knowledge *shared* between A and B or intersubjectively held knowledge.

of understanding of meaning is graded and ranges from perfect understanding to almost perfect misunderstanding (the limit being unintelligibility). The second is that rule-following is an *activity*, not a frozen analytical snapshot of what is going on. Thus it is predicated on non-abstract meaning, meaning manifest in a concrete activity or what Oakeshott and Wittgenstein called 'meaning in use'. We shall say more about this later, but for now, the gist of the idea of meaning in use is simply that rules, as meaningful propositions governing action, acquire their meaning in *the course of being used*.

But, of course, if the rules can be understood, they can also be misunderstood. This possibility of misunderstanding is indispensable for clarifying the concept of rule-following. In the words of Wittgensteinian Peter Winch, 'the notion of following a rule is logically inseparable from the notion of making a mistake.'[4] The mistake, when recognised, reveals the rule's oblique presence. This elucidates a crucial point that may be overlooked – to wit, that a set of individuals count as participants in a common practice only when they have common knowledge of its rules. This knowledge consists in that they (or at least most of them) can *tell* when a rule has been misused. Knowledge here does not designate propositional knowledge, or 'knowing that', but competence, or 'knowing how'.[5] Oakeshott elucidates the distinction in the following way:

Doing anything both depends upon and exhibits knowing how to do it; and though part (but never the whole) of knowing how to do it can subsequently be reduced to knowledge in the form of propositions (and possibly to ends, rules and principles), these propositions are neither the spring of the activity nor are they in any direct sense regulative of the activity.[6]

---

[4] Peter Winch, *The Idea of a Social Science and Its Relation to Philosophy* (London: Routledge, 1958), p. 32. Winch derives this reading from Wittgenstein. A similar view is advanced by Crispin Wright, 'Wittgenstein on Following a Rule: Five Themes', unpublished manuscript, quoted in Paul A. Boghossian, 'Rules, Meaning and Intention: Discussion', *Philosophical Studies* 124 (2) 2005: 185–197, p. 186. Key articles on Wittgenstein's concept of rule-following are collected in Alexander Miller and Crispin Wright (eds.), *Rule-Following and Meaning* (Chesham: Acumen, 2002).

[5] The distinction was popularised by Gilbert Ryle, *The Concept of Mind* (London: Hutchinson, 1949), ch. 2 (pp. 25–61).

[6] Michael Oakeshott, 'Rational Conduct' (1950), in Michael Oakeshott, *Rationalism in Politics and Other Essays*, new ed. (Indianapolis: Liberty Fund, 1999 [1962]), pp. 99–131, p. 110.

A competent player knows how to recognise and how to correct a mistake, should one occur – this is what sets apart masters from novices. Should the novice falter, the master can step in and offer advice. In accepting this authoritative advice, the novice will be accepting the rules of the game. The advice is authoritative not because it has been uttered by a person of great virtue or wisdom but because it appeals to a procedure of validity which sorts out valid from invalid moves. A game, at a minimum, is a logical space that has boundaries: it comprises all the valid moves potentially open to its players. This is why a mistake, diagnosed as an invalid move, is always a mistake *within* the logical space of a game: it is an internalist notion.

Practices resemble games in that both present rule-governed domains of interaction. A simplified chess model can help us convey the basic idea of rule-governed action or action that has enabling conditions in the form of rules. For instance, the action 'moving the Rook' is properly described as rule-governed because the rules of chess define the identity 'Rook' (and similarly, 'Queen' or 'King') and thus the moves that this chess piece is permitted to make within the chess game. *The label 'rule-governed action'* (or rule-dependent action) *indicates that an action is logically dependent on rules for its performance.* We must know the rules first to be able to carry out the actions they specify. With regard to this kind of action, it is logically impossible to act and invent a rule to cover the action performed after the event.[7] Action that falls within a practice or game, then, should be differentiated from action that does not take place within a domain governed by rules. In Chapter 1, we distinguished simple action (action *simpliciter*) from a practice-dependent action (a special sort of rule-dependent action). A simple action may be described and understood without knowing how it fits into a background social context.[8] Examples of simple actions may include walking, riding a bicycle, roller skating or throwing a stone. In contrast, a *practice-dependent action* is bound to the domain of a practice, where participants interact by necessarily following intersubjectively shared standards, rules.

---

[7] International relations scholar Robert Jackson recognises this point. The rules of cricket cannot be guessed; they must be known in advance of the game. Robert Jackson, *The Global Covenant: Human Conduct in a World of States* (Oxford: Oxford University Press, 2000), p. 50.

[8] See our discussion of simple action in Chapter 1, 'Simple Action and Practice-Dependent Action'.

The closest analogue of a practice in this sense is a rule-governed activity such as a game.

The concept of making a *mistake* can now be defined more precisely, as the violation (often inadvertent) of known and accepted rules of a game. Here, 'game' is to be understood broadly, to encompass practices and the like. If either of these two conditions – knowledge of the rules (competence) and rule acceptance – is missing, then the agent would qualify not as a rule-follower but, at most, as an *external* spectator to a rule-following activity. Such a spectator is somebody who does not know or understand what the actions under observation mean. This distinguishes the internal point of view (of participants) from the external point of view (of observers). The notion of observation, however, is an intricate one.

So far, we have defined 'internalism' as a standpoint of understanding common to a number of individuals. However, 'common' is an ambiguous term. Here we restrict the internal point of view to a common knowledge of a domain (space) of rule-following activity – a game or a practice. But we may wonder, How do the rule-followers know themselves to be positioned *inside* this common space? That is, how do they know themselves to be *participants* in a common game or practice? We should resist adopting Aristotle's distinction between *praxis* (action) and *theoria* (observation),[9] which instructs us to classify automatically all observers as non-participants. The kind of practice theory we recommend breaks with this Aristotelian distinction and claims that under certain conditions, conditions which comprise the basic rules of the practice, some observers count as game participants. Consider professional chess tournaments, where the chess players' moves are observed by a third party, a referee. The referee does not act as an observer in the sense of an external spectator. Instead, he or she guards against *cheating*. Since cheating is akin to the making of a mistake, a competent referee, like any other competent player, must know what sort of action counts as mistaken within the game. Thus if a chess player refuses to accept the verdict issued by the referee – say, that 'd1 to e3' counts as a mistaken move of the White Queen or perhaps as cheating – we may doubt whether this player

---

[9] On the distinction between *praxis* (action in the broad sense) and *theoria* (observation, or 'contemplation', as it is often translated), see Chapter 1, note 6.

either knows or accepts the rules of chess.[10] It follows that all those individuals who jointly know and accept known rules of the game, acceptance disclosed in their actual conduct, adhere to the internal point of view – the standpoint which renders intelligible the rules constituting this particular game. As a result, a game can include a category of observers (e.g., referees, judges) *inside* its domain. Where the line between the inside and the outside of a particular game will be drawn depends not on a prefabricated taxonomy of agents or of rules but on the fact that a group of agents hold common knowledge of certain rules among themselves.

To generalise, individuals qualify as participants in a common space of a rule-following activity (a practice or game) whenever they jointly know and accept the standards determining what counts as a mistake within that space. In virtue of such intersubjective knowledge held in common, as an internal point of view, a collectivity of agents becomes a group. A special case is that of a class of observers who know the rules of the game but do not accept these rules as a guide to their *own* conduct. An audience of such knowledgeable observers who monitor how the players (and possibly the referees) interact would count as participants in the game in an extended sense of participation: they would be *participants* and not *players*. In short, without rules to be 'followed', there can be no game, and successful participation in the game depends on common knowledge of the relevant rules.

## Constitutive Rules and Regulative Rules

Previously, we mentioned that certain moves count as mistakes and that certain agents count as participants in a game. The concept of 'counting as' brings us to the topic of constitutive rules. In the introductory chapter, we made use of John Searle's definition of constitutive rules, and in Chapter 1, constitutive rules were compared with a class of rules (left unnamed) that constrain action.[11] Here we shall

---

[10] A chessboard contains sixty-four squares. Viewed from the position of White, it has eight rows or ranks (1, 2, 3, 4, 5, 6, 7, 8) and eight columns (a, b, c, d, e, f, g, h).

[11] See the introductory chapter, notes 55, 71 (in the text accompanying notes 55–57 of the same chapter, we distanced ourselves from Searle's residual physicalism); and Chapter 1, under 'Internalism, Externalism and Social Science'.

label this class of constraining rules 'regulative rules' and flesh out how they differ from constitutive rules. As Searle noted, a constitutive rule stipulates that doing 'X counts as Y in context C'.[12] In terms of our chess model, '*Moving an object laterally on unoccupied squares of the chessboard* (X) counts as *moving the Rook* (Y) within the context of *chess* (C)' is a constitutive rule of chess. It is called 'constitutive' because it constitutes or creates a type of activity which did not exist before the rule was introduced.[13] It is obviously possible to physically move a wooden piece on a wooden board, but this physical move would not *count* as 'moving the Rook' (as rule-governed action) in the absence of the constitutive rules of chess. A game is never just a set of physical moves or physical entities – such physical aspects are incorporated into the game through the meaning of its constitutive rules.

Constitutive rules should not be confused with regulative rules. To regulate action is to constrain it. A rule constrains the manner in which an action is performed – we are supposed to drive *on the left*, talk *politely* or engage in military action across borders *responsibly*. Rules, as Oakeshott avers, are 'adverbial qualifications of choices'.[14] The bare minimum required of any rule is that it is an action constraint. But even though all rules are regulative, not all rules are constitutive. Constitutive rules create new types of activity, whereas regulative rules can be invented *post factum* to regulate a pre-existing activity. One way to establish whether a rule is regulative or constitutive is to test whether changing the rule would render the action falling within its purview impossible to perform. In Japan, the UK and South Africa, rules of the road stipulate driving on the left, whereas in North America and Europe, on the right. Were the rules to be swapped, so that now Americans, Canadians and Europeans would have to drive on the left side of the road, it would still be possible for them to perform the action described as 'driving a vehicle'. This shows that rules of the road regulate action but do not constitute it: they are, therefore, regulative rules.

---

[12] John Searle, *Speech Acts: An Essay in the Philosophy of Language* (Cambridge: Cambridge University Press, 1969), p. 35. This is Searle's second definition of a constitutive rule.

[13] Searle, *Speech Acts*, p. 33. This is Searle's first definition of a constitutive rule.

[14] Oakeshott, *On Human Conduct*, pp. 55–57. See also Chapter 1, note 23.

Constitutive rules create a new type of activity by defining what counts as such activity. They may be termed *defining* rules: they define and assign identities and rights to the agents performing the activity. In the game of chess, a constitutive rule assigns the identity 'Rook' to a certain chess piece, and this identity assignment determines what this piece may do (it may be moved vertically and horizontally on the chessboard). A constitutive rule, we might say, gives a set of rights which a player may use when contemplating what moves to make within a game. Thus a 'Rook' has the right (permission) of lateral movement. Such rule-dependent identities are not just theatre masks; for the players who endorse them, nothing more solid, true or objective lies behind these identities.

Rules can be thought of as conditions for performing an action in an appropriate way. In subscribing to rules, as Oakeshott and Rawls have suggested, agents subscribe not to common ends or goals but, rather, to common conditions.[15] These conditions are of two principal kinds. When their task is to constrain the manner of action, they present regulative rules. Conversely, constitutive rules are conditions that demarcate the domain of a concrete practice. These more exacting conditions not only define what counts as a valid, proper or correct manner of action within a concrete practice domain but do so by assigning statuses (identities) and thereby rights and obligations to its participants. To acquire the status of participants in a practice or game, a group of individuals must – this 'must' is a condition to be fulfilled – choose to recognise a common set of identities, together with the attendant rights and obligations, as binding in their mutual relations. They cannot sit on the fence with respect to that choice. Nor can they pretend to be acting *as if* they were abiding by the conditions of the relevant practice.[16]

One well-known difficulty, voiced by Wittgenstein, is that practices exhibit an extraordinary diversity.[17] (Wittgenstein's term for a practice is 'language-game'.)[18] The practice of tea drinking differs from university teaching, and both differ vastly from that of waging war. Should we infer from this that the puzzle of rule-following defies theoretical

---

[15] Oakeshott, On *Human Conduct*, pp. 61, 79, 119–120; Rawls, 'Two Concepts of Rules', p. 25.
[16] Rawls, 'Two Concepts of Rules', p. 24.
[17] Wittgenstein, *Philosophical Investigations*, §§65–71.
[18] Wittgenstein, *Philosophical Investigations*, §§23, 65–83.

integration, as advocates of the practice turn claimed in Chapter 2? Wittgenstein and practice-turn scholars seem to agree that a practice *theory* cannot be forged because practices lack a common foundation. One of the central theses of this book is that a coherent practice theory can be constructed without resort to foundations. We adopt a non-foundational approach of *practice differentiation* which distinguishes between various domains of rule-following, including international and global practices (Chapters 4 and 5). As a first step on the road to practice differentiation, we shall clarify how practices differ from cognate forms of rule-governed activity and particularly from games.

## Games versus Practices

In setting out to differentiate practices from games, we develop two broad arguments. The first is that games represent *rule-governed action*, whereas practices represent *rule-following*.[19] So far, our simplified chess model assumed that the categories of rule-governed action and rule-following are equivalent. Strictly speaking, however, rule-following is a special case of rule-governed action which hinges on a special notion of meaning ('meaning in use', analysed in the next section). Second, we argue that the 'moves' made within games lend themselves to abstract descriptions (chess being a quintessential example), whereas making sense of actions within practices requires descriptions that are substantive and concrete.

Here we use the concept of a 'game' as a term of art. It covers the idea of an interactive engagement among multiple players that is governed by rules. Game theory, to which we turn in a moment, has developed a special vocabulary to capture the congruence or conflict of interests among players. Chess, poker and boxing are 'games of pure conflict' in game-theoretic terms, where the losses of one party are gains for the other. In 'games of coordination', the players have overlapping interests, and in 'games of competition' such as the Prisoner's Dilemma, they simultaneously hold mutually conflicting and overlapping preferences. What differentiates games from practices? Games have a determinate beginning and end, and they can be played

---

[19] The converse, general claim, that *all* instances of rule-governed action are games or that *all* instances of rule-following are practices, is not taken up and is, in any case, implausible.

repeatedly, in matches, tournaments, bouts, galas, rubbers and hands. Practices, by comparison, have ongoing 'histories' and cannot be terminated or exhausted by a series of completed matches. Another peculiar trait of games is that they are rule-governed activities freely entered into. A player may enter a game for reasons of recreation or pleasure. New games may be invented at will. But certain types of practices, such as the civil state, present domains in which individuals find themselves participating whether they wish it or not. Practices of this kind are not the deliberate inventions of their participants but transformations of earlier historical forms.

The differentia between games and practices has two further facets that have a special bearing on the present discussion. The first is normativity. Games normally do not include normative injunctions. The game of chess, for instance, has no rule stipulating that the players *ought* to play chess. However, in certain practices of non-instrumental character, paradigmatic among which is the civil state, each participant *ought to* take into account what other participants in the practice do, so that the notion of making a mistake supposes normatively interlocking choices. The relation established between practice participants is normative in character (see Chapter 1). The second aspect of the notable difference between games and practices concerns the possibility of change. The defining rules of an actual living practice can gradually transform over time (think of the emergence of the welfare state), whereas changing the constitutive rules of chess means that we are no longer playing chess but some other game. Henceforth, the term 'practices' will be reserved for domains of rule-following which allow for normative relations between actors as well as for rule change and 'games' for artificial domains of rule-governed activity which lack the elements of normativity and change.

The contrast between games and practices is apposite for another reason that we illustrate with a brief discussion of game theory, a branch of mathematics that studies games of strategy. Choices are 'strategic' in the sense of being 'interdependent' – the outcomes in a game of strategy cannot be determined by a single player acting alone but reflect the interdependent choices of all the players.[20] From its very

---

[20] A standard definition by Zagare reads: 'Game Theory is formally a branch of mathematics developed to deal with conflict of interest situations in social science ... When game theorists use the word "game," they are referring to any social situation involving two or more actors (players) in which the interests of

inception in the mid-1940s, game theory was related to international politics. During the Cold War, game theoretical research in the United States sought to devise strategies for defeating the USSR and was sponsored by the RAND Corporation in Santa Monica and Princeton University.[21] We offer a brief overview of the game theoretic approach because it is representative of what we refer to as abstract games but also because game theory has become dominant in the disciplines of Political Science and IR in US academia.

Game theory covers games of interdependent choice whose typology varies depending on factors such as uncertainty, information, availability of agreements and the number of players.[22] Here we consider a two-person game of pure conflict (a two-person zero-sum game), the logical model for which is chess.[23] Game theorists have applied this and similar models to study international conflict, but our aim is not to discuss such applications.[24] The point is more basic: it is that the logic of a practice, as we have defined it, is fundamentally at odds with the logic of abstract games (such as chess) discussed within game theory. What matters is not that chess is a zero-sum game but that it presupposes a particular relation between the rules of the game and the players' attitude towards the rules – this attitude is purely instrumental. Our presentation is simplified to account for a typical abstract game (chess) to be compared with a typical practice. As will be shown, whereas a chess model can elucidate *some* of the analytical elements of a practice, it cannot elucidate *all* of its core elements, and we need to know why this is so.

---

the players are interconnected or interdependent.' Frank C. Zagare, *Game Theory: Concepts and Applications* (Newbury Park, CA: SAGE, 1984), p. 7.

21  Famous books on game theory published under the auspices of the RAND Corporation are J. C. C. McKinsey, *Introduction to the Theory of Games* (New York: McGraw-Hill, 1952); and Melvin Dresher, *Games of Strategy: Theories and Applications* (Englewood Cliffs, NJ: Prentice-Hall, 1961). Thomas Schelling spent a year at RAND before producing his classic, *The Strategy of Conflict* (New York: Oxford University Press, 1963).

22  One of the best overviews is Robert J. Aumann, 'Game Theory', in John Eatwell, Murray Milgate and Peter Newman (eds.), *The New Palgrave: Game Theory* (London: Macmillan 1989), pp. 1–53.

23  For a non-technical introduction, see Anatol Rapoport, *Two-Person Game Theory: The Essential Ideas* (Ann Arbor: University of Michigan Press, 1966).

24  The early applications of game theory to international relations were restricted to zero-sum games – for example, part 4 of Morton A. Kaplan, *System and Process in International Politics* (New York: Wiley, 1957).

What makes chess an attractive model of strategic interaction is its parsimony. Despite its enormous surface complexity, the game of chess can be reduced to four key premises: (1) a pair of players or camps ('Black' and 'White'); (2) a single domain of interaction ('chessboard'); (3) constitutive rules defining valid moves within that domain, known in advance by the players and (4) a no-change stipulation – constitutive rules cannot be changed while the game is being played. Game theorists often supplant this idealised chess model with assumptions borrowed from neoclassical economics.[25] Modern neoclassical economics or microeconomics is a science of *choice* under constraints (information and budget constraints). This emphasis on decision-making makes it directly compatible with game theory and rational-choice methodology.[26] The explanation of the mechanism linking actions to preferred outcomes, sought by the rational actor, is provided by a theory of utility.[27] Modern microeconomists use money as a standard of value for measuring utility. The assumption is that money is 'fungible' (translatable across diverse sectors)[28] and that it can serve as a universal metric to determine the price of qualitatively different classes of objects, including actions. Game theory does not impose restrictions on what sort of actions can have utility. In the sphere of politics and international relations, utility can be assigned to actions such as citizens' voting in an election, presidents dispatching troops or

[25] Consider the 'grandfathers' of game theory: von Neumann was a mathematician and Morgenstern an economist. John von Neumann and Oskar Morgenstern, *Theory of Games and Economic Behavior*, 60th anniversary commemorative ed. (Princeton: Princeton University Press, 2007 [1944]). In IR, Kenneth Waltz's seminal *Theory of International Politics* (Boston, MA: McGraw Hill, 1979) combines the microeconomic premises of a price mechanism with the methodology of game theory to explain the structure and functioning of the international system.

[26] An illuminating philosophical discussion of the difference between game theory (interdependent choice under constraint), rational choice (principles of rationality and utility maximisation) and social choice (choice aggregation strategies) is Gerald F. Gaus, *On Philosophy, Politics and Economics* (Belmond, CA: Wadsworth, 2008). The roots of game theory can be traced even deeper – to decision theory dealing with decisions under uncertainty or risk.

[27] On utility theory as positing a mechanism linking actions to outcomes, see Morton D. Davis, *Game Theory: A Non-Technical Introduction* (New York: Dover, 1997), p. 61.

[28] On fungibility in IR, see David A. Baldwin, 'Power and International Relations', in Walter Carlsnaes, Thomas Risse and Beth A. Simmons (eds.), *Handbook of International Relations* (London: Sage, 2013), pp. 273–297, p. 278.

a congress committee selecting a leader. In summary, the methodology of game theory assumes that monetary equivalents ('pay-offs') can be assigned to a set of ordered outcomes (in a ranked and transitive order), that each player has preferences over outcomes and that each chooses an action that picks the highest-ranked outcome from the set (utility maximisation). In a game theoretic sense, a 'game' presents a space of moves determined by initial states of the world, the distribution of outcomes and the feasible set of strategies enabling each player to win by acting so as to obtain the potentially highest pay-off. A strategy for a player is a complete plan, formulated in advance, for playing the game from beginning to end.[29]

At this juncture, we draw attention to two of game theory's standard conceptual pillars – chess (as a basic model of interdependent choice) and money (as a uniform metric of choice). By stipulating that disparate types of action can be measured through a uniform metric, the problem of action – to do something or not to do it – is recast as a decision-making problem concerning the price of alternative choices, also known as 'cost-benefit analysis'.[30] The strength of this analysis lies in its potential for generalisation. Its principle limitation is its inability to account for actions constituted by rules, especially rules which confer identities and rights. Consider identities first. If we wish to understand why, after the end of the Cold War, the majority of Eastern European states began to see themselves and act as genuinely independent (sovereign) states and no longer as satellites to a Soviet empire, a cost-benefit analysis would not help us: agents may hold on to an identity ('sovereign state') and often do, despite there being no pay-off (measurable in monetary terms or otherwise) for doing so. Now consider rights. Suppose that a state has proclaimed its commitment to the rule of law but that, in actuality, it started to resolve disputes over

---

[29] As Melvin Dresher writes, 'To simplify the mathematical description of a game, we introduce the concept of a "strategy." In the actual play of a game, instead of making his decision at each move each player may formulate in advance of the play a plan for playing the game from the beginning to end ... We may think of a strategy of a player as a set of instructions for playing the given game from the first move to the last.' Dresher, *Games of Strategy*, p. 2. The normal (matrix-type) form of representing a game emphasises outcomes and strategies. The extensive (tree-type) form allows a representation of the available information at each move and the timing of the moves.

[30] See David Schmidtz, 'A Place for Cost-Benefit Analysis', *Noûs* 35 (suppl. 1) 2001: 148–171.

rights on the basis of cost by allowing court cases to be adjudicated in favour of the highest bidders. Clearly, the logic of cost-benefit analysis clashes with the logic of rights. For once granted and recognised, a right – and analogously, an identity – forms a 'jurisdiction', in Oakeshott's terms.[31] The jurisdiction of rights and identities is indivisible (we either have rights or identities or we do not), and it extends over the person as a whole. It is misconstrued to treat them as if they were bundles of divisible goods that have price tags attached to them.

Seen from this perspective, game theory is an attempt to theorise action by dispensing with the language of rights and identities and thus with constitutive rules that define rights and identities. On game theoretic premises, the rules of the game are tools for attaining a uniform, instrumental purpose: the maximisation of pay-offs. Such purely instrumental rules are identity-free: they can be reproduced by any agent conceivable – a human being, an animal, a machine – or any process, including evolutionary processes and computer algorithms.[32] But certainly, if we compare the competition between pigeons with that between people, the differences will turn out to be far more perspicuous than the similarities, even if we grant that both types of agents engage in maximising behaviour. The significance of this conclusion is that game theory and practice theory, as articulated here, diverge in spite of having isomorphic starting premises (interaction constrained by rules) because they conceptualise rules in ways that differ in principle.[33] The game theorist employs a concept of a rule modelled on the notion of a *strategy*.[34] Strategic action, as a form of instrumental action, does not factor in actors' identities. But such identities present a central postulate of practice theory where certain rules – constitutive rules – operate as identity-conferring and rights-conferring devices.

[31] Oakeshott argues that a rule has a 'jurisdiction' or a domain of application. Oakeshott, *On Human Conduct*, p. 125. However, *mutatis mutandis*, his argument also applies to rights and statuses.

[32] At the limit, the players in a game can be computer strategies. A classic example of such an evolutionary game theoretic approach with relevance to international relations is Robert Axelrod, *The Evolution of Cooperation* (New York: Basic Books, 1984).

[33] The reason for this divergence is that game theory is a consequentialist theory of action (emphasising 'outcomes'), whereas practice theory belongs to the family of right-based and rule-based theories. For a distinction between goal-based, right-based and duty-based (rule-based) theories of politics, see Ronald Dworkin, *Taking Rights Seriously* (London: Duckworth, 1977), pp. 171–172.

[34] See note 29.

What is more, as a consequence of their commitment to economic micro-foundations, game theorists end up adopting a rather narrow conception of games themselves. A proper understanding of the game of chess (or any other game) requires knowledge of its constitutive rules, the rules specifying the identities of the pieces and the permissible moves. Cost-benefit analysis, however, assumes – and indeed, must assume – these identities away (it treats them as exogenously given).

Last but not least, another limitation of the game theoretic approach can be noted. It is that its abstract model of rule-governed action, represented by chess, does not approximate in an adequate way rule-following carried out in actual social practices. One aspect of this mismatch is empirical. Modern human society comprises a staggering number of individuals, not just two players, Black and White (violating chess premise 1). But since models do not purport to be empirically veridical, this is the least cogent objection. A more plausible criticism that draws its force from Pierre Bourdieu's social theory (Chapter 2) is that in modernity, human conduct unfolds on various chessboards, or 'fields' in Bourdieu's vocabulary – economics, ethics, aesthetics, politics and so on (violating chess premise 2). On this view, it is erroneous to assume that the economic domain must be primary with respect to human relations. Insofar as this objection is quasi-empirical, it is not potent enough. The final and arguably decisive objection against the attempt to view abstract games as approximations of concrete practices is conceptual: it concerns the category of constitutive rules. None of the constitutive rules of chess can be changed without thereby destroying the game. The rigidity of constitutive rules in games like chess has two sources. One is that chess is mapped over a single, logically closed domain of interaction – an eight-by-eight chessboard – where the identity of each player is defined by a single criterion, its permissible moves within this same domain. Another source of rigidity is the premise that both players in a chess tournament know, in advance of each move, what all the moves have been up to that point as well as how the game may be ended (either by the rule of checkmate or stalemate). In mathematical jargon, chess is a finite game of complete information.[35] But since in actual human conduct, rule-following

---

[35] Herbert Gintis writes, 'A finite game is a game with a finite number of nodes in its game tree. A game of perfect information is a game where every information set is a single node and Nature has no moves.' Herbert Gintis, *Game Theory Evolving: A Problem-Centered Introduction to Modeling Strategic Interaction*

takes place on multiple, not always clearly delineated chessboards, it is hardly possible to know how, or even whether, this multi-dimensional 'game' might end: the future is open. Since human beings participate simultaneously in many different practices, and since the circumstances in which these operate are subject to ongoing change, it is often necessary for participants to consider modifying some of the rules of their practices to avoid contradictions, tensions and identity crises. This is particularly salient in the international sphere, where people are participating in 'macro practices' – that is, practices encompassing other practices – a theme pursued in the Conclusion of the book.

The discussion in this section may be summed up by noting that the conception of a social practice contradicts all except one of the four basic premises of an abstract game such as chess. This is the premise of constitutive rules, the sole premise shared across practices and games (chess premise 3). Therefore, even though chess is useful as an initial model for explicating the concept of constitutive rules, for the reasons just mentioned, it cannot be profitably deployed for investigating the constitutive rules *of practices*, for the constitutive rules of a given practice may undergo change without thereby destroying the practice.

This, then, raises the problem of practice transformation. Certain practices may gradually wither away (such as duelling) or come into being (such as divorce). Yet the practice of divorce emerged not *ex nihilio* but modified the already established practice of marriage, rendering it revocable. Even when practices appear to be new, they are never completely fresh: they represent modifications of earlier ones. We may call this differentiation amidst continuity. For such internal practice transformation to take place, some of the constitutive rules of an earlier practice would have to be conserved, and some would have to be abandoned. Which ones will stay and which will go is a question that can only be answered after the fact, but we must not forget that the very possibility of having constitutive rules that may be altered is the unique trait of concrete practices which sets them apart from abstract games.

The upshot is that rigid rules may collapse under the pressure of change, and the more rigid and abstract they are, the easier their

(Princeton: Princeton University Press, 2000), p. 33. 'Nature' is an imaginary player whose moves represent stochastic events, and a 'node' is a segment of a decision tree at which a player must choose a move (pp. 10–11).

demise. Unlike abstract games, practices can absorb change so long as their participants still know how to make sense – or 'know how to go on', in Wittgenstein's expression – in a practice that is undergoing modification.[36] That practices can undergo internal modification with respect to their constitutive rules is a fact of particular importance when it comes to questions of ethics and politics. As so often happens in human affairs, certain participants in a practice might come to dispute the worth of the currently accepted constitutive rules and may urge that these rules be changed – this is the point at which political action commences. On our Oakeshottian definition (see Chapter 1), politics is not only a conflict of interests, although it is also that, but an attempt to rewrite the constitutive rules of a practice. In turn, ethics and normative discourse ask whether the rules *ought to* be rewritten. Such normative questions are addressed briefly in the final section and in subsequent chapters.

## The Understanding of Meaning within a Practice

Before venturing into questions of normativity, an interlude is required to elucidate a premise that was implicit in the foregoing argument – the idea that certain agents count as practice members by virtue of common knowledge. But what is it that the participants in a practice know in common? How do they know how to differentiate the boundaries of their common practice from other practices? These issues must be clarified for our argument to be coherent. Notice that with regard to practices, the proper epistemological category is not knowledge (whose criterion is truth); it is understanding (whose criterion is intelligibility). What is to be understood is meaning – not just the meaning of action, but the meaning of practice-dependent action or action located within the internal domain of a given practice.

Our brand of internalism relies on an intersubjective account of meaning. According to it, an expression (or action) has meaning for one interpreter because it necessarily has meaning for multiple interpreters. Meaning, in this sense, is 'public' or communicable between subjects.[37] Some philosophers take the question of whether meaning is a private and subjective or, conversely, public and intersubjective to be

---

[36] Wittgenstein, *Philosophical Investigations*, §§151, 179.

[37] See Wittgenstein's argument against the possibility of a private language (of pain sensations) in *Philosophical Investigations*, §§244–384.

an open question. Charles Taylor writes, 'Meaning is for a subject: it is not the meaning of the situation *in vacuo*, but its meaning for a subject, a specific subject, a group of subjects, or perhaps what its meaning is for the human subject as such.'[38] For Taylor, meaning can be generated and understood by an isolated thinker but, equally, by an interpreter surrounded by a community of interpreters.

Our premise of intersubjective meaning implies a particular model of how meaning is transmitted. It is incompatible with a model where a solitary actor attempts to understand a meaningful event so that the meaning transmission flows from the event to the observer. Instead, it involves a communicative model of meaning, where meaning consists in a *message* exchanged between subjects: a speaker and a recipient.[39] Both parties are assumed to possess sufficient communicative competence: speaker competence (most messages would be uttered in an intelligible format most of the time) and recipient competence (most messages would be deciphered by the intended recipients most of the time). Occasionally, an agent might misunderstand a message. To take an example from international relations, State A may be increasing its armaments for defensive purposes, yet State B may misinterpret that increase as a hostile action and begin to increase its own armaments in response. In the IR literature, this situation is known as a 'security dilemma'.[40] The idea is that even misunderstanding, as long as it does not collapse into unintelligibility, is a manifestation of understanding.

Turning from the meaning of action to the meaning of practice-dependent action, we can see why it is apposite to speak of understanding rather than knowledge. An analogy between a practice and a language spoken by proficient users may be helpful. A proficient language speaker not only *knows* the standard ('propositional') meaning of an expression for a language but is able to *understand* – to recognise and reconstruct – the meaning of a partially incorrect expression uttered by a not-yet proficient speaker of this language. *Mutatis mutandis*, a competent participant in a practice can recognise (understand) a mistaken action which violates the constitutive rules of a practice. The analogy is

---

[38] Charles Taylor, 'Interpretation and the Sciences of Man', *Review of Metaphysics* 25 (1) 1971: 3–51, p. 11.

[39] On speaker meaning, see H. P. Grice, 'Meaning', *Philosophical Review* 66 (3) 1957: 377–388.

[40] A classic paper is John H. Herz, 'Idealist Internationalism and the Security Dilemma', *World Politics* 2 (2) 1950: 157–180.

almost perfect, since the proficient speaker understands the meaning of an utterance the same way a competent practice participant understands the meaning of an action covered by practice-defining rules. Either way, understanding is inscribed within a context – be it a particular language or a particular practice.

We have just compared a practice to the structure of language, but the reverse also holds: language can be seen as a practice reproduced within an actual linguistic community. Stated differently, the term 'language' covers both the notion of an abstract grammatical structure and that of a concrete living practice of language speakers. This distinction allows us to differentiate an abstract system of rules from a practice. For, as Oakeshott noted, a human practice cannot be compressed into abstract rules without remainder:

But it is only in fantasy that a practice appears as a composition of rules claiming obedience which to learn is to acquire a familiarity with injunctive propositions and to understand is to know one's way about a rule-book.[41]

Oakeshott's point is that practices resemble vernaculars: they are not grammar books.[42] This argument is grounded in the notion of 'meaning in use', which is central to Oakeshott's and Wittgenstein's theories of meaning. As Oakeshott writes, 'customs, principles, rules, etc., have no meaning except in relation to the choices and performances of the agents; they are *used* in conduct and they can be used only in virtue of having been learned.'[43] And Wittgenstein similarly observes, 'For a *large* class of cases – though not for all – in which we employ the word "meaning" it can be defined thus: the meaning of a word is its use in the language.'[44] Because meaning is revealed in its use, in learning a rule, we must simultaneously learn the context of its proper application. For instance, the proposition 'The sun rises' uttered in the middle of the night misfires, for according to accepted usage, the rule governing the meaning of the word 'sun' does not apply to this context (midnight). It is not as if we first learn the rule and then learn to apply it in a second step. The doctrine of meaning in use stipulates that we must learn both steps at once. This identifies a basic distinction between abstract rules which can be severed from their context of application

---

[41] Oakeshott, *On Human Conduct*, p. 91.
[42] Oakeshott, *On Human Conduct*, p. 78.
[43] Oakeshott, *On Human Conduct*, p. 58, original emphasis.
[44] Wittgenstein, *Philosophical Investigations*, §43, original emphasis.

without becoming meaningless (as in chess) and rules which are meaningful only when they are being used in a context (i.e., a language-game or a practice). Chess rules and abstract rules more generally fit the category of *rule-governed action*, whereas rules that must be learned in the course of being actually used fit the distinct category of *rule-following*, as an activity characterising ongoing human practices. So whenever we speak of the 'rules' of a practice, the proviso is that we mean rule-following.

Now we are in a position to provide a full definition of a practice as *a distinctive domain of rule-following activity, defined by concrete constitutive rules and espoused as common understanding by a group of participants.* Although some of the rules constituting the practice may be explicitly stated, for the most part, they would be followed tacitly. Competent participants need not explicitly invoke the constitutive rules of a practice they understand any more than proficient language speakers need explicitly refer to the grammar of a language they are able to speak. The category of rule-governed action, including that of constitutive rules, is analytical as opposed to phenomenological. It responds to the demand for conceptual clarification: it discloses the boundaries of a practice in cases where they have become uncertain or contested. Nonetheless, the constitutive rules of a practice should in principle be open to being stated in language ('It is a rule that doing X counts as Y in context C') to ensure that the majority of participants in a practice follow the same rules and know that they are doing so.[45]

The premise of a community is crucial. A practice cannot materialise unless a number (typically, a large number) of agents adopt and follow its constitutive rules jointly. A rule serves as a *standard* of conduct because it is upheld by more than a single individual. If each separate individual were the authoritative maker and interpreter of one's own rules of action, the result would not be a shared domain of rule-following, a practice, but what Thomas Hobbes called a 'state of nature' – a deregulated interaction domain wherein individuals float about like atoms.[46] In consequence, no single participant in a practice

---

[45] Joseph Raz, *Practical Reason and Norms* (London: Hutchinson, 1975), p. 53.
[46] Hobbes's state of nature is described by Howard Warrender, *The Political Philosophy of Hobbes: His Theory of Obligation* (Oxford: Clarendon Press, 1957), as a 'moral vacuum' (p. 5). Here we describe it as an interaction domain lacking *common* rules. On the state of nature, see Thomas Hobbes, *Leviathan*,

can be an authority unilaterally entitled to interpret it. The talk of authority presupposes criteria of validity.[47] A practice is defined by its constitutive rules and validated intersubjectively, by and within a community, which rules set the basis for its interpretation. Therefore, no one can, without contradiction, claim a unilateral exemption from the constitutive rules of a practice to which one has subscribed. As Rawls says,

> If one wants to do an action which a certain practice specifies then there is no way to do it except to follow the rules which define it. Therefore, it doesn't make sense for a person to raise the question whether or not a rule of a practice correctly applies to *his* case where the action he contemplates is a form of action defined by a practice. If someone were to raise such a question, he would simply show that he didn't understand the situation in which he was acting.[48]

In sum, a practice binds a group of agents to its defining rules so that these rules count as common.

But a practice is a unity of multiple rules. Its character is such that it cannot be exhausted by a single rule. 'There is ... no point,' Joseph Raz observes, 'in following just one rule of etiquette relating to conduct at formal parties, say. This will only make one look all the more ridiculous.'[49] Raz's remark brings out another contrast between practices and abstract games – namely, that it is possible to imagine a one-rule-only game (say, a child bouncing a ball against a wall) but not a one-rule-only practice. Indeed, a practice integrates a multiplicity of understandings which are rules as well as judgments and sensibilities that accompany the rules. It is a world intelligible in its totality, Wittgenstein's 'form of life'.[50] To become practice participants, then, a group of agents should have learned to understand that such-and-such manner of action is appropriate for the domain of the practice in question, and this demands this domain to be understood as a meaningful whole. A proper understanding of a practice is holist.

---

ed. C. B. MacPherson (London: Penguin 1968 [1651]), chs. 13 (pp. 183–188) and 14, esp. pp. 189–190.

[47] See H. L. A. Hart's argument about the authoritative determination of the validity of rules making up a legal system in Chapter 1, under 'Constitutive and Authoritative Practices'.

[48] Rawls, 'Two Concepts of Rules', p. 26.

[49] Raz, *Practical Reason and Norms*, p. 114.

[50] Wittgenstein, *Philosophical Investigations*, §§19, 23, 241.

We start with the 'whole' (the practice as a multifaceted domain of interaction) and then proceed to identify its 'parts'.

The answer to the previous question – what agents know when they know a practice – is that a sufficient mass of competent participants must already understand the basic standards constituting the practice. A practice does not begin its life as a *tabula rasa*, where no understanding whatsoever is available; it begins in *medias res*. That much must be granted. Practice-defining standards, as noted, are reflected in the summary notion of making a mistake. Mistakes may arise from misunderstanding a known rule or from its misjudgement. To misjudge is to misunderstand the importance of a rule on a scale of values, a difficult question that will be glossed in what follows. We should be vigilant not to conflate mistakes with computational errors. Mistakes arise solely within the internal space of a practice (or more broadly, game), given the premise that the agents who accept the practice are able to understand it as a meaningful whole. Only those agents who reason and act from *within* the practice count as its participants, and they are located inside its domain by virtue of their ability to understand and, occasionally, misunderstand its constitutive standards or rules.

If a practice is a *whole*, its 'parts' can themselves be practices, soft conventions (rules of etiquette) or rigid institutions. For convenience, we may label all of these rules, so a practice can be seen as a system of rules. Considering that a practice is not just a whole but a *meaningful* whole, its domain would be delineated by the agents' ability to understand the meanings of more than one practice at a time. This is not a desideratum but a requirement. Without meeting it, we cannot hope to respond to the second question raised in this section: How do agents know where the domain of a particular practice begins and ends? The only way to pinpoint the internal domain of a specific practice is to juxtapose its meaning with that of other practices: this motivates our project of practice differentiation. To determine what the practice of church going is, for instance, the meaning of its constitutive rules would have to be compared with those of kindred practices such as promising and perhaps with remote practices such as buying and selling. This procedure of practice differentiation implies that partially overlapping practices differ in non-trivial ways, as we shall illustrate in Chapters 4 and 5 by examining the practice of global civil society and the practice of the society of states.

It is crucial to acknowledge that the possibility that different practices may overlap does not validate externalism, an invariant realm that subsists outside all conceivable practices and where the agents can allegedly find an ultimate refuge. Instead, it is fully compatible with the internalist argument that agents are participants standing *inside* multiple practices at any time.

There is, then, an unavoidable circularity when it comes to an explanation of action from the internalist standpoint of practices. (To 'explain', on our account, is the same as to 'understand from the inside'.) If we wish to establish why certain participants acted by following the rules of a particular practice, we can only make sense of their actions by referring back to the practice, as Rawls remarked.[51] This restriction is inherent in the internal point of view. To refer to something more basic (objective truth, reality, reason) than the practice itself would be to commit the error of reductionism. For if we were prepared to reduce rules to something *else*, we would be admitting that rules do not matter after all – and this is a conclusion we wish to resist. Moreover, the circularity implicit in an explanation of practices is of a non-vicious sort. Since every practice contains a 'historical' element, meaning that its participants can invoke its past resources to act in the present or to make sense of *new* social facts, the circularity involved does not entail vicious regress.

## Norms and Practices as Normative Domains

Thus far, we have sketched four of the analytical components of a practice: the internal point of view, rule following, constitutive rules, and meaning. We now turn to its final component, normativity. At the outset, we claimed that to qualify as participants in a practice, certain agents must have common knowledge of its constitutive rules (the so-called rules of the game) and must accept these rules as binding. But to say that some individuals accept the core rules of a practice may mean two different things – either that they accept the practice as a social fact (which provides terminus without reference to some further justifying reason) or that they accept it for some reason, say, *because* they value it. With this, we have crossed over into the realm of value and normativity. In philosophical parlance, value concerns the problem of the good or goodness. Neo-Humeans, for example, take desire (or preference) to be

---

[51] Rawls, 'Two Concepts of Rules', pp. 26–28.

the root of value – desire leads us to whatever objects may have value for us.[52] In adopting this approach, contemporary economists and rational-choice theorists define welfare in terms of preference satisfaction. Such neo-Humeans adhere to a monistic theory of the good, since all good is taken to issue from a single source: preference or desire (whatever its objects may be). Conversely, non-Humean approaches such as Kant's moral theory or virtue ethics hold that the good is not what we desire but what is *worthy* of desire or some similar standard of positive evaluation. The idea here is that the good qualifies as good only if it meets a prior standard of evaluation.[53] Thus a person who has a desire to tell an indiscreet joke may, upon reflection, come to see this desire as unworthy and may refuse to act on it. Neo-Humean approaches and Kantianism are both monist because they appeal to a single standard of evaluation – respect for persons, in Kant's case. But a value theory can accommodate a plurality of evaluative standards.

Objects worthy of value presuppose a background evaluative *standard* – or 'normativity' for short. A diverse range of objects such as knives or umbrellas, human character and actions can all be objects of evaluation.[54] In this study, we are concerned with action and therefore with evaluative standards of action. It is conventional to refer to such standards as *norms*.[55] This term should not be taken to mean 'whatever turns out to be the usual course of action', for which the appropriate term would be 'normal' and not 'normative'. Rather, a

---

[52] See R. G. Frey and Christopher W. Morris, 'Value, Welfare, and Morality', in R. G. Frey and C. W. Morris (eds.) *Value, Welfare and Morality* (Cambridge: Cambridge University Press, 1993), pp. 1–12.

[53] Elizabeth Anderson writes, 'To value something is to have a complex of positive attitudes toward it, governed by distinct *standards* for perception, emotion, deliberation, desire and conduct'. Elizabeth Anderson, *Value in Ethics and Economics* (Cambridge, MA: Harvard University Press, 1995), p. 2, emphasis added. Anderson distinguishes valuation (the experience of finding something good or valuable) from evaluation (the judgement that something *merits* valuation, a judgement hinging on a standard; pp. 2–3).

[54] Judith Jarvis Thompson, *Normativity* (Peru, IL: Open Court, 2008), is a metaethical study of the terms used for evaluation such as 'good', 'must' and 'ought', which attach to objects, actions and characteristics of human beings. Thompson argues that 'good' is an attribute rather than a predicate, so an object is not simply good but good in a certain respect. Being good in a certain respect is a property which attaches only to objects of a 'goodness-fixing kind' such as umbrellas and knives but not pebbles.

[55] Norms pertain to what Anderson calls evaluation (value standards), not to valuation (value experiences), see note 53.

norm is a standard of conduct chosen by the agents in the sense that the agents intentionally follow the norm. In its function of a *standard* of conduct, any rule operates as *a norm*. In this connection, recall Winch's argument about mistakes and rule-following. Mistakes disclose that a standard of conduct is at work, since for any particular instance of rule-following, it is possible to distinguish mistaken from proper conduct. By default, rule-following is normative in this sense. This species of normativity that characterises any rule as a standard of conduct may be termed *baseline normativity*.

One special group of norms are known as 'prescriptions'.[56] They are statements telling the agent what he or she *ought* to do. When prescriptions are formulated as rules, they constitute rules that are 'action guiding' rather than merely action constraining.[57] A prescriptive rule postulates that a given action falls under a constraint (the constraining element found in any rule *qua* rule), and at the same time, it *prompts* the agent to perform the action (the action-guiding element) covered by the rule. This action-guiding component is an emblem of what we refer to as *strong normativity*. For example, the moral injunction 'Promises ought to be kept', addressed to the agent, is equivalent to the prescription 'You ought to keep promises', to be distinguished from the purely descriptive statement 'There is a rule which says that promises ought to be kept'. This prescriptive aspect is very often absent from rules that

---

[56] Technically, prescriptions (ought statements) such as commands and imperatives are distinct from rules as *standing* orders (see note 44 in the introductory chapter). However, it is permissible to treat these categories as compatible, since commands and imperatives can be expressed as rules and given that the primary task in this section is to explicate the connection between rules and norms and not to provide a full theory of rules.

[57] One famous meta-ethical account of the language of prescriptions is R. M. Hare, *The Language of Morals* (Oxford: Clarendon Press, 1952), esp. pp.1–3, 129 and chs. 2, 7, 11. Hare argues that a prescription such as a second-person imperative 'Do A!' addressed to P (where P is a person and A an action) is entailed by the (universalised) prescriptive judgement 'A ought to be done'. Although Hare's moral theory is utilitarian (it is a utilitarian form of universal prescriptivism), it borrows premises from Kant and Kant's concept of the autonomous will of the individual. Morality for Hare is a matter of *individual* reasoned choice of prescriptive (action-guiding) principles. Because for Kant 'the individual' stands for *any* individual, and because reason is universal, individual principles of reasoning are universalisable (the subjective is transposed into the objective). On our premises, if a practice theory contains a prescriptive component, this component must embody *intersubjective* (rather than objective) action-guiding principles.

define games. The rule of chess 'The Bishop moves diagonally on the chessboard' does not prompt the chess player to move the bishop on the chessboard; it just states that this move is available as a valid move within the game. But although games have a baseline normativity, a large number of human practices are normatively modulated in a strong sense.

The notion of norms enables us to get a firmer grasp of social practices as normatively bounded domains. Imagine that somebody questioned the validity of the rules of chess. The only way to remove the difficulty is to explain to him or her the rules of the game all over again (the Rook moves like this ... the Queen moves like this ... and so on). This explanatory strategy, however, will falter if the object of contention is a practice – and specifically, the endorsement of a practice – as when a critic or a reformer challenges practice participants to give reasons for accepting the rules of their practice. To respond to the critic's challenge, the participants would have to justify this practice as a worthy one to have by adducing some normative reasons. Simply repeating what the rules of the practice state, as an analytical enterprise, would not suffice as a response to the critic, since it is not the *validity* of the rules but their worthiness that has been called into question. This amounts to a contrast between (analytical) explanation and (normative) justification. Normative justification usually appeals to evaluative standards such as prescriptions or values that go beyond the normative baseline. Normally, practice participants follow the rules of their common practice without questioning them. Under normal conditions, when a participant acts within the practice, the problem of justifying the practice as a whole does not arise. This is what Rawls was getting at when he said that we make sense of an action that falls within a practice, as a system of rules or norms, by referring back to those rules and norms.[58] In the less common situation of a crisis or political turmoil, the justification of the practice as a whole (and not merely of particular actions falling within it) becomes an issue.

To make headway on these questions, it should be possible to measure the 'pull' that a particular norm exerts on action. To this end, we introduce the concept of normative force. It discloses the deontic requirement – strong, mild or weak – attached to a given norm. One way to proceed is conceptual, by comparing the category of prescriptive rules (strong norms) with that of non-prescriptive rules

[58] See note 48.

(weak norms). An alternative, implicit in Hart's analysis, is to treat the normative force of rules not as a categorical distinction but as a matter of degree. Hart argued that unless the majority of practice participants regard instances of rule violation by other participants as blameable, no common practice can be said to unite them.[59] (In the Introduction to this book, this procedure of assessing reactions to rule violation was called a 'normativity test'.) The important implication is that an adverse reaction to rule violation can reveal the *degree* of normative force characterising a set of practice-defining norms. Their normative force will vary depending on the particular kind of practice they define.

Another way to make the same point is to say that certain, though not all, human practices are *normative* domains in a strong sense of normativity. Consider a prosaic practice such as driving a vehicle on the road. Its constitutive norms exhibit mild normativity because, if a driver drove without a license, thereby violating the rules, this mistake would most likely provoke slight criticism by other drivers. It would seldom provoke outrage. Once we move into the realm of practices associated with law and morality, the picture changes dramatically, the criticism for rule violation becomes much more acute and its implications for the delinquent party, more severe.

The practices of law and morality, including international morality and international law, are strongly normative by default. Strong normativity is an indicator that breaking the rules of practices of this sort would be vehemently criticised by their insiders. At the limit, the risk of being ostracised from the practice provokes an existential crisis for the delinquent participant – at stake here is the agent's self-identification, as a member of a practice, and not merely the loss or forgoing of benefits accruing from continued practice participation.

One of the distinctive features of morality and law is their coercive character. Morality is coercive in the sense that moral criticism can compel agents to follow rules prohibiting the infliction of harm, stealing and lying. Law, as a system of legal rules, is even more coercive, as it often sanctions the use of physical force to ensure observance of the rules.[60] But if this is the case, the relation between coercion and rule-following within practices such as law seems to generate tension.

[59] Hart, *The Concept of Law*, pp. 82–88.
[60] See Arthur Ripstein, 'Authority and Coercion', *Philosophy & Public Affairs* 32 (1) 2004: 2–35.

Coercion allows for the application of physical force, and force is an external constraint on action, imposed from 'the outside'. Conversely, rule-following operates without external duress, as it presupposes an 'internal' attitude of rule acceptance. (Here, 'internalism' and 'externalism' are construed as normative rather than as epistemological positions.) Should we conclude from this that coercive  institutions have no place in a practice theory based on the internal point of view? As Hart observes, while coercion is a precondition for, it is not the gist of law as a social practice. Law qualifies as a proper social practice illuminated by the internal point of view as a normative standpoint only if the majority of its participants follow its rules and do not merely obey the rules for fear of punishment.[61] Hart identifies a chasm between *obedience to rules* (predicated on the external point of view) and *rule acceptance* (predicated on the internal point of view).[62] To *obey the rules* is to agree to adopt them as an external constraint on action, for fear of adverse consequences, whereas to *accept the rules* is to follow the rules for their own sake – because they are rules. Hart accounts for the normativity of rule-following (rule acceptance) within social practices by pointing not to foundational norms or principles but, rather, to social facts (it is a social fact that the rules of practice P have been accepted in society S). Other philosophers may account for rule acceptance by linking it to the constitution of identity. Wittgenstein's remark 'When I obey a rule, I do not choose. I obey the rule *blindly* '[63] seems to suggest that the activity of rule-following has become part of the agent's identity. Still others, like Hegel, may ground rule acceptance in fundamental, non-instrumental values such as freedom. Regardless of whether social facts, identities or values are invoked, it is important to bear in mind that they are not mutually exclusive components but aspects of internalism, as a normative standpoint of rule-following.

## Conclusion

In concluding this discussion, we wish to draw attention to the normative significance of internalism. It is not enough to invoke the internal

---

[61] Hart, *The Concept of Law*, pp. 23–24, 85–88, 197.
[62] Hart, *The Concept of Law*, pp. 86–88.
[63] Wittgenstein, *Philosophical Investigations*, §219, original emphasis.

point of view in its basic, epistemological sense, where it marks the common intersubjective *understanding* shared within a group of individuals that enables them to jointly follow rules and thus to be participants in a common practice. Any account of rule-following within social practices is bound to remain incomplete if it excludes the normative aspect of the internal point of view. As we have seen, this aspect is revealed in the fact that a living practice, unlike an artificial game, cannot persist for long without its participants' willingness to accept its core rules as guides to conduct. Those practices that have particular salience in our common moral and political life are distinguished by strong normativity. Chapter 4 takes us to the sphere of international relations to articulate a neo-Hegelian practice theory which is normatively infused in this strong sense.

# PART II

# Practices in International Relations

# 4 | Two Core Practices in International Relations

## A Neo-Hegelian Perspective

In Part I, we questioned the dominant sociological approach to practices in contemporary International Relations (IR), which assumes the validity of the external point of view. Our philosophical analysis redirected the argument by disclosing the importance of the *internal point of view* (internalism). In Chapter 3, we argued that a practice exists when a group of participants in an activity, defined by a system of rules, understand themselves to be jointly following the rules – this understanding is what internalism amounts to. But the internal point of view is not only an epistemological standpoint of rule understanding. It is also, and indeed must be, a normative standpoint of rule acceptance. Without this component, no practice would ever be a full-blooded 'form of life'. The constitutive rules of a practice represent norms (standards of conduct) that guide its participants and accord normative identity to the practice as a whole. Failure to accept these norms by certain participants might indicate either a lack of competence necessary for proper participation in the practice or an attempt to flout the practice. If we ask, Why is it that participants accept certain rules and norms as binding to begin with?, the short answer is because they attach value to these rules, construed not simply as rules but as a system of rules or a practice. These values are not absolute but internal to the practice in question.

In this Part II, our philosophical enquiry turns to the contemporary realm of international and global relations to consider its constitutive practices. The central thesis of the present chapter is that this realm is constituted by two core practices – the practice of sovereign states and the practice of global rights – both of which embody the value of freedom or 'anarchy'. *Anarchy* understood as a relation between formal equals, states, is a cardinal concept in the study of international relations.[1] However, here we emphasise the connection between

---

[1] On anarchy as a fundamental concept to the discipline of International Relations, see Helen Milner, 'The Assumption of Anarchy in International Relations

anarchy as an international order and anarchy as a value of freedom actualised within social practices. We develop our argument by re-examining Hegel's account of social practices such as the state and civil society from *The Philosophy of Right* and his notion of freedom as grounded in mutual recognition from *The Phenomenology of Spirit*.[2] The result is a neo-Hegelian theory of practices in international and global relations.[3] This is one possible practice theory compatible with the philosophical template of practices developed in Chapter 3. The predicate 'neo' shows that we have modified Hegel's original account of freedom – which, in the modern world, is realised as rights-holding within civil society and the state – by introducing a parallel concept of freedom, as equal freedom in an anarchical social order between states. Concretely, our thesis consists of two parts: (1) internationally, we are constituted as rights-holders by virtue of being citizens of a state that participates in the anarchical practice of free states, and (2) globally, we are constituted as rights-holders by virtue of being participants in global civil society defined as a global practice of rights. Our analysis distinguishes three levels – domestic (relations inside the state), international (state-to-state relations), and global (supranational relations above state-to-state relations).

## Hegel and the Question of Freedom

The argument that follows is not an exegesis of Hegel's writings. It is a reworking and extension, to international relations and global ethics, of two of Hegel's main theses for freedom: (1) freedom as grounded in mutual recognition and (2) freedom as the holding of individual rights inside the institutions of civil society and the state. Hegel said relatively

Theory: A Critique', *Review of International Studies* 17 (1) 1991: 67–85; and Brain C. Schmidt, *The Political Discourse of Anarchy: A Disciplinary History of International Relations* (Albany: SUNY Press, 1998).

[2] G. W. F. Hegel, *Hegel's Philosophy of Right*, trans. T. M. Knox (Oxford: Oxford University Press, 1967 [1821]); henceforth '*The Philosophy of Right*'. G. W. F. Hegel, *Hegel's Phenomenology of Spirit*, trans. A. V. Miller (Oxford: Oxford University Press, 1977 [1807]). Hegel's concept of recognition is explored in Robert R. Williams, *Hegel's Ethics of Recognition* (Berkeley, CA: University of California Press, 2000).

[3] An earlier articulation of neo-Hegelian theory as constitutive theory by one of the book's authors is Mervyn Frost, *Ethics in International Relations: A Constitutive Theory* (Cambridge: Cambridge University Press, 1996).

little about international relations, which he associated primarily with interstate war, and his account of freedom differs significantly from our extension of it. While for Hegel, different kinds of freedoms can be ordered in a hierarchy of value, anarchy – the master concept of IR – captures the notion of equal freedom paradigmatically represented by the anarchical (horizontal) relations established between formally equal sovereign states. We begin with a sketch of Hegel's views on freedom before turning to the anarchical practices of sovereign states and the practice of global rights.

In *The Philosophy of Right*, Hegel discusses three basic, hierarchically arranged institutions, understood as social wholes or practices – the family, civil society and the state. Taken together, they comprise the sphere of Hegel's 'Ethical Life' (*Sittlichkeit*).[4] Each is constitutive of the identity of the individual as an ethical being, and each is associated with an appropriate form of freedom. For example, in the family, we are constituted as ethical beings who are loved and valued by other family members who love and value us in return. The bonds formed do not reflect self-conscious choice; they are ties of affection. Within this institution, we are not fully free, independent beings, but rather parts of a unity – the family unit.[5] This is overcome in the next institution, civil society, in which particularised, mutually independent identities emerge for the first time.[6] This independence of the subject from other subjects is the fundament of the concept of a right, as *subjective* freedom. Right (without an indefinite article) is the *objective* principle which determines and organises the distribution of rights within a common domain of rights-holding.

For Hegel, civil society is roughly coextensive with the free market. 'Roughly' is a useful qualification, since Hegel includes under the heading of civil society offices which nowadays would count as elements of the state – a basic legal framework for the regulation of property relations and prevention of crime ('administration of justice') aided by public administration (the civil service), plus a public authority ('police') providing order as well as basic infrastructural services.[7]

---

[4] Our analysis in this section is based on Hegel's argument for *Sittlichkeit* ('Ethical Life'), which is part 3 of Hegel, *The Philosophy of Right*.

[5] Hegel, *The Philosophy of Right*, §158.

[6] Hegel, *The Philosophy of Right*, §238.

[7] Hegel's 'police' is not the same as our contemporary notion of police – a public authority of law enforcement. By this term, Hegel means the public authority

In this category are included various 'estates' (the civil service, landed aristocracy and the manufacturing estate), where the latter two form the social base for political representation.[8] Individuals from various estates are free to associate into professional groups and guilds. The most distinctive feature of Hegel's civil society is that its members – 'civilians', as we shall call them – enjoy the freedom of voluntary association, enabling them to enter into self-chosen transactions and contracts. The idea of contracts freely entered into is central to the status of a free rights-holder in a society composed of other equally free rights-holders. But even though the exercise of freedom of contract is potentially open to all civilians, it does not bring about equality. Over time, free-market competition produces structural inequality. However, this is not the only drawback generated; another one is the fact of rivalry and alienation. As a result, civil society suffers fragmentation into self-serving interests that fail to realise the interest of society as a whole.[9] These drawbacks are finally overcome in the third principal institution, the state, where all citizens are granted equal rights under the law and where, represented on the basis of estates, they exercise self-government. For Hegel, the state is not exclusively an impartial umpire which keeps its citizens from injuring or interfering with one another, as it is for social contract theorists such as Hobbes and Kant.[10] It is a constitutional order rooted in shared customs and history – as such, it is a source of a political identity for its citizens, held together by ties of affection, patriotism. Hegel's ethical state anticipates Tönnies's notion of *Gemeinschaft* (community) to be contrasted with *Gesellschaft* (voluntary association) – the sphere of civil society.[11]

The insight we adopt from Hegel concerns the constitution of agent identity. Although the three principal social wholes which make up 'Ethical Life' disclose progressive development, they are not mutually

responsible for street lighting, bridge building, fixing of the prices of daily necessities, and public health. Hegel, *The Philosophy of Right*, §236A ('A' stands for 'Addition').

[8] On the three estates, see Hegel, *The Philosophy of Right*, §202.

[9] Hegel, *The Philosophy of Right*, §§157(B), 195, 200.

[10] Thomas Hobbes, *Leviathan*, ed. C. B. Macpherson (London: Penguin, 1968 [1651]); Immanuel Kant, *The Doctrine of Right* (pt. 1), in *The Metaphysics of Morals*, ed. Mary Gregor (Cambridge: Cambridge University Press 1996 [1797]), pp. 3–138.

[11] Ferdinand Tönnies, *Community and Association* (*Gemeinschaft und Gesellschaft*) (London: Routledge, 1955 [1887]).

exclusive. They generate a triad of compatible institutional identities – family member, civilian, and citizen. Each identity has value for its holder as well as for those granting it – it is an institutional *status* that can only be realised within the relevant practice. The general thrust of Hegel's argument is that certain core practices are constitutive of our identity as free individuals. These practices are constitutive in the sense of being identity conferring. An identity, realised as a concrete ethical status within a practice, has intrinsic value for its participants. Here 'intrinsic' means non-instrumental. Stated differently, the status accorded within the relevant institution counts as *ethical* not because it appeals to certain moral standards of action but because it is constitutive of the agent's identity. Moreover, this kind of status is assumed to have intrinsic value for all bona fide practice participants as a social group, apart from having value for each individual member – ethical statuses and identities represent social relationships. In his earlier work, *The Phenomenology of Spirit*, Hegel had identified mutual recognition as a prototype social relationship through which ethical statuses are created and maintained.[12]

Let us examine in greater detail how mutual recognition, ethical status and intrinsic value fit together. In Hegel's scheme, institutionally dependent ethical statuses are maintained by an elaborate system of mutual recognition. The idea of recognition presupposes a relationship binding self-conscious actors. Because recognition must be *mutual*, it cannot be established unilaterally. It has to be granted on the basis of criteria (such as the norms and rules constituting a practice) which the candidate who seeks recognition would have to satisfy and which would have to be recognised as valid by the granting party. Recognition is a relationship between *free* persons, and its ground cannot be coercion. It cannot be realised through the deployment of power, force, bribery or fraud. It is a relationship of mutuality freely entered into.[13]

---

[12] On recognition in *The Phenomenology of Spirit* (where it is central to Hegel's account of the master-slave relationship) and in *The Philosophy of Right* (where it is implicit), see Jürgen Lawrenz, 'Hegel, Recognition and Rights: "Anerkennung" as a Gridline of the Philosophy of Rights', *Cosmos and History: The Journal of Natural and Social Philosophy* 3 (2) 2007: 153–169.

[13] A useful analogy is the mutual recognition that exists within a friendship. One recognises another as a friend when the other person, in demeanour and action, meets the criteria internal to the relationship of friendship. Neither party to such a relationship can unilaterally defend or protect it. What is required is a

Such relationships are 'ethical' in Hegel's terms or 'practical' (practice-dependent') in our terms.

Like any other ethical relationship, mutual recognition has degrees of realisation. It is fully realised only when freedom is actualised as equal freedom. The ethical standing sought by a candidate party can be achieved only when it is conferred by other parties of equal standing. It has to be a recognition as an equal from equals. The point is illustrated by the master-slave dialectic Hegel set out in *The Phenomenology of Spirit* as a struggle for recognition between master and slave, as self-conscious actors.[14] The recognition a slave confers on his or her master cannot constitute the master as properly free because it comes from one who is dominated (owned) by the master. Translated into the discourse of contemporary international relations, this suggests that sovereign states do not seek recognition simply of their freedom but of freedom appropriate to equals. From the neo-Hegelian perspective adopted here, the *sine qua non* for participation in the practice of sovereign states is that states recognise one another as having *equal* sovereign freedoms or rights. Only this kind of recognition can confer on a candidate state full sovereign status.

## The Practice of Sovereign States

The contemporary practice of sovereign states is not a recent invention. It descends from the older notion of international society – a society whose principal members are states. The idea was originally pro-pounded by early modern European jurists and political thinkers such as Hugo Grotius, Samuel Pufendorf, Christian Wolff and Emmer de Vattel, who used it to capture the disintegration of *Christendom* into a plurality of mutually independent units – 'a system of states', in Pufendorf's phrase.[15] Over the next three centuries, international

---

reciprocal process of what might be called 'attunement' or conduct with a particular kind of orientation and empathy towards the other partner. Unilateral ploys or the threat of force cannot do the trick.

[14] Hegel, *The Phenomenology of Spirit*, ch. 4 ('Self-Consciousness'), which includes the discussion of the master-slave relationship (Miller translates it as 'bondage-lordship' relationship).

[15] Hugo Grotius, *The Rights of War and Peace*, 3 vols., ed. Richard Tuck (Indianapolis: Liberty Fund, 2005 [1631]); Samuel Pufendorf, *Eight Books on the Laws of Nature and Nations*, trans. C. H. Oldfather and W. A. Oldfather (Washington, DC: Carnegie Institution, 1964 [1688]); Christian Wolff, *Jus*

society spread out geographically to encompass the globe.[16] While we acknowledge the historical component of the practice of sovereign states, our primary task is to discern its current analytical boundaries. Metaphorically, we might say that we are focussed on examining its logical architecture, leaving aside its history. Pivotal to our discussion is the argument that the society of states represents an anarchical international order centred on the value of freedom. A similar view was put forward in the twentieth-century approach to IR theory known as the English School, popularised by Hedley Bull in his influential book *The Anarchical Society*.[17] We contend that Bull's view of freedom as basic to the international anarchy exhibits a tension, and we show how it can be remedied by our neo-Hegelian account.

Bull portrays international society as a social arrangement among states under conditions of anarchy. Anarchy is a condition where states interact without being governed by a global sovereign.[18] But even in the absence of a higher ordering body, the relations of states are still ordered, Bull claims. He identifies five central institutions for maintaining international order: the balance of power, international law, war, diplomacy and great powers. In the words of Barry Buzan, they represent 'the fundamental institutions of international society' – its elementary, constitutive rules.[19] These rules simultaneously constitute

---

*Gentium Methodo Scientifica Pertractatum*, trans. Joseph H. Drake (Oxford: Clarendon Press, 1934 [1749]); Emer de Vattel, *The Laws of Nations*, ed. B. Kapossy and R. Wahtmore (Indianapolis: Liberty Fund, 2008 [1758]). The phrase 'system of states' is from Samuel Pufendorf, *On the Duty of Man and Citizen according to Natural Law*, trans. Michael Silverthorne, ed. James Tully (Cambridge: Cambridge University Press, 2000 [1673]), bk. 2, par. 13, p. 144.

[16] See Hedley Bull, 'The Emergence of a Universal International Society', in Hedley Bull and Adam Watson (eds.), *The Expansion of International Society* (Oxford: Clarendon Press, 1984), pp. 117–126; Adam Watson, 'The European International Society and Its Expansion', in Bull and Watson (eds.), *The Expansion of International Society*, pp. 13–32; Adam Watson, *The Evolution of International Society: A Comparative Historical Analysis* (London: Routledge, 1992).

[17] Hedley Bull, *The Anarchical Society: A Study of Order in World Politics*, 3rd ed. (Houndmills: Palgrave, 2002 [1977]).

[18] Hedley Bull, 'Society and Anarchy in International Relations', in Herbert Butterfield and Martin Wight (eds.), *Diplomatic Investigations: Essays in the Theory of International Politics* (London: Allen and Unwin, 1966), pp. 35–50, p. 38; Bull, *The Anarchical Society*, pp. 55–56, 59.

[19] Barry Buzan, *From International to World Society? English School Theory and the Social Structure of Globalisation* (Cambridge: Cambridge University Press,

and constrain (regulate) the interactions of the participant actors: states. Viewed as constraining devices, institutions impose limits on conduct. This means that states as members of international society cannot act as they see fit but must pursue their self-chosen goals within the procedural constraints imposed by the common rules of international society. The rules of war are there to ensure that wars are less destructive and that harm to non-combatants is limited, the rules of diplomacy protect the persons of diplomats from being injured or killed during interstate war and the rules of the balance of power prevent the emergence of a global empire by limiting the ambitious of states for world domination.

Let us now consider the constitutive facet of international rules. As it may be remembered from Chapter 3, when rules and institutions are construed as standards, they represent *norms* of conduct. The basic constitutive norm of international society is sovereignty. In Bull's account, it is linked to anarchy (in a second sense): 'anarchy' here does not designate the absence of an overarching sovereign; it is a manifestation of the formal equality established *between* sovereign states, participants in international society.[20] This entails a third, strongly normative sense of anarchy, where it stands for the *value* of equal freedom and, concretely, freedom as mutual independence. According to Bull, states value their membership in the anarchical society because it is a *free* society of equals. So far, we are in full agreement with Bull's position on the value of 'anarchical' freedom.

However, Bull goes on to say that what matters ultimately is the freedom of the society of states, as a collectivity, and not the freedom of its members *qua* individuals.[21] The difficulty with this is that the concept of sovereignty presupposes precisely the notion of individual freedom: it is the *individual* state who is sovereign (independent or free) from other, equally independent states. So essentially, Bull retracts his initial commitment to sovereign equality and anarchical freedom. The reason for this 'switch' is that, at the end, he sees the institution of balance of power (which serves to thwart the emergence of global empire) as more fundamental than the institution of international law (which supports the

2004), pp. 167–176. Bull discusses the fundamental institutions of international society in *The Anarchical Society*, pp. 65–71.

[20] On Bull's view of anarchy in the second sense, see Bull, *The Anarchical Society*, p. 17, and on the primacy of sovereignty for international society as articulated by early modern jurists, see pp. 30, 35.

[21] Bull, *The Anarchical Society*, pp. 17, 103–105.

norm of state sovereignty). In a well-known passage in *The Anarchical Society*, Bull writes that maintaining the balance of power by waging war against a rising hegemonic state is necessary to ensure the freedom of international society as a collective body of states, irrespective of whether the target hegemonic state has infringed the rules of international law or not.[22] The logic of Bull's argument is utilitarian, and this, we suggest, is problematic.

Utilitarianism is a species of consequentialist moral theory which determines the morality of an action by assessing its outcomes. Notably, the collectivity and not the individual is the basic unit of moral concern. An action counts as moral if, on balance, it generates the best overall outcome for the relevant collectivity affected by it. Consequentialism exhibits an aggregative logic, since it asks which action produces the highest amount of *overall* good for all those concerned. In turn, the basic principle of utilitarianism *qua* maximisation device demands that the good or the welfare of the social group should be *maximised*.[23] However, it leaves out of consideration whether this good is distributed equally or fairly among individuals, or whether it is achieved at the expense of certain individuals. As a result, utilitarian reasoning discounts justice and individual rights (and the equal freedom presupposed by rights).

It is evident that Bull's premises are utilitarian as he argues that it is permissible and indeed necessary to sacrifice an individual state for the general welfare of the society of states. Bull associates this welfare with the absence of global empire. But to follow Bull's recommendation and to wage an anti-hegemonic war on a state that has not done wrong (e.g., broken the rules of international law) is to commit a wrong. Notions of *right* and *wrong* – the distinctive vocabulary of non-utilitarian ethical theory – are not employed by Bull at all. A standard limitation of utilitarian approaches is that they do not incorporate considerations of

---

[22] Bull, *The Anarchical Society*, pp. 104, 138. An insightful discussion of the tension between the balance of power and international law in Bull's account is Ronnie Hjorth, 'Hedley Bull's Paradox of the Balance of Power: A Philosophical Inquiry', *Review of International Studies* 33 (4) 2007: 597–613.

[23] As the pioneer of utilitarianism Jeremy Bentham put it, what needs to be maximised is 'the greatest good of the greatest number'. This is Bentham's 'fundamental axiom'. It states, 'It is the greatest happiness of the greatest number that is the measure of right and wrong'. Jeremy Bentham, *A Fragment of Government*, ed. J. H. Burns and H. L. A. Hart (Cambridge: Cambridge University Press, 1998 [1776]), p. 3.

rights and justice. This sheds light on Bull's famous utilitarian conclusion that achieving international *order* (the good) is separate from, and takes priority over, the task of achieving international *justice* (the right).[24] Yet it is doubtful whether the problem of international order can be severed from international justice in this way – after all, the question is to what extent the prevailing international order is just or unjust.[25]

Against Bull's utilitarian account of freedom in international society, we put forward a neo-Hegelian proposal that makes the idea of mutual recognition and the value of equal freedom central to state relations. Even though our argument is value-based, it is not consequentialist or utilitarian. In a Hegelian vein, we conceive of freedom as an intrinsic, non-instrumental value attached to valued ethical statuses. To the extent that Hegel's perspective is value-based, it is concerned with the good. But unlike utilitarianism, this perspective does not prioritise the good of the collectivity over that of its individual members.

Because Hegelian ethical statuses are social relations, they presuppose a social group of some sort. But this group is not an aggregate or collectivity; it is a *social whole* constituted by common rules. Hegel's concept of the good (value) cannot be severed from the right, and the right points to rules and duties which determine ethical statuses.[26] As Hegel writes, in modernity, statuses have come to possess intrinsic value for their holders in lieu of the capacities they accord to the conscious *individual*. It is the benchmark of the modern world that ethical statuses, based on 'objective' (i.e., social, in Hegel's terms) rules or duties, simultaneously accommodate rights *qua* 'subjective' (i.e., individualist) entitlements which individuals hold against one another – inside the sphere of 'Ethical Life'. A specific, characteristically modern status to be enjoyed by the individual men and women in civil society and in the state – and, as we argue, by the state as an international

---

[24] Bull, *The Anarchical Society*, pp. 83–94, 308. It is sometimes suggested that towards the end of his life, Hedley Bull became more sensitive to the project of international justice, particularly in the 1984 Hagey Lectures, reprinted in Kai Alderson and Andrew Hurrell (eds.), *Hedley Bull on International Society* (Basingstoke: Macmillan, 2000). A close study of these lectures does not support this revisionist thesis.

[25] Terry Nardin, 'Justice and Coercion', in Alex J. Bellamy (ed.), *International Society and Its Critics* (Oxford: Oxford University Press, 2005), pp. 247–264.

[26] On duty as a substantial determination of Ethical Life see Hegel, *The Philosophy of Right*, §148.

actor – is the status of a rights-holder.[27] Yet neither these rights nor the duties associated with them are vestiges of an eternal moral order – they are recognised within institutions and practices, manifest as concrete, historically determined social forms. For Hegel, then, agents (be it human individuals or states) identify themselves and are identified by others as holders of rights and duties within common social practices in a given historical epoch. Transposed to the current context of international relations, our Hegelian hypothesis is that any state, as a bona fide participant in the existing practice of sovereign states, values its status as a free individual surrounded by like individuals. Its standing cannot be realised unless it is recognised by other equally free members of the society of free states.

Having clarified these preliminaries, we can now proceed to outline the determining features of the contemporary practice of sovereign states and that of global rights. Before we specify them positively, we start with a negative point. These practices are *not* purposive associations.[28] That is, they are not the outcome of a voluntary transaction or a contract, and they are not set up with a view of achieving some external goal or goals that pre-exist the practice under investigation. Consider, first, the society of sovereign states. The participant states (and the citizens within them) do not understand their state and the society of states to be the product of a contract made on a specific occasion establishing an association of states directed towards maximising global wealth, providing specific services to some race of people or upholding the will of one or another god. Nor do they understand their state and the society of states to be 'mutual-protection associations' whose single purpose is to protect them more efficiently than could be done by private security companies.[29] Citizens in modern states in general expect (but do not always get) a lot more from their states than a simple protection service. So asking 'What is the purpose of the society of sovereign states?', understood as a question about goal(s) that pre-exists this practice, would be an off-target question.

---

[27] As Hegel puts it, 'In the ethical realm, a human being has rights in so far as he has duties, and duties in so far as he has rights'. Hegel, *The Philosophy of Right*, §155. On the emergence of rights in the modern world, see §182.

[28] See our discussion in Chapter 1, under 'Purposive Association and Practical Association'.

[29] On mutual-protection associations, see Robert Nozick, *Anarchy, State, and Utopia* (New York: Basic Books, 1974), ch. 2, esp. pp. 12–25.

The practice of sovereign states, as a social whole, has no purpose. This is not to say that its individual members, sovereign states, have no goals or, conversely, that as participants in a society, they must have shared goals. Clearly, individual states differ in capabilities, power and the diverse purposes they might wish to pursue – the same way citizens inside states espouse different life plans. What needs to be better understood is that the society of sovereign states presents a special kind of social practice which binds its participants to its common rules without thereby binding them to a common goal or purpose. A practice of this sort is not a purposeful association designed for instrumental reasons; it is a 'constitutive' practice, as we outlined in Chapter 1.

Evidence that participants in the practice of sovereign states value it, non-instrumentally, is the almost complete absence of any group of citizens, anywhere in the world, urging that the practice of statehood be abandoned. Similarly, participants in the practice of global rights do not agitate for the abolition of their rights or the practice within which they enjoy them. Quite the contrary, in most places in the world, rights-holders argue for better protection of their basic rights. Such high value is ascribed to both practices because they are *constitutive practices*, a class of practices that create ethical statuses or standings. To reiterate, these statuses carry value for their participants – not just any value, but value of fundamental ethical importance. A status of this sort qualifies as 'ethical' because it determines the bearer's core identity; it is not just a contingent aspect of ever shifting interests and goals.[30]

It follows that protecting one's ethical standing in any constitutive practice cannot be done in a purely self-regarding fashion, for the standing involved is *a social standing* and, furthermore, an *ethical standing* within a practice. This practice-centred view departs from the conception of individuals as atomistic units familiar from Hobbes's 'state of nature'.[31] Hobbes's metaphor of a state of nature has been focal to realist theory of international relations, where sovereign states are depicted as self-regarding Hobbesian units. From the alternative standpoint of constitutive practices, participants are assumed to have as much regard for their own standing in the practice

---

[30] For an outstanding discussion of identity and the social formations in which it is established, see Richard Ned Lebow, *The Politics and Ethics of Identity: In Search of Ourselves* (Cambridge: Cambridge University Press, 2012).

[31] Hobbes, *Leviathan*, chs. 13 and 14.

concerned as for the practice itself. Thus while self-regarding concerns are present in the sense that participants *qua* distinct individuals have goals and purposes of their own, they cannot be detached from other-regarding concerns. This means that participants are severely *limited in the proper means* that they are permitted to deploy in the pursuit of self-chosen goals. These limits rule out means such as fraud and wanton violence. One well-known objection, voiced by realists, is that in inter-state relations, and particularly in times of war, all is permitted – *inter arma silent leges*.[32] But there is evidence that states exert themselves to justify the waging of war. Such justificatory arguments characteristically draw on the vocabulary of justice and rights and are addressed not only to an international audience of states but, increasingly, also to a global audience of citizens.

Against the atomist view of the agent, constitutive theory portrays agents as social beings whose identities are constituted within practices from the start. The status each individual holds presupposes self-consciousness, as when the self understands (and appreciates) one's own ethical standing as a participant in a social practice, a self-understanding which must be ratified by peers. If this view is applied to state relations, it would mean that an injury to any one state in the practice of sovereign states would be seen by the rest as an injury against themselves – and indeed, against the entire practice. In international relations, the salience of other-regarding concerns is illustrated by systems of collective security such as the United Nations (UN), which is a system of mutual aid. In contradistinction to a security community in which aggression among member states has become inconceivable, a system of collective security allows for the possibility of aggression.[33] When an act of aggression occurs, the other members of the collective security system are required to aid the victim. Nearly all currently existing states are members of the UN, an international organisation committed to the preservation of international peace and security in the entire system of sovereign states.

---

[32] See Michael Walzer, *Just and Unjust Wars: A Moral Argument with Historical Illustrations*, 2nd ed. (New York: Basic Books, 1992), p. 3.

[33] On the distinction between collective security and a security community, see Alexander Wendt, *Social Theory of International Politics* (Cambridge: Cambridge University Press, 1999), pp. 300–302; and Emanuel Adler and Michael Barnett (eds.), *Security Communities* (Cambridge: Cambridge University Press 1998).

Another even more prominent manifestation of the care states have for the society of states as a whole is reflected in the commitment of advanced states with developed, representative political institutions and relatively strong economies – Rawls's 'well-ordered societies' – to help improve the conditions in weak, failed or 'quasi-states'.[34] The latter are branded 'weak' or 'failed' states because they neither adequately protect the rights of their citizens nor ensure the bare social minimum we typically expect of modern states. This minimum includes protection against external aggression, internal protection against terrorism and crime, the collection of taxes for public infrastructure and some modicum of public welfare.[35] On our analysis, policies of developmental aid directed to alleviate the condition of failed states are not discretionary acts of charity but acts *required* of sovereign states who claim to be members in good standing in the practice of states. The language in which these requirements are expressed is also the language of justice and rights. Support for this line of reasoning is found in the actual conduct of failed and quasi-states, many of which are located in Africa. For the citizens of these states and for their governments, a primary objective is that they should cease to be failures and that they should advance to successful statehood. Citizens in weak states aspire to have their citizenship rights fully realised in properly functioning, modern democratic states.[36] This is true even of those groups of citizens involved in secessionist and irredentist movements who make the case not for the abolition of states and the system of states but for the creation of a state of their own.[37]

---

[34] John Rawls, *The Law of Peoples* (Cambridge, MA: Harvard University Press, 1999).

[35] On failed states, see Robert H. Jackson, *Quasi States: Sovereignty, International Relations and the Third World* (Cambridge: Cambridge University Press, 1993).

[36] This sentiment was conspicuous in the events of the Arab Spring that began in Tunisia in December 2010. What matters here is not whether the movement has been successful but what it shows about people's self-understandings.

[37] The validity of this point is not undermined by a case such as the Crimea in 2015, where a group of Crimean citizens sought secession from Ukraine in order to accede to the Russian state. While this case is disturbing considering the coercive military interference of Russia in this process, the point is that this group was not seeking colonial status under imperial rule or the termination of the system of states but a fully-fledged membership inside a sovereign state.

## The Global Practice of Rights

So far, we have focussed on the practice of sovereign states. It is time to consider its companion – the practice of global rights. At the outset, we defined global civil society *as a practice of global rights*.[38] To be sure, there is no consensus on how civil society should be defined and in what sense it may count as 'global'. Michael Walzer defines domestic civil society as the sphere of voluntary association, including associations in the 'marketplace and the political arena'.[39] He notes that other theorists might wish to exclude market relations and corporations from this definition. Still others identify civil society with transnational social movements, so that civil society is global by default.[40] We adopt Hegel's notion of domestic civil society – as a sphere of free-market and civil enterprise located inside the public realm of the state but representing an independent check on it – and 'globalise' it to capture the notion of a borderless area of free enterprise which supervenes onto the international society of states. A central feature of global civil society so understood is that it protects the rights of individuals as private parties – or 'civilians', in our terms – regardless of location.

At this juncture, we must pause to spell out our conception of rights. There is a rich, sophisticated and enormously complex philosophical discourse on the nature of rights, which we cannot engage in detail. What we can do is to locate our position on the map of this discourse. In the paradigm case, a right is a *relation between* (ideally two) *designated persons*, where the obligation-bound (duty-bound) person is required to perform certain action whose recipient is the right-holder.[41] The action, object of the right, is obligatory and not merely

---

[38] See Mervyn Frost, *Constituting Global Rights: Global Civil Society and the Society of Democratic States* (London: Routledge, 2002).

[39] Michael Walzer, 'Equality and Civil Society', in Simone Chambers and Will Kymlicka (eds.), *Alternative Conceptions of Civil Society* (Princeton, NJ: Princeton University Press, 2002), pp. 34–49, p. 35.

[40] Richard Falk, 'The Global Promise of Social Movements: Explorations at the Edge of Time', *Alternatives* 12 (2) 1987: 173–196; R. B. J. Walker, 'Social Movements/World Politics', *Millennium: Journal of International Studies* 23 (3) 1994: 669–700.

[41] A. I. Melden writes, 'To have a right is to stand in a moral relation with respect to some one or more persons, and that relation does not simply disappear when, in recognition of it along with other relevant considerations, it is deemed

discretionary. This indicates that, logically, a right is a duty correlate.[42] The morality of rights, then, includes only that part of morality concerned with interpersonal relations. Relations in terms of rights are necessarily individuated in the sense that if Alan holds a right against Brenda, as a designated person, he does not thereby hold a right against Sally, even though, as it happens, Brenda and Sally have the same ethical status or social role. Thus by making rights central to modernity, Hegel was suggesting that a normative system defined only by duties (rules) such as the Ten Commandments is fundamentally distinct from a system in which duties are correlated to rights.

Closer to our time, American legal theorist Wesley Hohfeld showed in his landmark study that claim-rights alone qualify as rights proper in the requisite sense of correlativity (where the claim-right of one person implies a corresponding duty for another). They must be distinguished from three cognate relations between persons that resemble rights: 'privileges' (liberties), immunities and powers.[43] We are using the term 'rights' in the inclusive sense, which includes these cognates. In modern constitutional democracies or, more precisely, in rule-of-law states, citizens hold rights against one another (Alan's claim-right to receive an object he has bought from Brenda) but also against institutions and the state. The right of free speech, the right of association and the right not be detained without a court procedure all have the logical structure of Hohfeldian immunities. Although they represent citizens' rights 'against' the state, they are protected ('immunised') from violation by the state itself as part of its civil constitution – or a 'bill of rights', in the context of the US Constitution.

To the extent that the perspective of global rights proposed here concerns rights of free association or free speech, it fits into the tradition of global constitutionalism.[44] This presupposes that a global bill

appropriate to infringe or to refuse to accord a person his right'. A. I. Melden, *Rights and Persons* (Berkeley: University of California Press, 1980), p. 15.

[42] A critical examination of the correlativity thesis is David Lyons, 'The Correlativity of Rights and Duties', *Noûs* 4 (1) 1970: 45–55.

[43] W. N. Hohfeld, *Fundamental Legal Conceptions as Applied in Judicial Reasoning* (New Haven, CT: Yale University Press, 1919).

[44] Closest to our stance is Cohen's argument for global constitutionalism, understood as a global rule-of-law account which prioritises international law over the idea of global governance and decentralised global law. Jean L. Cohen, 'Whose Sovereignty? Empire versus International Law', *Ethics & International Affairs* 18 (3) 2004: 1–24. See also Martti Koskenniemi, 'Constitutionalism as

of rights has been established, at least in the segment of global civil society which might be called mature. This segment amounts to a global practice of rights which includes, apart from the 'bedrock' right of security of the person (including bodily integrity), the following representative sample of basic rights: rights to property, rights of free association and rights of free speech, plus rights to free movement across state borders, especially refugee rights. The domain of the mature global practice of rights supervenes onto the domain of mature international society. Empirically, this includes all those states who uphold basic rights – not just that of their own citizens, but also those of citizens of any other state or even stateless people. This 'mature' domain is roughly coextensive with the trans-Atlantic society of states, though it is not strictly limited to it.[45] For example, in 2017, millions of Syrian refugees displaced by civil war in their homeland were hosted by EU states and particularly by Germany.

States members of the mature international society recognise global rights to free association, free speech and free contract. They do not deny these rights to foreign citizens or stateless persons who enter their borders legally. Of course, the protection of such basic rights is far from uniform around the globe. States such as Saudi Arabia, for example, do not recognise the freedom of association of their own citizens, nor grant it to foreigners.[46] Analogously, during the Cold War, states from the Soviet bloc severely circumscribed the rights of their citizens to associate or hold private property, rendering the right of free contract ineffective. It has to be underlined that the individual right to free contract is never completely free. Rule-of-law states impose limits on it such that one is not free to sign a contract whose end is the murdering, maiming or injuring of a person (even when the person consents). Here the ground for limiting the scope of rights that can be legitimately held by one individual is the equal protection of the

Mindset: Reflections on Kantian Themes about International Law and Globalization', *Theoretical Inquiries in Law* 8 (1) 2007: 9–36.

[45] Brown lists Canada, the United States, the European Union, Norway and Switzerland as members of the trans-Atlantic society of states, and we may add Japan. Chris Brown, 'Cosmopolitanism, World Citizenship and Global Civil Society', *Critical Review of International Social and Political Philosophy* 3 (1) 2000: 7–26, p. 18.

[46] See US Department of State, 'Country Reports on Human Rights Practices for 2014', www.state.gov/j/drl/rls/hrrpt/humanrightsreport/#wrapper (accessed 10 March 2016).

rights of all individuals – the right of the security of the person, in this case. In the former Soviet bloc, the situation was different. The right to free contract was curtailed not with a view of protecting rights but in order to consolidate the total authority of the socialist state over its citizens as private parties. The socialist state, as an all-encompassing public authority, had become totalitarian, leaving no space of private initiative to its citizens freely to make (non-rights-violating) contracts or to associate for voicing political opinions critical of the state.

What this indicates is that civil society can only flourish alongside a particular type of state – Hegel's ethical state.[47] If the state is too weak and unable to limit the domination of large commercial or criminal interests, the resultant society it encompasses would be an epitome of these interests – it would be uncivil as opposed to civil. Conversely, where the state is too strong, as happened in totalitarian and authoritarian states, it fuses with society. Such fusion dispenses with the idea of civil society as an independent sphere of private freedom whose *raison d'être* is to protect the rights of civilians against encroachment by the state. Totalitarian structures engulf everything into the public realm of the state. Authoritarian structures, in contrast, reduce the state and the rest of society into the private property of an authoritarian leader – Kant branded this kind of government 'despotism'.[48] In analysing civil society, we use two distinctions: mature/immature and civil/uncivil. For now, the emphasis is on the former, returning to the latter in Chapter 5.

It is noteworthy that the neo-Hegelian view presented here is non-foundational. That is, we do not start by building a bedrock theory of morality – and a theory of rights as part of this theory – from the bottom up and for which we then seek confirmation in actual social facts. Our practice-based analysis operates in the reverse – it starts with the interpretation of social facts and seeks to render these facts coherent (this hermeneutic procedure does not imply a sharp separation between interpretation or 'theory' and facts). We contend that the right of security of the person; rights of free contract, free association, free speech and refugee rights are *recognised*, as a matter of social fact, in

[47] Brown, 'Cosmopolitanism, World Citizenship and Global Civil Society', pp. 12–13.

[48] Kant sees despotism as a fusion of executive and legislative power. Immanuel Kant, *The Metaphysics of Morals*, ed. Mary Gregor (Cambridge: Cambridge University Press, 1996 [1797]), 6:317.

the contemporary global realm.[49] This is a representative (non-exhaustive) list. Such a social-facts approach is required because the rights on the list do not fit a single analytic criterion. They cannot be described coherently, as a set, as negative rights or liberties (the right of contract demands positive protection by institutions such as courts and police) or as claim-rights (the right of free association and free speech are immunities). It is better to leave open the question of which actual right corresponds to which Hohfeldian position (claim-right, liberty, immunity, power) or cognate analytic category and instead analyse rights by distinguishing between concrete *domains of rights-holding.*[50]

Our central thesis is that the practice of global rights (global civil society) comprises two such parallel domains – mature and immature ('rudimentary'). In territorial terms, global civil society is a borderless social form, and in normative terms, it constitutes a normative domain (sphere)of rights-holding (referred to as a 'domain' or 'sphere' for short). While rights that fall within this mature sphere are well established or secure, such rights are threatened inside the immature sphere. What is more, the baseline for the mature global civil society involves a 'thicker' set of rights when compared to the 'thin' set of rights (linked to security of the person and perhaps to basic subsistence) typical of its immature counterpart.[51] So although people around the world claim certain basic rights, frequently by appeal to the Universal Declaration of Human Rights (1948), in many places, states and other social actors fail to make their claims realisable. So far, the right of free contract and free association, along with the right of refuge that gives rise to a duty

---

[49] It is important to differentiate the claim that rights are *created* within institutions from the claim that rights, however created, are *recognised* as valid within such institutions. See Rex Martin, 'Human Rights and the Social Recognition Thesis', *Journal of Social Philosophy* 44 (1) 2013: 1–21. That the social recognition of a moral right matters does not cancel out the separate point that a moral right counts as moral by virtue of some moral principle of justification.

[50] Each actual right, when analytically construed, is a complex 'bundle' of Hohfeldian positions. See L. W. Sumner, *The Moral Foundation of Rights* (Oxford: Clarendon Press, 1989). One of these positions forms the kernel of the right. For example, the right to freedom of speech, as an actual right, is analysable into a kernel comprising an 'immunity' against the state (an institutional party) plus an additional component of a 'liberty' against private parties.

[51] One famous argument for basic global rights of liberty, security and subsistence is offered in Henry Shue, *Basic Rights: Subsistence, Affluence, and U.S. Foreign Policy*, 2nd ed. (Princeton, NJ: Princeton University Press, 1996).

to provide asylum, have received recognition as basic global rights inside the mature global society. Inside the domain of the immature global civil society, although many rights are claimed, few are fully realised and protected beyond the bedrock right of security of the person. Even this basic right is sometimes violated by states who turn against their own citizens. When such delinquent states commit acts which, in Michael Walzer's phrase, 'shock the moral conscience of mankind', other states have a right to intervene and stop the atrocities.[52] This is the root of the doctrine of humanitarian intervention.[53]

The upshot of the argument so far is that the main agencies which recognise and protect basic rights globally are states. Not just isolated states, but a society of states. At present, this society incorporates norms such as humanitarian intervention and the granting of asylum to refugees which are now embodied in international law. Because the beneficiaries of these norms, protected by states, are individuals, the question is whether our position is cosmopolitan.

*Moral cosmopolitanism* holds that the rights of individuals are normatively prior to the rights of states.[54] The 'cosmopolis' constitutes a borderless, truly global realm of rights whose bearers are individual persons. Here rights are understood to be 'human rights' – pre-institutional rights that are not created by states or other institutions. For moral cosmopolitans, states may be useful for the realisation of human rights, but since such rights can be realised by alternative institutional means, states are dispensable, though perhaps not immediately.

Like cosmopolitans, we construe the global practice of rights as a borderless social form. Yet we depart from the (extreme) version of

---

[52] Walzer, *Just and Unjust Wars*, p. 107.

[53] Key essays on the contemporary doctrine of humanitarian intervention are collected in J. L. Holzgrefe and Robert O. Keohane (eds.), *Humanitarian Intervention: Ethical, Legal, and Political Dilemmas* (Cambridge: Cambridge University Press, 2003). See also Nicholas J. Wheeler, *Saving Strangers: Humanitarian Intervention in International Society* (Oxford: Oxford University Press, 2002); and Terry Nardin and Melissa S. Williams (eds.), *Humanitarian Intervention: NOMOS XLVII* (New York: New York University Press, 2006).

[54] The basic distinction within cosmopolitanism as a philosophical outlook is between *moral cosmopolitanism* (which treats the individual human person as the fundamental object of moral concern) and *political or institutional cosmopolitanism* (which demands the creation of global institutions). Key articles on both variants of cosmopolitanism are collected in Garrett W. Brown and David Held (eds.), *The Cosmopolitanism Reader* (Cambridge: Polity Press, 2010).

moral cosmopolitanism just noted in postulating a tight relationship between the international and the global. The rationale is that the two core practices, the practice of global rights and the practice of sovereign states, each provide an important vantage point that enables moral criticism of the other. Thus neither the global nor the international has normative priority – their relationship is dialectical (more on this in Chapter 5).

Concretely, we follow Walzer in defining 'moral criticism' as judgement of actual social practices by a social critic who is an insider to the practices.[55] Walzer focusses on the standards of criticism used by the social critic. These do not reside in immutable principles of value such as natural law (a set of universal precepts binding on all rational beings by virtue of reason alone) or natural rights exemplified by Locke's famous triad of rights to life, liberty, and 'possessions' (property).[56] Rather, social criticism is undertaken from within social practices and institutions. As such, it is 'an internal argument' spoken in the vernacular of the participants under investigation.[57] While our analysis invokes(global) rights as a critical standard for judging practices, it falls back on an institutionalist conception of rights as required by our Hegelian premises. If certain institutional rights supply a standard of moral criticism, that is because we have *learned* to use the language of rights properly.

The element of learning distinguishes our practice-based (institutionalist) view from its naturalist counterpart. To substantiate this point, let us return for a moment to the example of humanitarian intervention. Originally developed in the middle ages, the doctrine re-gained prominence in international affairs in the 1990s in the aftermath of massacres in Kosovo, Somalia and Rwanda. Its gist is that it qualifies the previously unconditional right of states to non-intervention, stemming from their basic rights to territorial integrity and sovereign independence. Two parallel arguments can be made. One is naturalist: its basis is natural

---

[55] Michael Walzer, *Interpretation and Social Criticism* (Cambridge, MA: Harvard University Press, 1987), pt. 2 ('The Practice of Social Criticism').

[56] A classical text on natural law is John Finnis, *Natural Law and Natural Rights* (Oxford: Oxford University Press, 1980). Locke uses 'property' as an umbrella term for three basic natural rights –life, liberty and possessions (the latter designates 'property' in present-day terms). John Locke, *Second Treatise of Government*, ed. C. B. Macpherson (Indianapolis: Hackett, 1980 [1690]), §§6, 9.

[57] Walzer, *Interpretation and Social Criticism*, p. 39.

law, and it appeals to the moral right of the innocent not to be killed.[58] The other is institutionalist: it points to the fact that a state (as an institution of positive law) has an obligation to protect the life and rights of its citizens.[59] Whenever the state fails to protect its citizens by enslaving or massacring them, humanitarian intervention by other states is permitted and, indeed, required. The naturalist and the institutionalist arguments reach this same conclusion regarding the moral necessity of humanitarian intervention, but the grounds for their conclusions are different in each case – absolute moral norms (naturalism) versus practices that presuppose moral learning (practice-based accounts). In the twentieth century, we may say, members of the mature society of states have learned to respect the rights of their citizens – at a minimum, the right of the security of the person. This is not the image enunciated by early modern writers such as Wolff, who held that inside international society states alone enjoy rights as (artificial) persons.[60] In its contemporary variant, international society and particularly its mature domain integrates both the rights of states and the rights of human persons (not to be massacred or subjected to exodus).

In the late twentieth century, the recognition of the basic rights of human persons by states has generated global norms of responsible state conduct. Figuratively speaking, these norms continue to 'diffuse' from the mature normative domain of the society of states towards its immature domain. Citizens of states who find themselves in the latter, normatively rudimentary domain inhabit a world without much respect for basic rights. But whenever these citizens seek to improve the institutional landscape of their own domestic state and society with a view of incorporating such rights, they seldom appeal to some abstract set of rights – rights to life, liberty and property – found on

---

[58] See Terry Nardin, 'The Moral Basis of Humanitarian Intervention', *Ethics & International Affairs* 16 (2) 2002: 57–70.

[59] This is Walzer's version of the argument for humanitarian intervention, which places special emphasis on the rights of citizens as members of a self-determining political community. As he puts it, 'When a government turns savagely upon its own people, we must doubt the very existence of a political community to which the idea of self-determination might apply'. Walzer, *Just and Unjust Wars*, p. 101.

[60] For a brief but insightful sketch of Wolff's conception of the society of states, see Charles Beitz, 'The Moral Standing of States Revisited', *Ethics & International Affairs* 23 (4) 2009: 325–347, p. 329–330nn17, 18. Beitz refers to Wolff, *Jus Gentium Methodo Scientifica Pertractatum*, §§7, 16.

the pages of foundational documents and constitutions. Above all, they appeal to rights that are *actualised* – visibly recognised and realised within the mature sphere of the society of states – on a global scale. From the Tiananmen student protests of 1989 to the Arab Spring of 2010, global rights have been the impetus behind the quest for freedom of association, freedom of speech and equal political participation.

But even though we make an *institutionalist* case for global rights, it is not a defence of *political cosmopolitanism*. Proponents of political cosmopolitanism advocate the creation of political institutions of a global reach – be it a global state or, less ambitiously, supranational institutions that wield coercive authority over the society of states as a whole.[61] In proceeding to 'globalise' Hegel's original argument for civil society, we do not push it to its logical conclusion. Hegel saw the domestic states as the framework that encompasses and regulates domestic civil society, but we do not claim that, analogously, a global state must encompass and regulate global civil society today (Hegel was sceptical of a global state). Considered as a domestic institution, the Hegelian state is supposed to ameliorate the negative effects of alienation and fragmentation that plague domestic civil society. But the global case presents a disanalogy, since the defects of *global* civil society are not such that they can only be remedied by the creation of a global state. On the contrary, we claim that an *international* authority – the society of sovereign states – is more apt for remedying such defects.

What makes a global state a bad option for overcoming the ills of global civil society? One famous consideration is Kant's worry that a single global political structure would most likely be inimical to individual freedom.[62] To reassert the value of freedom, we endorse global anarchy. As mentioned earlier, the practice of sovereign states is 'anarchical' in two distinct senses: first, it represents a social arrangement not governed by a global sovereign, and second, its institutional form is one of a 'flat', horizontal order of formal equals to be

---

[61] A Kantian argument for a global federation of republican states is Pauline Kleingeld, 'Approaching Perpetual Peace: Kant's Defence of a League of States and His Ideal of a World Federation', *European Journal of Philosophy* 12 (3) 2004: 304–325.

[62] Immanuel Kant, *Perpetual Peace: A Philosophical Sketch*, in Immanuel Kant, *Political Writings*, trans. H.B Nisbet, ed. H. Reiss (Cambridge: Cambridge University Press, 1991 [1795]), pp. 93–130, p. 113.

contrasted with a hierarchical order of superordinate and subordinate units. There is a third, axiological sense of anarchy referring to the value of equal freedom that both states and participants in the practice of sovereign rights may enjoy. What deserves attention is that anarchy in the third sense (anarchical freedom) depends on having an anarchical (flat) social form or anarchy in the second sense (a society of equally free states). Notice that while the value of anarchical freedom is a strictly normative notion, the other two conceptions of anarchy can be invoked either descriptively or normatively. The descriptive case was presented by Kenneth Waltz in his influential neorealist analysis of the anarchical international system, which he compared to a quasi-automatic market mechanism, and the normative case by Bull in his theory of the anarchical society.[63] Bull takes anarchy to be a normative notion, both in the sense of a horizontal relation between formal equals and as the obverse of global hierarchy. We concur with Bull's portrayal of international society as a practice with normative ramifications. This implies intentional action on the part of its participants who act to reproduce their common practice, as we suggested in the concluding pages of Chapter 2. On this normative reading, states, members of the anarchical society, deliberately act to thwart the rise of a global empire and maintain the formal equality between themselves.

The desirability of a global sovereign, be it a global empire or a super state, is what differentiates the practice of sovereign states from that of global rights. Anarchy, defined as a lack of a global state or empire, is a necessary presupposition of the practice of free states. In sharp contrast, the practice of global rights is compatible with a global state as much as with global anarchy. It is significant, then, that we link the realisation of global rights to the condition of global anarchy and thus to the agency of international society.

## Freedom and Anarchical Practices

One objection to our neo-Hegelian argument might be that states do not have values, only thinking and choosing human individuals do. So far, in considering the practice of sovereign states and the practice of global rights, we have espoused a view from 'above', from

---

[63] See Bull, *The Anarchical Society*; Kenneth N. Waltz, *Theory of International Politics* (Boston, MA: McGraw-Hill, 1979), chs. 5 and 6 (pp. 79–128).

the international and global realm. But if we adopt a view from 'below', as individuals living inside states, the thesis becomes that we, men and women, participate in two core 'anarchical' practices that constitute us as *free* actors or actors with specific sets of rights. As participants in the society of sovereign states, we are constituted as citizens of free states related to other states within a common domain of sovereign freedom (the society of free states). As participants in global civil society (the practice of global rights), we are constituted as rights-holders enjoying a specific set of freedoms. In the contemporary world, then, the freedoms of sovereign states and the freedoms of individual rights-holders are statuses valued by all bona fide participants – this is the general thrust of our normative position. These statuses are valued against an earlier historical background in which political formations (precursors of states) and individual men and women were not recognised as free in these ways and where empire, tyranny, serfdom and slavery were the norm.

If the freedom manifest in the two core practices we have been discussing has become integral to our identity as modern individuals, it cannot be seen as identical to Hobbes's 'right of nature'. By this expression, Hobbes meant unlimited freedom which grants the agent a full licence to act in the external world and whose ground is self-preservation. But self-preservation is a boundless notion, covering any of the means necessary to perpetuate one's life, such as shelter, food – all the way up to physical harm, including the killing of another person who might be an obstacle for maintaining one's life.[64] Because morality or ethics is a matter of observing limits in conduct, neither self-preservation nor the right of nature qualify as proper moral or ethical concepts. While our Hegelian concept of ethics (*Sittlichkeit*) is less restrictive in scope than Kantian morality (morality based on principles), both imply that conduct is subject to normative limits and, indeed, on internally imposed limits that the agent recognises without external duress. Hobbes's right of nature is a symbol of a world purged of normative limits: physical obstacles to one's freedom of action are the only constraints present in it. In such a world, there is no room for ethics or morality.

For certain realists in IR, this Hobbesian image of social interaction beyond the purview of morality and ethics is the correct description of

---

[64] See Hobbes, *Leviathan*, ch. 15, pp. 212, and ch. 21, pp. 268–269.

international relations.[65] Notice that 'social' need not be synonymous with 'moral' or 'ethical'. If 'social' is taken to mean involving *regular interaction*, then Hobbes's state of nature qualifies as a social condition: it is as an interaction domain where agents, using their uncurbed freedom to act, regularly collide and harm one another. Viewed from the vantage point of the Hegelian ethics as interpreted here, the world of international relations is distinctively different – it is a social world structured around ethical relationships and statuses. Because these statuses are constituted within practices, these constitutive practices themselves are assumed to have value for their participants. From this angle, the contemporary practice of sovereign states, insofar as it embodies the value of equal freedom, cannot be equated to an instrument for protecting pre-existing rights in a Hobbesian world of self-regarding states. Instead, these rights and freedoms must be seen as internal to the practice and therefore to the identity of its members.

More generally, it is incoherent to think of any constitutive practice in instrumental terms as a vehicle for achieving external goals that could have been achieved more efficiently by alternative means. Two sets of literatures in IR have offered arguments to this effect. One is the literature on global hierarchy. Its best-known advocate, David Lake, has argued that in the name of cost efficiency, weak states are prepared to make contracts by exchanging some part of their sovereign freedom for obtaining goods such as international security from a group of powerful states in the international system – great powers.[66] The resultant picture of global hierarchy, dominated by the great powers, treats sovereign freedom as a good to be traded off against other goods in the international marketplace. However, on our account, far from being a good that can be bargained away, sovereign freedom is a highly valued identity. Losing one's identity is not simply a matter of cost but something deeper – its loss would precipitate an identity crisis (see Chapter 3). A state that traded away its sovereign freedom would no longer see itself and would no longer be recognised as an independent

---

[65] Offensive realist Mearsheimer holds that the structural factors sufficient to explain what is going on in the international system include 'anarchy' (a Hobbesian state of nature) plus the distribution of power among the great powers in the system. John J. Mearsheimer, *The Tragedy of Great Power Politics* (New York: W. W. Norton, 2001), p. 10.

[66] David A. Lake, *Hierarchy in International Relations* (Ithaca: Cornell University Press, 2009), esp. pp. xi, 3–4, 8, 96, 123–124.

state by other members of the society of free states – it would have become a dominion, a 'satellite' or a colony of another state.

Another argument that appeals to efficiency stems from the literature on the privatisation of security. Here security is treated as a private, divisible good that can be provided by private companies rather than as a public good whose provision is entrusted to public authorities such as states and state military forces.[67] Private security companies, the claim goes, supply a faster, cheaper and more efficient solution to the problem of military intervention on the ground in war-torn zones, particularly in quasi-states where it is impossible to rely on cooperation with local authorities of public law enforcement. One defect of this recommendation for the privatisation of security is that no overarching public global authority exists impartially to adjudicate cases of abuse by personnel of private security firms.[68] Private security companies exercise global rights of contract across state borders or within the global rights practice. This shows that this practice has its dark side.

## Conclusion

In light of this last observation, which points to the ambiguity of practices, it would be misleading to assign fixed essences to the practice of sovereign states or the practice of global rights. For, as we claim, their identities do not exhibit an essence; they are *dialectical*. In Chapter 5, we take up the question of the dialectical transformation inside each of these two core practices as well as between them.

---

[67] On the privatisation of security, see Robert Mandel, *Armies without States: The Privatization of Security* (Boulder, CO: Lynne Rienner, 2002); Christopher Kinsey, *Corporate Soldiers and International Security: The Rise of Private Military Companies* (London: Routledge, 2006); Lindsey Cameron and Vincent Chetail, *Privatizing War: Private Military and Security Companies under Public International Law* (Cambridge: Cambridge University Press, 2013).

[68] Brown, 'Cosmopolitanism, World Citizenship and Global Civil Society', p. 17.

# 5 | The Dialectic of Global Practices

The previous chapter outlined the key features of the two core practices in contemporary international relations – the practice of the society of sovereign states and the practice of global rights. For reasons of presentation, we discussed them as if they were static. In fact, both practices are dynamic, or 'dialectical', as Hegel would say. By this term, Hegel meant a process of change of an identity triggered by one or more internal contradictions.[1] In what follows, we complete our neo-Hegelian analysis by examining the dialectical character of each of these core practices considered singly as well as their mutual relationship which, we contend, is itself dialectical.[2] Part of our task is to assess the fact that both of these practices have become global. Obviously, the contemporary *global* practice of rights is global by default. And although the practice of sovereign states counts as *international* insofar as states (colloquially, 'nations') continue to be its primary actors, during the last century or so, it has come to encompass all parts of the globe. Such globalisation has implications that are not merely geographical but ethical or normative. As before, we draw

---

[1] Hegel's notion of contradiction runs through his entire corpus of works. One example is the section on contradiction in G. W. F. Hegel, *Hegel's Science of Logic*, trans. A. V. Miller (Atlantic Highlands, NJ: Humanities Press International, 1989 [1812–1816]), pp. 431–443.

[2] Hegel scholars continue to debate specific points of interpretation that arise from a close reading of G. W. F. Hegel, *Hegel's Philosophy of Right*, trans. T. M. Knox (Oxford: Oxford University Press, 1967 [1821]) – henceforth referred to as *The Philosophy of Right*. See, for example, the essays collected in Z. A. Pelczynski (ed.), *Hegel's Political Philosophy: Problems and Perspectives* (Cambridge: Cambridge University Press, 1971); and Z. A. Pelczynski (ed.), *The State and Civil Society: Studies in Hegel's Political Philosophy* (Cambridge: Cambridge University Press, 1984). Recent contributions include Alan Patten, *Hegel's Idea of Freedom* (Oxford: Oxford University Press, 1999); and Thom Brooks, *Hegel's Political Philosophy: A Systematic Reading of Hegel's Philosophy of Right* (Edinburgh: Edinburgh University Press, 2012). We do not engage this scholarship but present our own interpretations of Hegel's ideas.

attention to the value of freedom as a primary value that animates the practice of sovereign states and the practice of global rights.

The exposition has three parts. After briefly elucidating Hegel's dialectic, we go on to consider the challenges and opportunities each of these two dialectically related practices creates for its participants: individual rights-holders or states. The proposed account illuminates the problem of change in the current global realm and shows it to be permeated by tensions with negative ethical repercussions.

## Freedom and Hegel's Dialectic

Let us start by recalling a central argument in this book: a coherent understanding of contemporary international relations requires that we comprehend its core global practices properly – as meaningful social wholes within which the identities of international actors are constituted. In Chapter 4, we suggested that inside this duo of practices, men and women are constituted as free agents – as 'civilians' (civil society actors) within the global rights practice and as citizens within the global society of states. This raises the difficult question of freedom. Our point of departure is Hegel's idea that in modernity, freedom is manifest as a status of rights-holding based on mutual recognition between self-conscious actors. What is important is that the rights-holders recognise one another not just formally but in actuality – in all the complexity of the life choices each has made through the use of their rights. The same logic applies to the practice of sovereign states. A state cannot fully actualise its internal sovereignty (its ultimate legal right to rule inside its jurisdiction) without receiving proper recognition from the other sovereign states in the practice of states who must acknowledge its external sovereignty (its right to be independent from the juridical authority of another state). The sovereignty of the state epitomises a particular (juridically grounded) form of freedom *qua* rights. It has two aspects: (1) the right to freely (without undue interference) enter into external relations with other states on an equal footing and (2) the right to freely determine its internal constitutional order, national traditions and political culture. In a broader sense (not limited to the state), the term 'sovereignty' conveys the idea of a free and autonomous individual. Because Hegel did not envisage a society of states, we put forward a neo-Hegelian interpretation that couples the idea of an anarchical society of sovereign states with Hegel's notions of freedom as right-holding, dialectic and actuality.[3] As will be shown in the next section, apart from its manifestation as rights-holding, freedom for Hegel is a value espoused by self-conscious actors.

Our main aim, then, is to examine the internal dialectical change *within* and *between* the global practice of rights and the global practice of states as concrete, dynamic social wholes inside which participants seek fully to actualise the value of freedom.

Hegel's dialectic, as we understand it, comprises a process with two closely related but distinct aspects. The first captures the way in which, in the long run, the activities of participants in a social practice bring about unintended outcomes that threaten to undermine both the rules of the practice and the ethical statuses established within it, statuses which constitute the identities of its bona fide participants. The cumulative effect of such outcomes is to erode the ethical values embedded in the practice. We refer to this dialectical process as 'ethical erosion'. Ethical erosion captures the paradox of freedom, which is that the exercise of freedom over time comes to threaten freedom itself. Where this happens, practices may be said to have generated a *self-undermining* momentum or what Robert Williams has branded a process of 'self-subversion'.[4] This is the first aspect of the dialectic.

The second aspect of the dialectic discloses how, over time, higher-order constitutive practices emerge which remedy the subversion (or erosion) of freedom just mentioned. Such ethically remedial higher-order practices do not cancel out the former practices but preserve them, while mitigating their negative effects. The faulty part is taken up in a subsequent whole that provides an antidote to the fault. Hegel's term for this process is *Aufhebung* ('sublation' or 'overcoming').[5] The term 'dialectic' in this (second) sense indicates how an ethically corrosive feature of a constitutive practice is subsequently overcome

---

[3] See our discussion of the anarchical society under 'The Practice of Sovereign States' in Chapter 4.

[4] Robert R. Williams, *Hegel's Ethics of Recognition* (Berkeley: University of California Press, 1997).

[5] On 'sublation', see Hegel, *Hegel's Science of Logic*, Vol. I ('The Objective Logic'), bk. 1 ('The Doctrine of Being'), pp. 106–108. See also G. W. F. Hegel, *Hegel's Phenomenology of Spirit*, trans. A. V. Miller (Oxford: Oxford University Press, 1977 [1807]), A ('Consciousness'), sec. 2 ('Perception: Or the Thing and Deception'), p. 68. Miller translates the term *aufheben* as 'supersede' rather than 'sublate'.

(*aufgehoben*) in a higher-order practice. Notice that the emergence of a higher-order practice is not to be explained as a causal sequence of events or as a purposeful activity directed at solving problems in the former practice. Rather, the interactions of a multiplicity of individuals, each engaged in their own self-conscious pursuit of ends, generates unintended cumulative effects that have negative consequences – these effects are best described as dialectical. With hindsight, the relationship between the two global practices that we are investigating can be seen as dialectal in the way just outlined.[6]

The sketch of the dialectic presented thus far is schematic. To supplant it with contents, it is best to return to Hegel's dialectical theses concerning the relationship between civil society and the state – the central political and economic institutions of domestic order in modernity. Hegel describes civil society as a 'system of needs'. Within its purview, the concrete person, as a *particular* individual, has needs that reflect 'a mixture of caprice and physical necessity'. But since this person, at the same time, stands in *relation to* other particular persons, such relations exhibit *universality*.[7] Further, the fact that unlike animals who lack reason, a human being is governed by rational thought and understanding leads to the multiplication of needs.[8] To satisfy their needs, individuals have to cooperate, and to make their cooperation efficient, they have to engage in a division of labour. The result is a highly complex system of mutual interdependence.[9]

Inside this 'system of needs', people use the freedoms they have constituted for themselves to pursue their *private* interests.[10] The particular/universal is transposed into the private/public. It is at this point that the first feature of the dialectic starts to emerge. Because the sphere of civil society is one of particularity, Hegel argues, differences between individuals 'have as their inevitable consequence disparities of individual resources and ability'.[11] Furthermore, 'men are made unequal by

---

[6] Regarding understanding certain social relations with hindsight, Hegel famously wrote, 'When philosophy paints its grey in grey, then has a shape of life grown old. By philosophy's grey in grey it cannot be rejuvenated but only understood. The owl of Minerva spreads its wings only with the falling of the dusk'. Hegel, *The Philosophy of Right*, 'Preface', p. 13.

[7] Hegel, *The Philosophy of Right*, §182.

[8] Hegel, *The Philosophy of Right*, §190.

[9] Hegel, *The Philosophy of Right*, §198.

[10] Hegel, *The Philosophy of Right*, §187.

[11] Hegel, *The Philosophy of Right*, §200.

nature, where inequality is in its elements, and in civil society the right
of particularity is so far from annulling this natural inequality that it
produces it out of mind and raises it to an inequality of skill and
resources, and even to one of moral and intellectual attainment.'[12]
Thus when each actor inside civil society proceeds to exercise his or
her freedoms, *without any deliberate wrongdoing*, the unintended
outcome for civil society as a whole still turns out to be negative, with
great inequalities in social positions, power differentials and alienation.
In the shadow of these negative effects, the freedoms of those who
participate in civil society are shown to be abstract (purely formal or
nominal) instead of real ('actual', in Hegel's terms). In short, the
dynamism within civil society, as a practice within which private
individuals are constituted as free, comes to threaten the very freedoms
it creates. What is being disclosed here is a civil society in motion
producing elements of incivility.

   In the second aspect of the dialectic, these shortcomings of Hegel's
civil society are overcome – or 'sublated' (*aufgehoben*) – within a
higher-order institution, the state. The state, as Hegel presents it,
'sublates' the freedom-eroding features of civil society while preserving
the private freedoms constituted within this society. In simultaneously
gaining membership in the state, 'civilians' come to constitute one
another as occupiers of a higher status, that of citizen, which enables
them to enjoy a superior form of freedom than that available in civil
society. It is superior because of the unity of particularity and universality achieved within the state. As Hegel writes,

What is of the utmost importance is that the law of reason should be shot
through and through by the law of particular freedom, and that my particular end should become identified with the universal end, or otherwise
the state is left in the air. The state is actual only when its members have a
feeling of their own self-hood and it is stable only when public and private
ends are identical. It has often been said that the end of the state is the
happiness of the citizens. That is perfectly true. If all is not well with them,
if their subjective aims are not satisfied, if they do not find that the state as
such is the means to their satisfaction, then the footing of the state itself is
insecure.[13]

---

[12] Hegel, *The Philosophy of Right*, §200.
[13] Hegel, *The Philosophy of Right*, §265A ('A' is an 'Addition' from notes taken at
     Hegel's lectures).

The contrast between the state and civil society is stark. Participants in civil society are private actors pursuing private interests; they have no sense of belonging to a larger social whole – to the state as a public realm. The cumulative results of their individual private actions confront them as alien forces of nature. This is fundamentally different from the kind of relationship that exists between citizen and state. Citizens understand the state to be *their* state and know that the rights they possess, as citizens, are validated inside *that* particular state. They hold the state, as a public institution, to be responsible to and for them as individual actors. Correlatively, as individual actors, they understand themselves to be responsible for the actions of their state. Elaborating on his conception of the modern state and comparing it to earlier forms of political organisation, Hegel says,

In the state everything depends on the unity of universal and particular. In the states of antiquity, the subjective end simply coincided with the state's will. In modern times, however, we make claims for private judgement, private willing, and private conscience. The ancients had none of these in the modern sense; the ultimate thing with them was the will of the state. Whereas under the despots of Asia the individual had no inner life and no justification in himself, in the modern world, man insists on respect been paid to his inner life. The conjunction of duty and right has a twofold aspect: what the state demands from us as a duty is *eo ipso* our right as individuals, since the state is nothing but the articulation of the concept of freedom. The determinations of the individual will are given an objective embodiment through the state and thereby attain their truth and their actualization for the first time. The state is the one and only prerequisite of the attainment of particular ends and welfare.[14]

Hegel's state is distinctively an *ethical* state – a social whole within which individual citizens recognise one another as equally free. Even though Hegel was not a proponent of a democratic system of political representation on the principle 'one person, one vote', he insisted that the state must be understood as a social whole in which citizens feel at home. The 'ethical state' is not an alien, external force but a creation of the citizens that has to have concern not just for their individual interests but, above all, for their common good. Holding the status of citizen inside an ethical state is a prerequisite for overcoming the ethical defects of civil society manifest in the first phase of the dialectic.

[14] Hegel, *The Philosophy of Right*, §261A.

Thus whenever the ethical state passes legislation binding on its citizens in order to ameliorate the social inequalities arising within civil society, this is not an external imposition on their will but an act of self-government. It is an act of *their* state, which has concern for their interests and well-being. In present-day terms, the citizens are to regard the public welfare policies of the state aimed at the provision of any (or all) of the following – education, health, housing, pensions, tele-communications – as an act of the state, which is none other than a public agency comprising the citizens themselves. Within the ethical state, there is an identity of interest between citizen and state.[15] On a Hegelian reading, a contemporary democracy contains one basic element of the 'ethical state': the actualisation of freedom as self-government. For example, even those citizens who did not vote for the person or party currently leading the government understand it to be 'their' government, provided they have exercised an equal right to vote for political representatives in free and open elections. Self-government, as we shall see, is only one component of the fully actualised ethical state.

Hegel's 'ethical state' is a special form of public authority. It is instructive to contrast it with the alternative, 'minimal state' defended by libertarian philosopher Robert Nozick. Nozick reformulates the natural-rights tradition inaugurated by John Locke, where the state is created *via* a social contract between individuals who hold natural rights in an original condition ('state of nature') prior to the state.[16] The prerogative of Nozick's minimal state is restricted to enforcing the original rights of the individuals who have set it up. Citizens' rights here are simply coercively (juridically as well as materially) protected natural rights. The minimal state is not an agency authorised to *constitute* new rights but a custodian of pre-existing natural rights. Because it lacks 'constitutive' powers enabling it to make rights, it has no ethical significance (in Hegel's terms of ethics) as an institution: it is not a public realm distinct from the realm of natural rights possessed by sovereign individuals. In terms of the public/private distinction, the

---

[15] This is not to suggest that states cannot abuse their powers and thus abuse their own citizens. As we know, this is a common occurrence even in so-called mature democracies. The point here is to outline *conceptually* the ethical structure that links citizens to states and vice versa.

[16] John Locke, *Second Treatise of Government*, ed. C. B. Macpherson (Indianapolis: Hackett, 1980 [1690]); Robert Nozick, *Anarchy, State, and Utopia* (New York: Basic Books, 1974).

minimal state does not qualify as a proper public authority; it remains a larger-scale private authority whose institutional and material power suffices to keep in check the rest of the private parties inside its realm. This Nozickean model of private authority as a surrogate for public authority sheds light on the rise of similar agencies on a global scale, private military and security companies that we discuss later on in this chapter. Compared to Nozick's view of the state as a large-scale private authority, Hegel's great insight is to have articulated the modern sovereign state as a public realm. But this is not a public realm predicated on an impartial principle of non-interference between citizens, as in Kant's legal theory.[17] Hegel's ethical state is a public domain where a bond is forged between the state and its citizens.

So far, we illustrated how Hegel's dialectic works within domestic institutions, but the question pertinent to our practice theory is, Does the dialectic also work globally? The answer we provide is affirmative, with a host of qualifications. As it will become clear, the domestic sphere of the ethical state and civil society portrayed by Hegel differ in crucial respects from the contemporary global sphere, as constituted by the practice of sovereign states and the practice of global civil society. In the remainder of this chapter, we first discuss the global practice of sovereign states and examine the degree of its ethical self-erosion. Having identified its ethical defects, we then trace how they are partially overcome through its dialectical link to the practice of global rights. Finally, in a third dialectical movement, the practice of global rights reveals its shortcomings, which, we contend, can be remedied through the agency of states (and hence through the practice of sovereign states), though inconclusively.

## Ethical Self-Erosion in the Global Practice of Sovereign States

Hegel depicts the self as an agent constituted by attachments and values. To adopt this Hegelian premise with respect to a freedom-based practice is to grant that the free choice and autonomy of each individual inside the practice is not merely tolerated but positively valued by all its participants. In the context of our present analysis,

---

[17] Immanuel Kant, *The Doctrine of Right* (pt. 1), in *The Metaphysics of Morals*, ed. Mary Gregor (Cambridge: Cambridge University Press 1996 [1797]), pp. 3–138.

this implies that the participants in this kind of practice, be it states or human rights-holders, attach a positive value to individual freedom and diversity.[18] In this section, we focus on the practice of sovereign states. It is straightforward to see that by recognising one another as free and equal, states announce their commitment to diversity and pluralism. If a state has a *recognised* right to be a sovereign (autonomous) individual, it is entitled to espouse a domestic constitutional order of its own choice. Some states will adopt constitutions informed by religious doctrines, others will be thoroughly secular, some will be liberal and yet others will be socialist. Although states might disapprove of one another's political moralities – for example, secular states might criticise states grounded on Christian or Islamic principles – the presumption is that they all approve of the diversity that their common international practice makes possible. The Hegelian corollary to this conclusion is that pluralism and diversity are nurtured and not merely enabled within a practice whose core value is freedom.

The primary agency of the global practice of states is the society of sovereign states. In lieu of the priority it assigns to the value of freedom, we have been referring to it as an 'anarchical' society (borrowing Bull's expression).[19] Within its framework, each participant has the recognised standing of an independent authority – in this sense, each state is an equal and free (autonomous) individual. But, and this is the dialectical aspect, the exercise of sovereign autonomy by states has a dark side. It can become a trump against international criticism. Typically, a state would banish international media or nongovernmental organisations from its territory when it is guilty of abusing the rights of minorities or, more generally, the rights of its citizens, especially the bedrock right to bodily integrity and security. When an abuse on a mass scale takes place as in cases of genocide, enslavement, persecution or deportation of entire groups based on their race and ethnicity, it poses a dilemma for other states who, until recently, recognised the norm of non-intervention as a baseline in international society. A state is said to enjoy basic rights to territorial

---

[18] On this topic, see the outstanding essay by Andrew Buchwalter, 'Hegel's Conception of an International "We"', in Philip T. Grier (ed.), *Identity and Difference: Studies in Hegel's Logic, Philosophy of Spirit, and Politics* (New York: State University of New York Press, 2007), ch. 7 (pp. 155–176).

[19] Hedley Bull, *The Anarchical Society: A Study of Order in World Politics*, 3rd ed. (Houndmills: Palgrave, 2002 [1977]).

integrity and sovereign independence the same way a human person enjoys basic rights to bodily integrity and autonomy.[20] The right of non-intervention, the argument runs, represents a baseline for international conduct because it is the flipside of a state's right to independence, understood as external juridical sovereignty. But in the twentieth century, the idea that states hold an unqualified right of sovereignty, as a legal right, was questioned on *moral* grounds. When the state began to exterminate its own ethnic minorities, as in Srebrenica (1995) and Kosovo (1999), the international society of mature states invoked a moral right to intervene and save the innocent. This was the motivation behind the recent revival of the doctrine of humanitarian intervention. Sometimes the blame was not one of commission but one of omission, including by third parties. The international society of mature states failed to intervene to prevent the genocidal killings in Rwanda in 1994 and in Darfur in the Sudan in 2003 (despite the United Nations [UN] Security Council authorising sanctions). Such cases of genocide and ethnic cleansing led to the modification of humanitarian intervention into the so-called Responsibility to Protect (R2P).[21] The R2P was endorsed by the UN General Assembly at the Word Summit in 2005.[22] It marks a significant normative change: previously, states had a moral *right* to intervene in the territory of another state to halt grave human rights abuses; now, under the new rules, states have a *duty* – or responsibility – to do so.

Both doctrines of humanitarian intervention and the R2P have contributed to the process of modifying the legal norm of sovereignty in the name of human rights *qua* moral rights. But even though rights have become a standard in normative discourse, internationally and globally, no canon determines what rights are, what kinds of rights

[20] Charles R. Beitz, 'The Moral Standing of States Revisited', *Ethics & International Affairs* 23 (4) 2009: 325–347, p. 326.

[21] Notable here is the Report of the International Commission on Intervention and State Sovereignty, *The Responsibility to Protect* (Ottawa: International Development Research Centre, 2001). The Commission's work is analysed in Gareth Evans, *The Responsibility to Protect: Ending Mass Atrocity Crimes Once and for All* (Washington, DC: Brookings Institution Press, 2008). See Alex J. Bellamy, *Responsibility to Protect: The Global Effort to End Mass Atrocities* (Cambridge: Polity Press, 2009); and Alex J. Bellamy, *The Responsibility to Protect: A Defence* (Oxford: Clarendon Press, 2015).

[22] See United Nations General Assembly 2005 A/60/L.1 (World Summit Outcome); and United Nations General Assembly 2009 A/63/677 (UN Secretary General's Report on the Responsibility to Protect), both available at www.un.org.

have precedence over other kinds of rights (and why) or even over cognate normative principles (such as well-being or interest). It is worth reiterating that our Hegelian position entails a 'social recognition' thesis about human rights.[23] The idea is that human rights have the *nature* of moral rights (rights held by any human being as such) but that at least some basic moral rights matter because they have received *recognition* within social practices. That is, we are not interested in an ideal theory that may articulate abstract arguments about the nature and justification of rights but in their social role and significance as actualised within ongoing social practices. One basic moral right of the individual human being that is currently recognised within the global practice of rights is the right not to be massacred by one's own state. In this respect, the global rights practice offers a standpoint for criticising the practice of sovereign states. The former derives its critical force from the fact that local rights abusers are, as it were, brought to judgement at the bar of a truly global practice that transcends state (or any other) borders: its claimants are people everywhere.

Around the eighteenth century, the practice of states recognised only states as agents and their rights in relation to one another.[24] The gradual infusion of human rights into the sphere of this state-to-state practice has brought about its dialectical transformation, which has become palpable in the mid-twentieth century. The practice has been transformed without being rendered defunct, since states continue to be mutually related on the basis of rights such as legitimate self-defence against aggression, diplomatic rights for official state representatives, territorial integrity and so on. What is novel is that it is now a benchmark of the civilised practice of states that the sovereignty norm, which recognised the status of the state as an autonomous individual, is no longer treated as absolute but as *conditional* on the respect of

[23] This social recognition thesis about rights was the pivot of our position on rights in Chapter 4, under 'The Global Practice of Rights'. As Beitz insightfully puts it, if we grant the premise that human rights stand, broadly, for moral rights, it does not follow that moral rights must necessarily be *natural* moral rights.
Charles R. Beitz, 'What Human Rights Mean', *Daedalus* 132 (1) 2003: 36–46, esp. p. 41. Beitz's point is that *socially recognised rights* can count as moral rights.

[24] See note 60 in Chapter 4. This is the premise behind Bull's idea of the 'anarchical society' as a society of states, whose origins he associates with the early modern jurists Hugo Grotius, Christian Wolff and Emer de Vattel.

states for at least some elementary human rights.[25] At a minimum, this includes the right of citizens not to be exterminated through the action or inaction of their own government. This dialectical development can be understood in the light of the Hegelian analysis presented thus far. It suggests that most people in the contemporary world simultaneously participate in the society of sovereign states (by being citizens of a state which is an agent in the society of states) and in the global practice of rights. Hence the only way to maintain coherence between these two practices is to make the case that citizens have a right to demand of their states that they recognise and actualise certain basic human rights and to extend their protection to the territory of other states.

The upshot is that the practice of global rights is increasingly invoked as a moral corrective to the practice of sovereign states. In more general terms, this dialectical shift has ethical significance, for it points to a qualitative transformation in the *standing* of states inside international society. This society has changed from one where states alone hold rights and responsibilities against each other into one where not only states but also human individuals are bearers of rights and responsibilities. This fundamental *Aufhebung* affects the identity of the kind of state which deserves to be recognised as a participant in international society in good standing. At present, such a state is required to honour individual rights at home and abroad. This require-ment sets a novel standard of proper state conduct within international society (see Chapter 4), despite the fact that for the time being, it is predominantly realised within its mature domain.

## Ethical Self-Erosion in the Global Rights Practice: The Global Free Market

However, the dialectic warns us that the global practice of rights is saddled with tensions of its own. This practice contains multiple domains of rights within itself. While the most prominent one is the global market (including global financial markets and online share trading), many other civil-society activities have extended across the borders of states. Con-sider a few of the many things we may do with the freedoms we claim and usually exercise in global civil society: setting up transnational

---

[25] Mervyn Frost, *Global Ethics: Anarchy, Freedom and International Relations* (London: Routledge, 2009).

companies, travelling to foreign lands, engaging in global scientific exchanges, enrolling in universities abroad, participating in global cultural exchanges or in sporting activities and promoting global religious creeds. Such activities are encapsulated in the catchphrase 'We live in an increasingly globalised world'. It would be a mistake, however, to think that this phrase refers merely to an empirical state of affairs and to overlook the ethical dimension involved in the global rights practice. Participants in global civil society, as rights-holders, consider themselves to be *entitled* to engage in the aforementioned activities. They are ethically affronted when they are prohibited from pursuing such engagements. A fine example of such ethical outrage is the reaction of the white South Africans following their exclusion from international sporting events in response to their support for the policies of apartheid. This was specifically an ethical affront to their sense of *amour propre*. Russian leaders reacted in a similar way when their international travel rights were curbed in response to Russia's military involvement in Georgia in 2008 and in Eastern Ukraine in 2016.

In the global practice of rights, the process of ethical self-erosion is well under way. Through the legitimate use of their rights, billions of people worldwide are bringing about states of affairs that undermine the basic value integrating the practice – that of individual freedom exercised between equals. Some of these developments are profoundly negative from an ethical point of view, in a sense pertaining to the first phase of the dialectic introduced earlier. Here we discuss them in the most visible domain of the global rights practice: the global free market. Although during the Cold War it was plausible to claim that the free market was operative in some parts of the world but not in others (behind the Iron Curtain), this is no longer the case. It is now evident that the free market includes all countries and all people.[26] While not everyone everywhere is engaged in wage labour, most people in most places are parties to market relations ranging from major international corporate deals to the buying and selling of bare necessities by private individuals.

First, one of the major negative consequences of the emergence of the global labour market is alienation as a type of 'estrangement' between agents. This negative consequence of free-market relations was hinted at by Hegel and subsequently elaborated by Marx. Marx argued that

[26] Justin Rosenberg, *The Empire of Civil Society* (London: Verso, 1994).

ceaseless economic competition produces different forms of alienation – from the products of one's labour, from one's fellow labourers, from the entire species beings and, finally, from the very activity of labour which, as Marx claimed, constitutes the individual as a self-conscious, creative being.[27] Nowadays, workers participating in the global economy are becoming increasingly alienated from their fellow labourers and from the products of their work. Consider how this happens in globalised manufacturing processes. To begin with, if the product is an airliner, its components will be manufactured in many different sites spread around the world, meaning that those involved in making it will not experience the satisfaction of producing a completed product. Instead, they will understand themselves to be units of labour in a huge, widely dispersed and dehumanised production process. Next, as economic cycles oscillate, workers in manufacturing and other economic sectors will suffer the prospect of job insecurity. Those engaged in the globalised labour market are generally at risk from competition for scarce jobs from abroad. The fear of large-scale refugee displacements stems partly from a fear that these refugees will 'steal' jobs in the country they relocate to. Global factors that bring about unemployment will be experienced by the individual labourers as alien forces over which they have no control.[28] Finally, because workers are likely to perceive their fellows elsewhere as direct threats to their own well-being, they will not feel bound to them by ties of fraternity. Quite the contrary, they will tend to treat other workers, and in turn be treated by them, as if they were mere inanimate things.

Second, the millions of ethically legitimate market transactions taking place globally every day tend to produce dramatic social inequalities. The tendency is that the group of holders of disproportionately large amounts of wealth and capital is becoming progressively

---

[27] Marx's doctrine of alienation is developed in his *Economic and Philosophical Manuscripts of 1844*, partially reprinted in Karl Marx, *Early Writings* (New York: Vintage Books, 1975). The relevant section is 'Estranged Labour' (pp. 322–334). However, the theme for which Marx became famous, that the realisation of human capacities requires labour, was originally developed by Hegel.

[28] South Africans fear massive influxes of economic migrants from the poorer regions of Africa for just this reason. Workers all over the world fear the cheap labour available in India and China.

smaller.[29] What is objectionable is not wealth itself but its concentration in the hands of a select few, which tends to generate structural inequalities in society. Concerns of this sort have been voiced by philosophers such as Michael Walzer in his discussion of domestic civil society and by proponents of republican freedom as non-domination such as Philip Pettit.[30] For Pettit, the presence of structural inequalities means that the rich are in a position to set up a structural (non-contingent) relation of domination over the poor. Even though the poor are technically autonomous, they are not genuinely free because the scope of their choices is dominated, via discretion, by the affluent, who enjoy such discretion in lieu of preponderant power. For Walzer, the problem is that the accumulation of wealth, and the social power that stems from it, grants to its holders disproportionate access to the political process.[31] In effect, private parties are able to highjack a process that is supposed to be devoted to the protection of the public good. Here we extend Walzer's insight to the global domain of rights. At present, giant global corporations engaged in, *inter alia*, the production of armaments, oil drilling, computer software and pharmaceuticals command extraordinary power not only over individuals and other companies but also over states, especially weak ones. A distinctive feature of the power that accrues to this group of global wealth holders is that it is *private*. To be sure, in terms of the internal ethics of global civil society, they are entitled to their privacy, and therefore much of what they do is legitimately done in secret. But this poses serious problems, since these power holders are not officials or politicians whose actions are constrained by public oversight.

In sum, what the dialectic discloses is that the majority of the ordinary participants in the global market are trapped in a hostile web of endless competition and alienation, insightfully labelled 'turbo capitalism'.[32] Through the legitimate use of their rights, participants in

---

[29] Thomas Piketty, *Capital in the Twenty-First Century*, trans. Arthur Goldhammer (Cambridge, MA: Harvard University Press, 2014).

[30] Michael Walzer, *Spheres of Justice: A Defense of Pluralism and Equality* (New York: Basic Books, 1983); Philip Pettit, *Republicanism: A Theory of Freedom and Government* (Oxford: Clarendon Press, 1997).

[31] Walzer, *Spheres of Justice*, pp. 120–122.

[32] Edward N. Luttwak, *Turbo Capitalism: Winners and Losers in the Global Economy* (London: Weidenfeld and Nicolson, 1998).

the global rights practice, and the global market in particular, have brought about negative outcomes that tend to corrode the practice as a whole. That the disproportionate power of 'turbo' capitalists is huge and still growing indicates that the ethical erosion of this practice is advancing apace. In a more basic sense, the dialectic identifies a schism between the ideal and the actual: although individuals in the global rights practice continue to be rights-holders ideally (in the formal sense of equal freedom), what they can accomplish *in actuality* (by making use of their formal rights) is severely limited in the face of the ever-growing global inequalities; the rights they have remain somewhat hollow.

Third, the features of the ethical state that Hegel saw as ameliorating the harsh aspects of *domestic* civil society are largely absent from the contemporary *global* realm. Apart from the corporations or 'guilds' – such as trade associations, religious associations, learned societies and political clubs – Hegel also counts institutions such as the civil service, public authority ('police') providing basic welfare services, and the judiciary as part of his conception of civil society. These institutions, he thought, would temper the ethically negative repercussions of civil society because they represent an extension of the state, whose aim is to oversee and regulate the activities of rights-holders acting singly or within groups such as guilds. Such domestic mediating institutions are either absent from the global rights practice or their impact is negligible. Currently, no global state exists to control the uncivil manifestations of global civil society (the global rights practice), and as we argue, if it existed, it would be a cure that is far worse than the disease. But a condition of no global state also means that no global civil service, judiciary or institutionalised welfare scheme of global redistribution is available. The question remains open as to what institutional structure can mitigate the incivility of global civil society.

## The Global Practice of Sovereign States: An Incomplete *Aufhebung*

The ethical problems produced by the self-erosion of global civil society, we argue, can be 'sublated' by the agency of the society of sovereign states, even though, as a result of the dialectic, only piece-meal progress would be possible. Concretely, our thesis is that some of the more persistent global problems that plague the borderless global rights practice today can only be ameliorated by the concerted action of free states and their citizens acting as agents of a single society of states.

One such problem arises with respect to globally operating private security companies. For example, the American private security company Academi (formerly Blackwater) was contracted by the US government to supply protection services in the Iraq War of 2003. The controversy surrounding the use of such private contractors in war zones centres on their lack of public accountability as well as the paucity of procedures in public international law for enforcing sanctions in cases of atrocities perpetrated by the staff of private security companies in a foreign territory. The creation of the International Criminal Court (ICC; ratification in 2002) was a key advancement in this respect. The states' signatories acknowledged the principle that their own citizens can be tried by such an *international* institution for crimes such as genocide, crimes against humanity, war crimes and aggression committed abroad.[33] Unfortunately, however, the United States has not yet ratified the provisions of the Court.

Another possibility is to attempt to overcome the negative effects of the global rights practice through international organisations. The UN is one notable international organisation with global membership, but it is clear that it is not suited to the task of *Aufhebung* because it represents what Oakeshott referred to as an 'enterprise' association (see Chapter 1). This type of association is established for instrumental purposes. Since its inception in 1944, the primary purpose of the UN has been the maintenance of 'international peace and security', although subsequently, it has expanded its range of goals in many other directions. As an enterprise with a voluntary character, it does not have the capacity to constitute new ethical identities for the 194 sovereign states participating in it. Nor is it a body authorised to deal with the gross inequalities in global wealth distribution, including those generated by interstate market competition. Its achievements, and they are indeed considerable, continue to depend on the purposive agreement of the participating states.

---

[33] See Chris Brown, *International Society, Global Polity: An Introduction to International Political Theory* (London: Sage, 2015), pp. 81–85. As Brown notes, the ICC works on the principle of 'complementarity' or only in cases when the national courts do not wish or are unable to handle a given case.

Much more promising in ethical terms is the institutional arrangement of the European Union (EU), for this is more than a treaty-based association of states designed for purely instrumental purposes. Although it might well have started as that, it has evolved into something much more ambitious. Currently, the EU contains the nascent features of a common practice that promises to overcome the ethical contradictions associated with the first aspect of the dialectic permeating both global civil society and the society of states. This has been achieved through the creation of new roles and identities in an overarching, common European practice. The EU member states, taken together, form a 'we' or a whole that is required to protect the well-being of each member. Those member states who are weak and not fully able to flourish as free states are considered as having an ethical claim on the union for economic, political and scientific support. Thus when Greece, Spain, Portugal and Italy found themselves in dire financial straits after the economic crisis of 2008, the rest of the EU states cooperated in solving the problem. One of the EU's principal accomplishments is that in some measure, the negative repercussions of the vigorous economic competition between states that undermines the freedom of participants in the society of states has been overcome.

The global banking crisis of 2008 is an illustration of how the free transactions of private agents in the financial sector had broader, detrimental effects that undermined the fundamental notion of equal freedom constitutive of global civil society. The only agency that undertook the responsibility to install an institutional regime that will prevent financial crises spurred by private speculation in the future was the mature society of states. What bears emphasis in this connection is that the society of states is able to counteract the excesses of powerful private actors in global civil society because it is a kind of public authority governed by concerns with the common good.

But even though the agency of the mature international society is indispensable for overcoming the ethical defects of global civil society and the global market in particular, it is not a magic bullet. Three main considerations can be adduced as to why such as 'solution' would remain far from complete in the near future.

To begin with, what obstructs the effective agency of the society of states is the structure of the contemporary global political economy.

As John Stopford and Susan Strange have argued, the boundaries between states and firms, and between security (political) and economic issues, are not as firmly set as before.[34] To understand what is going on in the present global political economy, we can no longer rely on the traditional image of the state as a public realm concerned with internal law making, law enforcement and security provision against other, potentially hostile states. Rather, the state should be seen as an actor that must produce domestic wealth by interacting with global multinational companies. Recasting the orthodox juridical image of the state in this way has two main implications. First, states are no longer exclusively engaged in traditional state-to-state diplomacy; they also engage in diplomacy based on state-to-firm relations: 'No longer do states merely negotiate among themselves, they now must also negotiate – if not as suppliants, then certainly as suitors seeking a marriage settlement – with foreign firms.'[35] In other words, in the contemporary global political economy, the policy options available to states are constrained by the competition among powerful companies with a global reach. Second, powerful multinationals behave more and more like traditional states, and states behave more and more like firms or private agencies whose task is wealth generation.[36] In order to survive, states are compelled to compete for global market share (often in collaboration with foreign firms) the same way firms themselves have to compete in the global marketplace. Sovereign states, therefore, have begun to act like firms.[37] In the language of our argument, states conduct themselves as civil-society actors.

One consequence of this development is that all states have become extraordinarily vulnerable to global market forces. Particularly vulnerable are the weak and failed states, many of whom depend on the export of a single commodity, either grown or quarried from

---

[34] John M. Stopford and Susan Strange with John S. Henley, *Rival States, Rival Firms: Competition for World Market Shares* (Cambridge: Cambridge University Press, 1991), esp. ch. 1 (pp. 1–31) and ch. 7 (pp. 203–236).

[35] Stopford, Strange and Henley, *Rival States, Rival Firms*, p. 2.

[36] Stopford, Strange and Henley, *Rival States, Rival Firms*, p. 2. Firms act like states because they must build stable alliances with each other, and states acts like firms because they have to accumulate wealth-generating factors.

[37] See Stopford, Strange and Henley, *Rival States, Rival Firms*; and Susan Strange, *States and Markets*, 2nd ed. (London: Bloomsbury, 2015 [1988]), p. 15ff.

the ground. Thomas Pogge has drawn radical conclusions from this observation by claiming that an unjust global institutional order has been imposed on the third-world states by the developed states.[38] This argument resembles Pettit's republican thesis for freedom as non-domination, where the choices of the poor are constrained by the sheer power possessed by the affluent members of society.[39] By extension, the citizens of economically underdeveloped states, as subjects who are dominated, possess merely nominal rights and freedoms.

The second, principal reason why the society of states cannot be expected completely to resolve the ethical shortcomings of global civil society is that it is an anarchical society of *free* states.[40] Inside this kind of society, each member is recognised as having the ethical standing of an autonomous individual, surrounded by equally autonomous individuals, so no state can rightfully be coerced to adopt provisions against its will. But the exercise of autonomy is not always an unequivocally positive thing. As we saw, certain states did not endorse the authority of important international institutions such as the ICC, even though without such institutions, the crimes committed by private parties in the borderless realm of the global rights practice would go unpunished.

The incomplete *Aufhebung* of problems generated within the global rights practice by international society has a yet another, dialectical facet stemming from the fact that this society comprises two normative domains – mature and immature – that differ in the degrees of ethical commitment to certain basic normative principles and values. What distinguishes the mature society of free states from its immature counterpart (see Chapter 4) is that in the former, the states protect not just the rights of their own citizens but also the rights of foreign citizens and even stateless people. This respect for the value of individual freedom, actualised in the form of rights, shows that a mature or responsible state cannot curtail the free activities of agents inside the realm of its domestic civil society without thereby violating the principle of

---

[38] Thomas Pogge, *World Poverty and Human Rights: Cosmopolitan Responsibilities and Reforms*, 2nd ed. (Cambridge: Polity Press, 2008). Pogge argues that the existing structural inequalities in the global economy are caused by the developed states.

[39] See note 30.

[40] 'Anarchical' both in the sense that no overarching global authority is present to regulate state relations, and in the sense that the relations between states are 'horizontal' relations of formal equality.

freedom to which it is committed. It is a distinctive feature of freedoms and rights that they can be put to various uses, not all of which are commendable. If a state respects and promotes the value of individual freedom, it must permit various civil society groups within its borders to make use of their rights and freedoms as they see fit, even when their aspirations may be ethically questionable and as long as their actions do not contravene the law. The lawful pursuit of unbridled profit and the provision of private security services may be ethically unsavoury, but because it is lawful, it cannot be prohibited within a state that purports to respect rights and freedoms, such as a mature state.

The dialectical paradox of freedom, then, is this: mature states, by virtue of their commitment to individual freedom, are ill-equipped to thwart the emergence of uncivil society that brings exploitation, alienation and crime in its wake. It would be erroneous to suppose that the more the society of states matures, the more it would integrate within itself the positive effects of civil society, necessarily excluding the negative effects of *uncivil* society. Conversely, totalitarian states that show little, if any, respect for the value of individual freedom may be able to control such negative effects by the most efficient means available – by abolishing all the rights and freedoms individuals hold in a well-functioning civil society. This solution is indeed total, for what it abolishes is not merely some of the defects of uncivil society but civil society as a whole. In totalitarian states, no civil society exists as a sphere of free civilian initiative that mediates between the institutions of the family and the state, and in authoritarian and autocratic states, the sphere of civilian freedom is considerably truncated. Thus the price that we have to pay for enjoying freedoms (rights) as members of civil society is that we must accept hazards such as the possible misuse of freedom or incivility.

It follows that any attempts to abolish the core rights because, supposedly, they give rise to an uncivil society would undermine the very value of freedom that grounds the practice of civil society, both domestically and globally. Instead of rights abolition, therefore, the proper response to the emergence of incivility must be regulation and limitation of rights abuse. Some authors think that this aim can be achieved by embracing the international rule of law.[41] While this

---

[41] See Michael Oakeshott, 'The Rule of Law', in Michael Oakeshott, *On History and Other Essays* (Indianapolis: Liberty Fund, 1983), pp. 129–178. The rule of law concerns the moral basis of public legal authority. It is based on principles such as promulgation of the law of the state, prohibition of retrospective

perspective considers the fact of globalisation, it argues not for global law but for an *international* rule of law conducted between sovereign states. It acknowledges the spread of private authorities on a global scale where 'networks' composed of private actors such as firms, banks and professional organisations transact across state borders, challenging the public authority of states.[42] However, it cautions us that the process of global fragmentation of public authority into an array of not clearly identifiable, dispersed private authorities leads to democratic deficits and creates opportunities for rights abuse. In short, the envisaged rule of law must be international rather than global, since only a state-to-state law represents a public law (albeit in a decentralised form) with the capacity to regulate the actions of private parties, including globally active private parties.

We share the view that an international (as opposed to a global) public authority is the appropriate institutional structure for regulating the negative outcomes generated by global processes. It is vital that this authority should retain its character of an 'anarchical' society of free states that is distinct from a hierarchical, global institutional structure such as a global state. It is unnecessary to belabour Kant's well-known point that a global state, if ever created, would be inimical to the actualisation of individual freedom.[43] Thus our endorsement of globally extended international society should not be taken to imply that such a society is a provisional step on the road to a global state. On the contrary, the value of 'anarchical' freedom (equal freedom) can only be actualised through the anarchically organised society of free states as an *international* (state-to-state) normative structure. But while we concur with the proposal for an international rule of law, our Hegelian sensibilities point to an additional way of taming the negative effects

legislation and respect for citizen equality under the law (ruling out racial, gender and other types of discrimination). On the international rule of law, see Terry Nardin, 'International Pluralism and the Rule of Law', *Review of International Studies* 26 (5) 2000: 95–110.

[42] Terry Nardin, 'Globalization and the Public Realm', *Critical Review of International Social and Political Philosophy* 12 (2) 2009: 297–312. Nardin criticises Slaughter's global networks argument from the standpoint of the international rule of law. See Anne-Marie Slaughter, *A New World Order* (Princeton, NJ: Princeton University Press, 2004).

[43] This is Kant's position in *Perpetual Peace: A Philosophical Sketch*, in Immanuel Kant, *Political Writings*, ed. H. Reiss, trans. H. B. Nisbet (Cambridge: Cambridge University Press, 1991 [1795]), pp. 93–130. See also Chapter 4, under 'The Global Practice of Rights'.

of global civil society – through the practice of state building and the creation of full-fledged citizen rights *inside* immature states. This brings us to the third and final aspect of the incomplete *Aufhebung* analysed in this chapter.

Recall that for Hegel, all 'civilians' in civil society are also citizens of a state. In Hegel's account, the defects of civil society are to be overcome by the creation of the state and the institution of citizenship. Citizenship brings with it a higher form of freedom which preserves the autonomy of rational individuals capable of free choice (the benchmark of civil society) while giving each of them the sense of belonging to a larger social whole, as an equal surrounded by equals. If we apply Hegel's original model globally, the shortcomings of global civil society would have to be 'sublated' by the creation of a global state, a prospect which, as we have seen, is ethically unappealing (and practically unfeasible). Nonetheless, a modified neo-Hegelian argument that stops short of a global state can be developed.

Our proposal is first to look inside the institutional structure of the domestic state and then return to the international realm by considering how the domestic structure of the state can impact the relations between states. In many ways, this resembles Kant's republican peace view that only states with proper domestic constitutions ('republics') can be bona fide participants in an international society of free states (*foedus pacificum*).[44] But since our leanings are Hegelian, our concept of domestic structure differs from the Kantian one in two respects. First, by the term 'domestic structure', we have in mind not the general type of constitutional order a state may have ('republican' versus 'despotic', according to Kant) but the more specific institutional *relation* established between citizen and state.[45] Second, while Kant was preoccupied with the formal properties of human institutions, following Hegel, we are investigating their *actualised* properties – to wit, whether citizens inside a given state *enjoy* actual rights or whether these are merely rights on paper.[46]

---

[44] See note 43.

[45] Despotism for Kant amounts to a fusion of the executive and legislative office of government. Immanuel Kant, *The Metaphysics of Morals*, ed. Mary Gregor (Cambridge: Cambridge University Press, 1996 [1797]), 6:317.

[46] The idea that rights must be enjoyed and not merely held in a formal sense is central to Henry Shue's treatment of rights in *Basic Rights: Subsistence, Affluence, and U.S. Foreign Policy*, 2nd ed. (Princeton, NJ: Princeton University Press, 1996).

It is a commonplace that not all states in our present-day inter-national society have been successful in establishing fully realised rights and freedoms, despite formal claims to the contrary set out in constitutions and other formal documents. This discrepancy between the ideal and the actual is particularly acute in the segment of immature states such as unstable democracies, authoritarian states, totalitarian states and weak or failed states.[47] It may be remembered that in Hegel's 'ethical' state, citizens had actual access to the political process, enabling them to exercise self-government. Hegel, however, did not think that everybody qualifies as a participant in this process – only members of the 'estates' (the landed aristocracy and the manufacturing or business class) do. In contemporary democratic states, the principle of self-government has become universal, allowing all adults in society – regardless of race, class, gender or ethnicity – to vote and elect govern-ment for the state.[48] At the same time, it is significant that authoritarian states restrict even further the class of agents who are entitled to hold citizenship rights originally envisaged by Hegel. Such tendencies for rights restriction are prominent in certain (but not all) states in the Middle East, notably in autocracies such as the Kingdom of Saudi Arabia or in states with theocratic constitutions such as the Islamic Republic of Iran. There, formal citizens' rights to vote are acknowledged, but not everybody is entitled to vote (women are excluded), and not all

---

[47] The closest, though imperfect counterpart to our category of 'immature states' includes both what Rawls called 'burdened societies' (roughly, quasi-states) and 'benevolent absolutisms' (where basic rights are respected but consultation mechanisms for conveying citizens' demands to the government are absent). Both kinds of states differ from Rawls's 'illiberal societies' (outlaw states such as North Korea), which do not respect rights domestically or the rules of international law, but also from 'decent, well-ordered' societies (liberal democracies and 'decent hierarchical peoples'), which respect basic rights domestically, provide for political representation or consultation, and respect the rules of international law. To the category of 'immature states', we assign also some of Rawls's 'decent hierarchical peoples', which do not provide an adequate protection of religious rights and/or voting rights in the public realm of the state. See John Rawls, *The Law of Peoples* (Cambridge, MA: Harvard University Press, 1999).

[48] The right to vote for one's government is a basic citizenship right, but it is not the only one. In a proper freedom-respecting state, to this class belongs also the right to leave one's own state. See Silviya Lechner, 'Basic Rights and Global Justice: The Problem of International Coercion', in Matthew Happold (ed.), *International Law in a Multipolar World* (London: Routledge 2012), pp. 158–178.

issues can form the ground for political debate (religious issues cannot be put up for discussion, and there is no right freely to choose one's religious denomination).[49] Still, even in such states, the relationship between state and citizen is acknowledged to some degree. These states often go to great lengths to explain that there are alternative ways in which citizens can communicate their wishes to their government. For example, in Saudi Arabia, it is claimed that there is in place an ancient and well-established system of for citizens to petition the king.

Autocratic states in general deny their citizens the full spectrum of opportunities for self-government provided by proper democratic institutions. Often, such denials of citizenship rights are accompanied by the absence of a fully functioning civil society that accords to civilians actual rights such as the right of free association, including the right to form political parties. Analogous was the situation in totalitarian states in the Soviet bloc during the Cold War. While inside these states, the right to vote was formally universal, the *actual* option to form new political parties was non-existent, except on paper; in reality, the citizen had the choice to either vote for the Communist Party or not vote at all.

Beyond such democratic deficits which prevent large sections of the population from exercising effective self-government, there are other problems that frustrate the full actualisation of citizenship rights in states inside immature international society. For instance, in many weak (quasi) states, the connection between democratically elected governments and the citizens they serve has been bedevilled by systematic corruption. Both politicians and civil servants have become accustomed to extracting rents from their official positions. This is done by rigging the process of tendering for government contracts in such a way that companies owned by close friends and relatives are favoured as recipients of such contracts. In other states, the police service itself is corrupt.[50]

A further problem which occupied the advocates of freedom as non-domination is whether a certain basic level of economic development is a precondition for the realisation of political and social freedom.[51]

---

[49] In December 2015, women in Saudi Arabia were allowed to vote and run for office in municipal elections for the first time. See 'Human Rights Watch, World Report 2016: Saudi Arabia', www.hrw.org/world-report/2016/country-chapters/saudi-arabia.

[50] Alina Mungiu-Pippidi, *The Quest for Good Governance* (Cambridge: Cambridge University Press, 2015).

[51] On freedom as non-domination, see note 30.

In the context of the global practice of sovereign states, it pertains to the relations between mature states that typically have strong economies and weak or quasi-states that are economically underdeveloped.[52] It is an established norm in the current practice of mature sovereign states that weak states are entitled to receive a minimum of economic assistance, since without such international aid, they cannot realise their status of free, sovereign states. This policy of international aid has been criticised by Robert Jackson on paternalist grounds: weak states are not self-reliant and therefore genuinely autonomous, but they are artificially propped up as free states by external agents.[53] In essence, such states do not possess internal sovereignty – only external sovereignty based on the norm of mutual recognition between equal states that is pivotal to the contemporary society of sovereign states. One response to Jackson's argument is that it ignores the prospect for learning and identity change that learning entails, for treating a weak state it as if were a fully autonomous agent of international society may change its self-perception in a positive way and contribute to the development of internal sovereignty.

In summary, immature states, be they autocratic, totalitarian or weak (failed or quasi), deny their citizens the full value of their freedoms as citizens. The experience of citizens across this range of immature states will vary greatly. In spite of this, we argue that in all these states, with the possible exception of North Korea, citizens understand themselves to hold rights against the state, and the state understands that it has certain duties towards its citizens.

The major net effect of this incomplete implementation of citizenship rights around the world is that the negative consequences of the global rights practice cannot effectively be counteracted by all states in an equal measure, even if formally they all seem committed to the rules of the game of international society (the formal principle of sovereignty, the value of anarchical freedom and the norm of R2P). This allows us to understand the phenomenon of the 'immature' society of states, which comprises

---

[52] This is just a general trend. Many immature states with underdeveloped or undemocratic domestic institutional structures happen to be affluent – for example, certain autocracies found in the Middle East (as well as the Democratic Republic of China, where the label 'democracy' formally stands for self-government but in actuality comprises a one-party political rule).

[53] Robert H. Jackson, *Quasi-States: Sovereignty, International Relations, and the Third World* (Cambridge: Cambridge University Press, 1990).

precisely those states – autocracies, totalitarian states and failed states – in which the citizen-state relation is merely formal or nascent and where formally proclaimed citizenship rights (and often, civil society rights) are not properly actualised. Strong citizenship rights and democratic self-government may not be a panacea for all social ills, but in their absence, citizens have no way of determining their own fate; somebody else – the autocrat, the religious council or the party leadership – would make this choice *for them*. Nothing guarantees that this choice would protect the common good as opposed to the private interests of an unaccountable ruling elite. Moreover, given the fragile and merely abstract citizen-state relationship manifest inside this type of state, the immature society of states cannot effectively shelter their citizens from the adverse effects brought about by powerful global actors, as we suggested earlier.

Finally, the dialectical processes of ethical erosion operative in the global rights practice, taken together with the half-completed task of actualising citizenship rights and state formation in many places around the world, has one less-apparent but disturbing effect. Namely, this dialectical process tends to undermine the relationship of mutual recognition of equals by equals, which lies at the heart of the 'anarchical' society of sovereign states. The prototype of the ethical state, member of international society, is the mature state, where citizenship rights are fully actualised. The mutual relationship between such institutionally strong states is one of genuine recognition between equals. This relationship is not paternalistic. However, the potential for paternalism increases when an immature state seeks to establish relations with a mature state. The hazard is that institutionally strong states may take it upon themselves to engage in state building and democracy promotion exercises in ill-conceived ways, often with a military dimension, that override the self-determination rights of citizens to lead a common social and political life in a state of their own choosing.[54] Targets of such

---

[54] On the doctrine of democracy promotion, see Graham T. Allison and R. P. Beschel, 'Can the United States Promote Democracy?', *Political Science Quarterly* 107 (1) 1992: 81–98; Thomas Carothers, *Critical Mission: Essays on Democracy Promotion* (Washington, DC: Carnegie Endowment for International Peace, 2004); Thomas Carothers and Marina Ottaway (eds.), *Uncharted Journey: Promoting Democracy in the Middle East* (Washington, DC: Carnegie Endowment for International Peace, 2005); Jonathan Monten, 'The Roots of the Bush Doctrine: Power, Nationalism and Democracy Promotion in U.S. Strategy', *International Security* 29 (4) 2005: 112–156. We saw adventures of this kind in Afghanistan, Iraq and Libya.

paternalistic policies and their citizens can then quite rightly accuse the mature states of illegitimate interference in their domestic affairs.

## Conclusion

The foregoing pages exposed the dialectical contradictions permeating our common global practice with its duo of constitutive moments – the practice of global rights (global civil society) and the practice of sovereign states. Needless to say, the picture was painted in the bold strokes of the theorist and not with the detailed palette of the historian. The task of our practice theory, in any case, has been to provide a basic theoretical synthesis that would enable us to make better sense of social practices. The virtue of Hegel's dialectic lies in its complex, characteristically dynamic articulation of practical life that reveals it to be a life of ongoing struggle. In analysing the contradictions permeating the current global practice, this chapter focussed on the institutionalised (or 'practical', in our terms) relations between states (international level), between people and their state (domestic level) and between people regardless of location (global level). Nothing here implies an 'end-of-history' solution which will supposedly resolve once and for all social contradictions by establishing the primacy of the modern 'ethical' state or, correlatively, the international society composed of such ethical states – a view commonly but inappropriately attributed to Hegel.[55] And yet some partial progress is possible because identifying where the *concrete* problems lie with respect to the duo of global practices – in an unbridled global market, privatisation of global security services, institutionally weak states that have little concern for citizen and civilian rights – gives us a more coherent understanding, indeed self-understanding, of where we stand as actors directly engaged in these practices.

---

[55] In a contemporary setting, this allegedly Hegelian end-of-history view is often incorrectly attributed to Fukuyama. See Francis Fukuyama, *The End of History and the Last Man*, 20th anniversary ed. (New York: Penguin Books, 2012 [1992]).

# 6 | Practice Theory, Macro Practices and the Study of International Relations

This conclusion fleshes out the broader significance of the proposed practice theory for philosophy and the field of International Relations (IR). Most crucial is the novel theme of macro practices, which is our response to the present tendency to theorise international and global practices on the basis of micro foundations. The next central theme we examine is the prospect of practice theory transforming the landscape of contemporary IR theorising. In particular, we show where the theory stands in relation to scientific theory and normative theory and how its adoption would change the practice of teaching the academic subject of IR. Before doing this, we address a possible objection, which is that our account of practices is relativist.

## Relativism and Complex Social Facts

A core thesis of our project has been that the proper understanding of practices requires (practice) internalism. The term 'internalism' (internal point of view) captures the idea that a third-party observer or a social scientist who attempts to understand a practice that is not yet understood must adopt the standpoint of a practice participant – that is to say, adopt the language that participants themselves use in understanding their practice. Some contemporary moral philosophers approach the puzzle of understanding from 'the inside' differently – through the prism of relativism, as a metaethical position.[1] Thus the pressing question is whether the practice theory we have presented is a relativist argument in disguise.

Relativism, often labelled *cultural relativism*, is roughly the view that the standards for judging a certain action in one culture or society

---

[1] On the varieties of relativism, see Michael Krausz and Jack W. Meiland (eds.), *Relativism: Cognitive and Moral* (Notre Dame, IN: University of Notre Dame Press, 1982).

differ in principle from or are incongruent with the standards for judging that same action accepted in a different culture or society.[2] Because such standards often apply to issues of morality such as the infliction of harm, especially bodily harm and death, or restrictions of freedom and autonomy, many philosophers use the terms 'cultural relativism' and 'moral relativism' interchangeably.[3] Some add that the thesis of moral relativism is the thesis of cultural relativism plus the premise of truth.[4] This focus on truth-values and the meanings of moral terms indicates that the investigation takes place in the realm of metaethics. Precisely formulated, the thesis for relativism states that the proposition 'Action A is wrong' is true relative to society S1 but false relative to society S2.[5] Thus one and the same type of action, killing one's aged parents, counts as wrong in our Western-type modern societies but as right or at least as permitted in the Inuit society, where elderly parents are abandoned to die in the snow once they became too frail to fend for themselves. (Instead of 'cultural relativism' or 'moral relativism', henceforth the generic term 'relativism' will be employed.) The thesis rests on two general premises: (1) that *one and the same action* can be judged differently across different societies in terms of its normative value, or truth-value, and (2) that a given *standard for judging* the action internal to one society (S1) differs in principle or is incongruent with the corresponding standard internal to another society (S2, S3, etc.). Practice theory treats this second premise of relativism as a limiting case, since it accepts that at the limit (and there alone), two or more societies can represent domains that are disconnected and normatively incongruent. But in the paradigmatic case, as we shall

---

[2] The type of relativism we discuss is a species of *social* relativism dealing with social standards for (judging) action and not individual relativism pertaining to individual judgement. A relativist position in this sense is articulated by Robert L. Arrington, 'A Defence of Ethical Relativism', *Metaphilosphy* 14 (3/4) 1983: 225–239. See also the exchange between a pro-relativist (Harman) and a pro-objectivist in morality (Thompson) – Gilbert Harman and Judith Jarvis Thompson, *Moral Relativism and Moral Objectivity* (Oxford: Blackwell, 1996).

[3] For example, Arrington, 'A Defence of Ethical Relativism'.

[4] Richard T. Garner and Bernard Rosen, *Moral Philosophy* (New York: Macmillan, 1967), p. 168.

[5] Formulating the problem of moral relativism by reference to propositions and truth shifts the question from the realm of ethics to that of meta-ethics, where 'ethics' stands for the study of moral conduct. On our premises informed by Hegel and Oakeshott, 'ethics' is the realm of moral conduct understood as conduct constituted by non-instrumental practices.

see, the theory regards different societies as mutually connected and, often, as normatively congruent.

What practice theory, as we have articulated it, rejects altogether is the first premise of relativism, the idea that *one and the same type of action* is judged differently across different societies. The relativist supposes that what is judged differently by the Inuit and by us is the same kind of action: 'killing one's parents'. But it is misconstrued to postulate some alleged, practice-neutral term, 'killing', as a common denominator that underwrites the shared meaning of the two descriptions adopted by us and by the Inuit, respectively. That is, it captures neither the harsh moral meaning of 'patricide' nor the milder (non-moral) meaning of 'abandonment'. Our practice theory and particularly its normative descriptivism rejects relativism's first premise. The relativist assumes tacitly that we can identify an action by simply looking at it. Against this, in Part I we claimed that an action can only be understood under a description: determining what an action is and whether it belongs to the same type as another action requires a prior description.

But why speak of *normative* descriptivism and not just of descriptivism? A key theme running through our discussion has been that the relevant context which determines the relevant descriptions of actions is an entire social practice, defined as a system of rules accompanied by the usages and sensibilities requisite for following the rules. The descriptions that our practice theory picks out are descriptions not of action *simpliciter* but of rule-governed action – more specifically, of practice-dependent action. To describe a practice-dependent action is to describe it by appealing to the relevant rules, which constitute the concrete practice nesting the action. To the extent that these rules are standards of conduct, they represent *norms*, and some of these norms exhibit a stronger, prescriptive normative force.[6] Hence it is more apposite to label our position 'normative descriptivism' instead of plain descriptivism.

From the vantage point of practice theory, social scientists or third-party observers must seek the appropriate descriptions of action. At the outset of this project, we defined appropriateness in terms of relevance. To identify an action as a practice-dependent action of a certain type (as baptising a child, for instance), we need a relevant

---

[6] On normative force, see the final section of Chapter 3.

description – a description whose sources are the constitutive rules and norms of a practice as a concrete practice (that of baptising a child as opposed to some abstractly defined practice). So the procedure for understanding the identity of a putative action, hypothesised to be a practice-dependent action, is to commence by identifying the relevant practice as a whole and then identifying the particular actions falling within its domain. This reveals why we do not advocate a relativist position. Our procedure for determining the description of an action with a not-yet-determined identity is holist – it involves zooming out and considering the broader practice that inscribes the action. Relativists, conversely, adopt an atomist procedure of observation. They zoom into a given action and treat it as having meaning and normative implications as a self-standing entity, apart from any practice or its rules and norms. In this crucial respect, the normative descriptivism animating our practice theory parts ways with relativism.

The principal reason why the proposed theory is non-relativist has to do with the theory's first pillar – internalism. Recall the puzzle posed by the relativist: 'Why is it that an action that counts as proper (in the sense of relevant or 'true') according to standards accepted as valid in S1 counts as improper (in the sense of irrelevant or 'false') according to standards accepted as valid in S2?' So formulated, the puzzle paves the road towards (practice) externalism, which turns out to be an incoherent position, as we argued in Chapters 1 and 2. In this discussion, the term 'externalism' (external point of view) does not convey the trivial idea that some members of society will be outsiders or non-participants to at least some of its practices. For instance, in present-day, largely secular, Western societies, not everyone participates in the practice of church attendance. Rather, externalism designates any invariant standard of observation represented by certain forms of moral theory such as natural law, Kant's moral law, act utilitarianism and rule utilitarianism, scientific theory such as determinism and rational choice economic theory. Because the general observational standard is invariant by default, when it comes to the observation of normatively modulated action, it follows that the normative standards for evaluation must exhibit invariance as well – they must be standards external to any particular social practice. The idiom of invariance (colloquially, 'universalism') which underpins externalism is not inherent in relativism but stems from an attempt to respond to the relativist challenge. The relativist charges that since what is valid or true inside one society is not valid or true inside another society (assuming that these societies represent discrete normative domains), no genuine moral or normative conflict can ever arise *between* societies. The only way to refute the relativist, it would seem, is to invoke normative standards for judging conduct that are marked by universality or invariance – to wit, universal moral truths, basic facts about human nature or even basic facts about human society. But practice theory proper, as we have been arguing, denies the relevance of such invariant standards.

Instead of some fixed natural facts about human society, practice theory begins with the concept of complex social facts. This expression corresponds to what John Searle has called 'institutional facts'.[7] Compare a brute fact such as 'The cat is on the mat' with an institutional fact such as 'Signing an international treaty'.[8] Each fact is a *that* statement. The first fact here describes *that Murry the cat is sitting on the mat*; the second describes *that an act of diplomacy is taking place*, where 'diplomacy' refers to a social institution defined by rules. We can understand the meaning of the first description without reference to any social institution or practice. But this is logically impossible in the second case, for the description 'Signing an international treaty' has meaning only by reference to the constitutive rules defining the institution of diplomacy. The relation holding between an institutional fact and the constitutive rules of the corresponding institution (or practice) is logical and not merely contingent or causal. It is also an internal relation, since each individual practice is a normative domain, determined by its own practice-specific rules that have concrete meanings *inside* this domain. No set of rules has an external (universal) validity across all practices, as Wittgenstein reminded us with his dictum about 'family resemblances'.[9] Different practices presuppose different criteria of relevance for assessing the validity or truth of descriptions made inside their domains.

The upshot is that we cannot grasp an institutional fact or observe its occurrence unless we know, in advance of observation, what its *relevant* description is, and this description in turn is determined by the

---

[7] John R. Searle, *Speech Acts: An Essay in the Philosophy of Language* (Cambridge: Cambridge University Press, 1969), pp. 50–52; and John R. Searle, *The Construction of Social Reality* (New York: Free Press, 1995), pp. 27–29.

[8] This example is ours, not Searle's.

[9] Ludwig Wittgenstein, *Philosophical Investigations*, 3rd ed., trans. G. E. M. Anscombe (Oxford: Basil Blackwell, 1958 [1953]), §67.

constitutive rules of a practice, construed as a system of concrete meaningful propositions. Some examples of institutions include making a promise, getting married, signing a treaty or contract, and making an oath. The *leitmotiv* of practice theory is that a coherent understanding of social conduct demands reference to such institutions. The international and global realms, the focus of research for IR scholars, are governed by a set of distinctive institutions, a topic to which we return shortly.

Institutional facts are complex social facts. Each institutional fact exhibits complexity because its overt, summary description includes an array of implicit descriptions specifying the relevant actors, their roles as defined by the normative standards internal to the practice, these standards themselves and, more obliquely, the way the individual practice fits into a larger social whole. To be able to recognise the fact *that an act of signing an international treaty is being performed* (or was performed), we have to know who is authorised to sign international treaties (diplomats), who qualifies as a diplomat (official state representatives) under the constitutive rules of diplomacy as an institution, what these rules are (state representation across borders, the inviolability of the person of the diplomat, the system of embassy and its exemption from local jurisdiction, the secrecy of diplomatic post) and, finally, how the practice of diplomacy coheres into the relevant social whole, the practice of international society.

Another way of elucidating the character of social facts or institutional facts is by returning to David Hume's famous is-ought distinction.[10] As Hume pointed out in the *Treatise*, the realm of 'is' (facts) covers occurrences that exists independently from human thought or volition, whereas the realm of 'ought' (values) includes the evaluations we ourselves impose on the facts, which for Hume involved feelings of approval and disapproval.[11] So when we observe an action and recognise it as an act of cruelty (say, torturing a defenceless cat), it is not that we have discovered some deep metaphysical property called 'cruelty'; rather, 'cruelty' is a mark of the feeling of disapprobation we attribute to this sort of action, a feeling that is a product of social upbringing. Metaphysical properties or facts are found in the nature of things;

---

[10] David Hume, *A Treatise of Human Nature*, ed. L. A. Selby-Bigge (Oxford: Clarendon Press, 1888 [1739]), p. 469.
[11] Hume, *Treatise*, pp. 468–469.

evaluations, in contrast, are human creations. This is why Hume denied that we can move from the realm of facts into that of values.[12]

The view of practices as sources of descriptions which identify complex social facts redraws the boundary of the original Humean fact-value distinction. Social facts are positioned inside the realm of value so that in the locution 'social facts', the emphasis is on *social*, not on *facts*. On this view, the observation that actions falling within a certain class – paying with a money bill, making an oath, issuing a war declaration – have occurred count as social facts because they are constituted within social institutions (practices): the institution of money, oath making or waging war. Institutions, in Searle's sense, or practices in our sense, represent normative domains – they impose standards of appropriate conduct as well as rights and obligations on their participants. Because the descriptions of complex social facts acquire meaning within the framework of particular social practices, they cannot fall in the realm of mind-independent metaphysical properties; they belong to the human realm of value.

One major difference between social facts and natural facts is that they presuppose a different kind of relationship between a putative fact and the theory that explains it. When we observe a natural fact – a sunrise, for example – the observation ('There is a sunrise') is caused by the occurrence of a certain natural event (refracted light which has

---

[12] What Hume means is that statements of fact do not *entail* statements of value – there is no logical relation of entailment allowing us to move from facts to values. Prescriptivists such as Richard Hare have shown that it is possible to move from facts to values by adding a 'bridge' principle, which must be a normative or value-laden principle. This point resonates with contemporary discussions of practical reason which appeal to the so-called practical syllogism. Thus we can derive statements of value (in the conclusion of the practical syllogism) given a statement of fact (in the minor premise) plus a statement of a general normative principle (in the major premise). An example adapted from Hare is the following:

- All the boxes *ought* to be taken to the station (Major premise)
- This is one of the boxes (Minor premise)
- This box *ought* to be taken to the station (Conclusion)

The original example is found in Richard M. Hare, *The Language of Morals* (Oxford: Clarendon Press, 1952), p. 27. Hare is interested in the logic of imperatives (where the propositions of morality are one class of imperatives), so his major premise is 'Take all the boxes to the station' and the conclusion, 'Take this to the station'.

caused an image to appear on the observer's retina). The act of seeing requires the observer to take notice of and interpret the image as a sunrise and not as something else; in doing this, the observer may be said to deploy a theory. The theory (typically, physical theory) determines that what we see is a sunrise and not a sunset. In brief, when it comes to identifying natural facts, the orthodox position is that something (a natural event) must exist out there in a way that is independent of the theoretical interpretation imposed by the observer.[13] Contrariwise, any theoretical account of social facts is observer-dependent: *we* generate the relevant description of a social fact, not frivolously, to be sure, but by first invoking the constitutive rules of a practice understood from the internal point of view. The description then picks out the action under observation as a special kind of practice-dependent action and identifies the fact that a practice-dependent action of this particular kind is being performed – for instance, that a cheque is being signed or that an oath is being sworn.

To summarise the idea, the fact that a practice exists is not a natural or metaphysical fact to be established by a physical or metaphysical theory. It is a social fact – indeed, a complex social fact – that can only be understood from within the context of the social wholes within which it has been constituted. Whereas the standard scientific (or metaphysical) view posits a divide between the realm of facts and the realm of theory, on the social practice view, theory is the theoretical *aspect* of our socially acquired understandings. As such, it is condensed in a set of descriptions that have been rendered coherent and that rely on intelligible, non-abstract language. Understanding involves a relation between teachers and learners and does not have the character of abstract knowing by a solitary Cartesian Cogito. To learn how to recognise complex social facts through their relevant descriptions is what learning to participate in a social practice amounts to: it is a type of activity that is distinct in principle from the type of activity involved in the discovery of natural facts. For this reason, the *proper* observational perspective for making sense of practices must be located inside these practices.

---

[13] The orthodox position is realist in the philosophical sense. It has been famously articulated by Gilbert Harman in *The Nature of Morality: An Introduction to Ethics* (New York: Oxford University Press, 1977), ch. 1 ('Ethics and Observation'), pp. 3–10, as we explain later on.

## Why Macro Practices Matter

### Macro Practices and Their Role in International and Global Affairs

We now turn to the theme of macro practices and argue that the two global practices discussed in Part II represent macro practices.

It is convenient to introduce the idea of macro practices by returning to the second general premise of relativism, which portrays two societies, S1 and S2, as incongruent normative domains. People inside S1 accept one set of norms as valid, the relativist holds, whereas people inside S2 accept the validity of a completely different set. Since the normative sets are incongruent, no genuine normative conflict ever takes place *between* societies. That is, members of S1 speak a different language from members of S2, so argument between them is impossible; they merely talk past one another. Any dispute presupposes a common language, but according to the relativist, there is no such common language, since the interlocutors are locked inside discrete social worlds.

Relativists make a further point about normative cohesion. They portray each society as a cohesive, largely conflict-free zone where the majority of members agree on most of its normative standards most of the time – agreement and cohesion mark the baseline. If conflict ever arises, it is intermittent and quickly settled. But as our neo-Hegelian rendition of practice theory disclosed (Chapter 5), society is permeated by ongoing internal tensions and conflicts – by a dialectic. What is often disputed is not just the propriety of certain actions but the basic 'rules of the game' defining a given practice. Notice that the relativist argument for the intelligibility of normative standards and for normative cohesion applies at all levels of generality – to individual normative standards of conduct but also to an entire system of standards or society as a whole.

Our argument for macro practices is anti-relativist. It holds that the logic of society as a macro normative edifice cannot be reduced to the logic of its constituent normative standards. To support the thesis, it is key to distinguish the concept of society from a practice, as developed within practice theory. Unlike relativism, practice theory does not treat society as a monolith, nor does it define it as a self-contained, territorially bounded domestic community or culture. In one sense, a practice is a narrower category than society. Each domestic society may be viewed as a constellation of diverse practices such as trading on the local market, attending church, signing contracts, producing works of art, taking part in learned societies, participating in university life as a student or professor, participating in the civil state as a citizen and so on. In another, more specific sense, a practice can stand for a broader category than domestic society. Waging war, creating balances of power, conducting international diplomacy, participating in global music festivals and buying and selling goods and services on the global market are all practices that encompass more than a single domestic society – hence the label 'international' or 'global'. But even though the concept of macro practices includes that of international and global practices, it is not co-extensive with them. As we shall see, the domestic state is also a macro practice.

What, then, are the distinguishing features of a macro practice? Its first, most perspicuous feature is that it is a second-order practice which contains other types of practices within its normative domain. Macro practices are practices of practices. To get a grip on this idea, we should recall two key facets of practices: practice differentiation and practice integration. One suggests that society comprises a multiplicity of diverse practices; the other supposes that this multiplicity is loosely integrated into a social whole – Wittgenstein's 'form of life'.[14] Recognising the facet of practice differentiation guards us from committing the fallacy of supposing that practices are homogenous at base. Practices differ in scope (some are comprehensive and include all societal members such as the practice of the state, while others are restrictive, such as the practice of literary festivals), in extension (some are domestic, while others are international or global), in normative significance (some are quotidian, while others, such as the practice of citizenship, concern the fundamental structure of political society) and in voluntariness (some involve voluntary agreements, such as commercial partnerships, while others, such as the state, are non-voluntary). The importance of practice integration is that it protects us from another hazard, normative disintegration. If we treat practices as if they were mutually isolated entities, we shall lose sight of the larger social whole to which they belong. Searle's insightful argument for institutional facts is vulnerable on this count, as it takes up one institution or a

[14] Wittgenstein, *Philosophical Investigations*, §§23, 241.

practice at a time. In his 1964 article, Searle focussed exclusively on the institution of promising.[15] Thus Searle's account does not extend to practices made of practices.[16] But precisely this notion of macro practices brings out the just noted trait of integration among practices without neglecting the differentia of each distinctive practice.

This integrative aspect is reflected in the second core feature of macro practices: *comprehensiveness*. A comprehensive practice is one that includes as its participants everybody in a given domain – this domain can be domestic society, international society or some other normative arrangement. Moreover, 'participation' is meant in the strong sense of the term. As may be remembered from Chapter 3, actors participate in a practice in the strong sense when they understand its core rules and when they are committed to following the rules, whereas third parties or observers participate in a weak sense, which requires competent understanding without commitment. Promising qualifies as a comprehensive practice because it is assumed that *anyone* in society who sincerely makes a promise in the appropriate circumstances must not only understand the rule of promising but also honour it (or accept that the making of a promise entails an obligation to do what has been promised). But while promising is a comprehensive practice, it is not a macro practice, as it does not contain other practices within its normative domain.

A third feature of macro practices is that they are ethically fundamental for those participating in them. This means that from the point of view of participants, there is no option of leaving the practice without the loss of ethical standing, which is crucial to their sense of self-worth. For example, an individual sovereign state within the macro practice of sovereign states cannot resign from the practice and maintain its standing as a sovereign state. It might seem as if what we are claiming here is that there is a compulsory component to a state's participation in this practice. But a sovereign state is not an entity that could be compelled to participate in the practice of

---

[15] John R. Searle, 'How to Derive "Ought" from "Is"', *Philosophical Review* 73 (1) 1964: 43–58, reprinted in Philippa Foot (ed.), *Theories of Ethics* (Oxford: Oxford University Press, 1967), pp. 101–114.

[16] John R. Searle, 'Social Ontology: Some Basic Principles', *Anthropological Theory* 1(6) 2006: 12–29, esp. 28. For a discussion, see Frank Hindriks, 'Constitutive Rules, Language and Ontology', *Erkenntnis* 71 (2) 2009: 253–275, esp. p. 259.

sovereign states – because, as indicated in Chapter 4, the practice of sovereign states is 'anarchical' or freedom respecting. In a like manner, the macro practice of global rights cannot be said to be a compulsory practice which forces participation on people in the sense that it compels them to claim rights for themselves. Precisely because a rights-holder is a free agent, the notion of rights-holders being compelled to participate in this practice makes no sense at all.

Coercion presents the fourth central feature of macro practices. Since it is prone to be misunderstood, a longer exposition is warranted. We may distinguish between two concepts of coercion. A coercive act, in an agent-relative sense, is an act by A which effectively changes the will of B by means of a threat of force that negatively affects the cost of performing the action originally contemplated by B. A coerces B if A's threat succeeds in making B do what B would not have done in the absence of the coercive threat.[17] Beyond this, we have in mind coercion in an institution-relative sense, the paradigmatic example being the civil state. The idea here is not that the state has a coercive right to enforce its laws on its citizens (coercion in the first sense of enforcement) but rather that the state itself is a coercive institutional domain – a territorially bounded, closed society (coercion in the second sense of institutional closure).[18] In John Rawls's formulation, citizens have no choice in becoming members of the state: they are born into it and leave it by death.[19] Coercion in this institution-relative sense implies a lack of free choice on the part of the citizen in establishing or terminating a state-citizen relation. Paradigmatically, there is a no-entry

---

[17] This is, roughly, the sense of coercion of Robert Nozick's classic essay. Robert Nozick, 'Coercion', in Sidney Morgenbesser, Patrick Suppes and Morton White (eds.), *Philosophy, Science and Method: Essays in Honour of Ernest Nagel* (New York: St. Martin's Press, 1969), pp. 440–472.

[18] The laws of the state are coercive in the agent-relative sense because the state can be seen as an agent who can threaten and effectively force the citizens to pay taxes, to be conscripted in the military (for male citizens) or to be incarcerated and even killed for crime. Unlike other types of coercive agents, be it organised mafias or individual actors who exercise coercive threats, the state commands effective institutional means necessary for enforcement (police, prisons, courts) that can be deployed whenever coercive threats fail, based on its claim to hold authority over the means of legitimate coercion. These two features of institutionalised coercion make the state a special institution.

[19] John Rawls, *Political Liberalism*, pbk. ed. (New York: Columbia University Press, 1996), p. xlv.

clause (all citizens are born as members of a particular state) as well as a no-exit clause (no one can abdicate the role of citizen).

Let us see whether international and global practices count as coercive in this second, institutional sense of coercion. The domestic state, as we just saw, is a coercive institutional structure by virtue of having no exit as well as no entry clause for the individuals inside it – namely, its citizens. 'Political society,' Rawls writes, 'is closed: we come to be within it and we do not, and indeed cannot, enter or leave it voluntarily'.[20] The same logic seems to apply to the individual state participant in the contemporary practice of states. The default premise is that a state belongs to international society, unless it keeps on violating its common rules persistently and with impunity – but it is next to impossible to find examples of such persistent transgression. Even rogue states pay lip service to the settled rules of the game. So the question of entry does not arise; all states count as insiders to the society of states. The question of exit does not arise either, since this society has become globalised – its normative blanket covers all parts of the world. If a state were to persist in breaching the common rules in the practice of states, it would not be expelled from the practice (the notion of expulsion is out of place) but punished or ostracised *within* the practice.

To appreciate the importance of this institutional closure, let us assume for a moment that a participant wants to exit a practice. Here it is requisite to differentiate between cases where exiting (in whatever sense) is permitted by the rules of the practice from cases where it is not. This is a normative question which asks not whether one can leave but whether one is *permitted* to leave. In other words, is there an obligation to honour the rules of the practice even in cases where doing so would harm one's interests? The answer is affirmative for the class of non-instrumental practices, but it is negative for the class of instrumental practices (see Chapter 1). The latter type of practices are tools for forwarding the interests of their participants. Thus a participant in an instrumental practice is permitted to initiate and terminate one's membership in a practice at will – both options are open under the rules of the game. However, on Rawls's conception of the state, both options are blocked – this tenet makes the state a coercive, closed society.

So understood, the state constitutes a non-voluntary form of civil association, an idea present in the political theories of Hobbes, Kant,

---

[20] Rawls, *Political Liberalism*, p. 136.

Hegel, Oakeshott and Rawls.[21] On the opposite end of the spectrum, the voluntarist theory of the state propounded by John Locke and neo-Lockeans such as Robert Nozick, holds that societal members, while nominally called 'citizens', resemble private-market contractors who create an overarching managerial institution (a government) to more efficiently protect their rights and interests.[22] The identities and interests of such private parties are considered complete *before* they enter the state. On the non-voluntarist view, core identities and interests are defined *within* the domain of the state, so the rules of the game have a standing that is different in principle – the state here is not just a manager but a public realm inside which individuals acquire a new public identity as citizens. Given that these rules are identity conferring and not merely interest advancing, they possess a non-instrumental, intrinsic value for their participants, as our discussion of Hegel illustrated. But Hegel argued that in order to have non-instrumental value, the coercive laws of the state must be just or non-discriminatory against certain individuals or groups.[23] As he made clear, the political subjects of the modern state accept the rules of the game on rational grounds.[24] The fact that these rules must be rationally *justified* to the citizens shows that far from being an abstract institution, the modern state is a social practice that needs to be reproduced, an active reproduction that would be impossible without ongoing acceptance by its citizens. The upshot is that the enforcement powers of the state (coercion in the first sense) ultimately require legitimacy. On the Hegelian idea of *rational* justification, the citizens accept the coercively guaranteed rules of the game not out of necessity but because they are convinced that the game is fair – for example, that the rules guarantee their rights, that the rules do not favour those in power or that

---

[21] Thomas Hobbes, *Leviathan*, ed. C. B. MacPherson (London: Penguin, 1968 [1651]); G. W. F. Hegel, *Hegel's Philosophy of Right*, trans. T. M. Knox (Oxford: Oxford University Press, 1981 [1821]); Michael Oakeshott, *On Human Conduct* (Oxford: Clarendon Press, 1975). Rawls recognises the coercive aspect of the *state*, qua *political* society, but he defines *society* by reference to cooperation, as a 'cooperative venture for mutual advantage'. John Rawls, *A Theory of Justice* (Cambridge, MA: Harvard University Press, 1971), p. 4.

[22] John Locke, *Second Treatise of Government*, ed. C. B. Macpherson (Indianapolis: Hackett, 1980 [1690]); Robert Nozick, *Anarchy, State, and Utopia* (New York: Basic Books, 1974).

[23] See the famous paragraph 209 in Hegel's *Philosophy of Right*.

[24] Hegel, *The Philosophy of Right*, §§ 137, 260, 261A.

everybody has an equal set of rights. This sets apart Hegel's ethical state or rule-of-law state from an authoritarian or quasi-state.

Still, our neo-Hegelian argument does not just extend the non-voluntarist view of the domestic state to international and global affairs. The core practices that constitute our contemporary international and global realm – the practice of states and the practice of global rights – are not modifications of domestic ethics, law and politics; they are *sui generis* macro practices. Like the domestic state, they exhibit the core tenets of macro practices noted previously: they are second order, comprehensive, ethically foundational and coercive in the institutional sense. Nonetheless, they are 'anarchical' and as such non-coercive in the agent-relative sense.

Concretely, the two core global practices are macro practices with the following features. First, international society is a society made of various domestic societies; analogously, the global rights practice contains different regimes of rights within its domain – they are second-order practices. Second, both practices are comprehensive, as nowadays they include states and people everywhere, respectively. Third, both are ethically fundamental in that they accord valued ethical statuses to their participants – the status of a state inside international society and that of a rights-holder inside global civil society. Fourth, these global practices are coercive in the institutional sense because they contain no exit and no entry clause: all states – and all rights-holders – are trapped inside their normative domains. The chief difference between the state and these macro practices is that the latter do not incorporate coercion *qua* enforcement. While an individual citizen can be forced to abide by the laws of the state against his or her will, this enforced participation does not apply to states inside the practice of states or to rights-holders inside the global rights practice. The individual state ought freely to accept the common normative standards of international society and, correlatively, the rights-holder the common normative standards of the global practice of rights. This form of freedom is not freedom *from* obligation, as it is in the voluntarist tradition of instrumental practices; it is freedom within a common framework of obligations one shares with others.[25] A state,

---

[25] Here we offer only a bare outline of the argument underwriting the non-voluntarist tradition, which links freedom to coercion and obligation. Assuming a correlation between obligations and rights and thus a relation between an obligation-bound party and a rights-holder, the basic idea is that an obligation is

as a participant in international society, understands that it cannot walk away from its obligations, since having rights inside the practice presupposes having corresponding obligations.

On our view, the state is not the closed society described by Rawls. It is not a self-contained unit that may or may not maintain regular relations with other states, but it is a connected state, a part inside a larger whole – the macro practice of the society of states. Adopting this macro perspective means that citizens who live in a state *connected to other states* are no longer subject to the Rawlsian no-exit restriction: they now have the option of exiting the realm of their state and joining another. The citizen is permitted to sever the existing bond with a particular legal and political system even though setting up this bond was not a matter of free choice. This, we may say, is a 'soft' form of state coercion. It is noteworthy that the *mature* domain of international society alone contains rule-of-law states. Within its immature domain, autocratic and totalitarian states do not allow their citizens to leave state borders. This constitutes a 'hard' form of state coercion.

A further feature that distinguishes the connected state from the closed Rawlsian state is that the former maintains a normative link to the global rights practice. As a participant in the mature society of states, each state is required to respect and protect the rights of individuals inside its territory as well as abroad. This normative arrangement may be examined from different angles. From the point of view of a civilian in the global rights practice, this suggests that individual rights can be claimed against the state in which one holds citizenship or in another state that one is visiting. Rights-holders in the global rights practice may claim their rights wherever they happen to be – fundamental rights are not granted to people by states, although as we argued in Chapter 4, individuals may and do rely on states for the protection and actualisation of their rights. In sum, states members of international society are required to respect the basic rights of everyone in their territory but also outside it, whenever other states flagrantly

coercive in the sense that some action is *due* or required (from the party under obligation) and is not just a matter of charity. A contemporary view which claims that such coercive obligations (obligations of justice) bind only citizens inside the domestic state and do not extend globally is presented in Thomas Nagel, 'The Problem of Global Justice', *Philosophy & Public Affairs* 33 (2) 2005: 113–147.

abuse or fail to protect the basic rights of their own citizens (as the doctrine of the Responsibility to Protect [R2P] illustrated).

In some crucial sense, then, the practice theory of international relations presented in this book invites us to re-think the state-citizen relation postulated by traditional political theory. Under the proposed re-articulation, the coercive authority of the state no longer clashes with the principle which recognises the dignity of the individual citizen as a free agent and a rights-holder inside three normative orders: the domestic state, the international society of states, and the global realm of rights.

## The Challenge of Micro Practices in IR

Interpreting international relations in terms of macro practices as we have done seems to be out of tune with the prevailing attitude in the IR discipline, which favours micro practices. In this section, we point out the advantages of the macro perspective as well as the limitations of the micro perspective in general social theory and IR.

The idiom of micro practices has been imported into IR from the social theories of Michel Foucault and Pierre Bourdieu.[26] Because Bourdieu, whose ideas were examined in Chapter 2, categorises practices under the rubric of Aristotle's *praxis* and because practice-turn scholars in IR adopt Bourdieu's apparatus, they tend to associate practice with *praxis*. In Part I, we distinguished *praxis* (practical activity in the broad sense) from *a* practice (human institution) and showed that incoherence arises from conflating these two notions.

One difficulty that we have not mentioned so far is that by embracing micro foundations, practice-turn scholars inadvertently end up

---

[26] Pierre Bourdieu, *Outline of a Theory of Practice*, trans. Richard Nice (Cambridge: Cambridge University Press, 1977 [1972]); and Pierre Bourdieu, *The Logic of Practice*, trans. Richard Nice (Stanford, CA: Stanford University Press, 1990 [1980]). See also Michel Foucault, *Madness and Civilization: A History of Insanity in the Age of Reason*, trans. Richard Howard (New York: Vintage Books, 1988 [1961]); Michel Foucault, *The Birth of the Clinic: An Archaeology of Medical Perception*, trans. Alan M. Sheridan (London: Routledge, 1989 [1963]); Michel Foucault, *Discipline and Punish: The Birth of the Prison*, trans. Alan M. Sheridan (New York: Vintage, 1995 [1975]). In IR, see Nicholas J. Kiersey (ed.), *Foucault and International Relations* (London: Routledge, 2011); and Rebecca Adler-Nissen (ed.), *Bourdieu in International Relations* (London: Routledge, 2013).

examining social practices at both micro and macro levels. On the one hand, this group of researchers hold that the practices which international relations observers should study are *micro* practices – day-to-day actions of diplomats, foreign policy practitioners and security officials.[27] On the other hand, the leaders in the 'turn' to practice, Emanuel Alder and Vincent Pouliot, approach international practices *via* Bourdieu's theory of practice and its central categories: *habitus*, field and capital.[28] However, Bourdieu intends his key categories as *macro* categories – a field consists of relations in terms of agents' positions, determined by capital endowments (financial capital, educational capital, symbolic capital and so on) and measured within 'social space' as a totality of social relations. This reference to social totality indicates that Bourdieu views agents as representatives of large-scale formations (social groups, classes) and not as individual actors.[29] In effect, practice-turn scholars combine micro practices with Bourdieu's macro determinants, and this is analytically incoherent. To restore coherence and complete our defence of macro practices, we shall spell out in further detail the relation between micro and macro practices.

Practices are marked by enormous diversity, and one aspect of this diversity concerns their scope. The macro-micro distinction is one way to think of scope. According to Foucault, micro practices are everyday patterns of actions and interactions inscribed within institutions below the level of the state. As a theorist of power, Foucault seeks to explain power relations circulating within modern, post-eighteenth-century institutions such as prisons, mental asylums and hospitals.[30] Power relations have as their medium micro practices – they do not operate

[27] Emanuel Adler and Vincent Pouliot, 'International Practices', *International Theory* 3 (1) 2011: 1–36. See also Iver B. Neumann, 'Returning Practice to the Linguistic Turn: The Case of Diplomacy', *Millennium: Journal of International Studies* 31 (3) 2002: 627–651; Oliver Kessler and Xavier Guillaume, 'Everyday Practices of International Relations: People in Organizations', *Journal of International Relations & Development* 15 (1) 2012: 110–120.

[28] Adler and Pouliot, 'International Practices'; and Emanuel Adler and Vincent Pouliot, 'International Practices: Introduction and Framework', in Emanuel Adler and Vincent Pouliot (eds.), *International Practices* (New York: Cambridge University Press), pp. 1–35.

[29] This emphasis on social space as a macro entity is palpable in Pierre Bourdieu, *Practical Reason: On the Theory of Action* (Stanford, CA: Stanford University Press, 1998). For a detailed assessment, see our Chapter 2.

[30] Of relevance here are the writings of the early Foucault. See note 26.

through the top-down sovereign authority of the state but from the bottom-up, through the deployment of daily strategies of institutional-ised classification (people are classified as patients or inmates), discip-linary techniques (surveillance and control) and symbolic power (uniforms of doctors and guards). Like Bourdieu's penchant for the bodily manifest *habitus*, Foucault is preoccupied with modern discip-linary strategies that target the human body, disclosed in discourses of bodily disciplines as well as mental normality and abnormality (which differ from pre-modern notions of health and disease). For Foucault, the macro structure of society in modernity is constructed by discourses of rationality and disciplinary control set up in terms of exclusion and inclusion. The core of society includes the normal and the rational, whereas the abnormal and the irrational are relegated to its fringes.

It is notable that Foucault shies away from discussing politics, construed as a deliberation intended to alter the basic rules of associ-ation.[31] This is Oakeshott's construal of politics (Chapters 1 and 3). When some actors seek to modify these rules in a given direction and find themselves at odds with other actors who seek change in a differ-ent direction, they are practicing politics. Politics, in this Oakeshottian sense, is an activity taking place inside the bounds of settled rules and norms and is not merely a confrontational, interest-seeking conduct. Analogously to his bracketing of politics, Foucault refrains from address-ing problems of ethics – the strategies of discipline, surveillance and control in prisons and hospitals he describes never become the object of ethical evaluation, at least not in any conventional sense of ethics.

In contrast to Foucault, ethics has been pivotal to our investigation of practices. We defined it in Hegel's terms as *Sittlichkeit*, meaning mores, customs or human institutions. By default, such institutions and the identities they accord have non-instrumental value for their partici-pants. In earlier chapters, we reworked Hegel's triad of institutions – the family, civil society, and the state – into an account of the consti-tutive institutions of the contemporary international and global realm, and we have now argued that the state, the international society of states and the global practice of rights represent macro practices. Whatever the merits of our argument – the readers alone are to

---

[31] We alluded to Walzer's insight in the Introduction. See Michael Walzer, 'The Politics of Michel Foucault', in David Couzens Hoy (ed.), *Foucault: A Critical Reader* (London: Basil Blackwell, 1986), pp. 51–68.

judge – it affords clear criteria for distinguishing macro from micro practices, criteria which Foucault and Bourdieu do not spell out.

Foucault appears to regard macro discourses of power as the cumulative effect of everyday practices. He uses the term 'everyday practices' as a synonym for micro practices, and the same usage is adopted by Bourdieu. However, this conceptualisation is inadequate. Consider the practice of citizenship, a key component of the practice of statehood. It is comprehensive (by default, it includes everyone living inside a political society, where the status of non-citizen is outside the default position), it is ethically foundational (the status of citizen is not subject to trade-offs), it is coercive in the institutional sense (we may not walk away from our rights and obligations as citizens at whim) and it possesses a second-order character (other practices such as buying and selling and travelling abroad depend on what citizenship we hold). As citizens, we participate in this *macro* practice daily, so it is misleading to equate everyday practices to *micro* practices.

It is more illuminating to explicate the concept of micro by contrasting it with our conception of macro. Turning the tables, we obtain the following criteria for a micro practice: it is a non-comprehensive, non–ethically foundational, non-coercive and non-second-order practice. Examples include tea drinking, rabbit trapping, writing an academic essay, signing a cheque and buying vegetables on the local market. Agents can participate or opt out of micro practices whenever they wish to do so: participation in such practices is not ethically fundamental for them, nor is there an institutional closure which requires their ongoing participation (e.g., as is the case with the practice of citizenship). These possibilities are available because micro practices lack a second-order character (participation in them does not change the actor's status inside other practices), they are non-comprehensive (including only a limited number of societal members) and they are unlikely to affect the normative fabric of society at large. If we consider contemporary French society, we may notice that no general norm requires French people to drink tea, write essays, buy fruit and vegetables on the local market or trap rabbits. But if the relevant group were restricted to that of French academics and given that being recognised as an academic is ethically fundamental for them, then academic life would not, from their point of view, be a micro practice. A practice which is ethically fundamental but not comprehensive or institutionally coercive may be termed a meso practice. This reveals that the mirco-macro practice distinction, although basic, is not exhaustive.

One noteworthy implication is that it would be incorrect to pair a micro practice with local or domestic society, and a macro practice with international or global society. A practice, even if it is practiced around the globe (e.g., the global use of mobile phones), remains a micro practice as long as it is non-comprehensive, non-ethically fundamental, non-coercive and lacking a second-order character.

One final point to reiterate before we proceed is that all forms of practices that we have been discussing are *common practices*. A practice can be 'common' in two distinct senses. Compare two scenarios. Imagine first that British people develop a practice of tea drinking, and simultaneously but independently from them, Japanese people develop a practice of tea drinking as well. A third-party observer then concludes that since similarities exist between these two practices, a common practice of tea drinking binds the British and the Japanese. Now imagine a different scenario where certain Japanese and certain British people develop a practice of drinking tea *together* by following common standards *ab initio*. Under the first scenario, certain Japanese learn how to drink tea by considering what other Japanese tea drinkers do, a manner of tea drinking that *per accident* may coincide with British tea drinking. Under the second scenario, the Japanese learn the art of tea drinking by deliberately considering how the British drink tea, and correlatively, the British learn this art by deliberately considering how the Japanese drink tea. In our view, consistent with the second case, a practice counts as common if it covers a single normative domain. As such, it cannot be the outcome of an accidental overlap across standards drawn from multiple normative domains or practices. A common practice must rely on shared (not just similar) normative standards, and it must be deliberately (though not purposefully) pursued.[32] Thus individuals participate in a common practice whenever they deliberately take each other's actions into account under shared normative standards within a single normative domain, irrespective of whether this domain has a sub-domestic, domestic, international or global extension.

---

[32] Here 'deliberate' is used in the sense of 'intentional'. The concept of intentional action is not the same as purposeful action. An *intentional* action implies a plan of how to do something and is not merely automatic or unconscious.
A *purposeful* action is an intentional action that aims at a particular outcome. Intentional action therefore need not be purposeful action.

## Practice Theory and IR Theory

In the previous sections, we did not draw a sharp distinction between practice theory and practice theory of international relations. Now it is time to consider the potential of practice theory to illuminate the IR field. Can this theory redefine the contours of theorising in the field, or is it just another addition to the canonical menu of IR theories such as realism and liberalism and their contenders: constructivism, English School theory, critical theory and post-structuralism? As we pointed out in the introductory chapter, practice theory is not a substantive theory but a metatheory or philosophy which raises second-order questions about knowledge, interpretation, action and the status of (social) facts. Thus a proper rival to practice theory would have to be another kind of metatheory accepted within the current IR cannon. The relevant contrast here is between scientific theory and normative theory, construed as contending meta-theoretical positions. The point of departure for our argument in this section is the lamentable tendency among IR scholars to associate theory with *scientific* theory. But while our practice theory challenges scientific theory in the philosophically realist mode, it is fully compatible with scientific theory in the hermeneutic mode. Last, but not least, the practice theory presented in this book is not just a refurbishment of normative theory of international relations – it has an independent significance.

### Scientific Theory and Practice Theory

The motto of the practice turn in IR examined in Chapter 2 reads, 'Forget about theory!' The idea is that practices defy theoretical synthesis. Practice-turn scholars suggested that therefore, theory in the strict sense should be replaced with context-specific empirical generalisations. In the context of the Cold War, for example, the researcher can produce generalisations about the practice of deterrence or NATO-Russia diplomacy. But the cogency of this argument depends on how we understand 'practice' and 'theory'. Advocates of the practice turn take 'practice' to be practical activity in the sense of Aristotle's *praxis*, whose opposite is *theoria*. Actions consist of what we do, and what we do is intelligible apart from any theoretical ordering. This entails instrumentalism with respect to theory – theory is a filing device:

it arranges our observations of actions, but it does not enter into their descriptions. This instrumentalist view is problematic on two counts.

First, there is a reason why we cannot discard theory. It is that theory, defined as a set of statements or a theoretical language, creates an intelligible world, where a world is a system of objects and their relations. It does so by setting limits on the types of objects and relations that belong to a given world and determines the level of observation at which they can meaningfully be observed. In the absence of theory, we would not know *what* to observe or at what resolution to affix our observations. Consider classical physical theory, including Newton's theory of motion, Maxwell's electromagnetism, and Einstein's theory of general relativity. It postulates a world whose bedrock components are atoms and their properties (mass, momentum, velocity, position). The level of observation ranges from macro objects (galaxies, trees, stones) to micro objects (atomic particles) hypothesised to enter into causal relations. The theory of quantum mechanics portrays the physical world in a fundamentally different way. It is a world composed of micro (subatomic-level) quantum entities, where each entity is a half particle / half wave whose position and momentum cannot be simultaneously determined. Because of this indeterminacy, the universe of quantum mechanics cannot be studied in terms of nomic or causal relations; it only allows for the estimation of probabilities. Observation here is indirect: it comprises what one of the fathers of quantum mechanics, Werner Heisenberg, called 'observation in principle'.[33] We *infer* (probabilistically) the existence of quantum entities indirectly by directly observing macro objects in experimental settings. Thus the presence of a proton is inferred by observing a trail in a Wilson's chamber. The corollary is that it does not make sense to ask what the physical world without further qualification is like; posing the question properly requires the framework of a *specific physical theory*. It is equally pointless to invite researchers to observe action without further qualification – the proper approach is to observe a specific (type of) action under a specific description of it.

The second defect of instrumentalism is that it ignores the relation between descriptions and theoretical context. Let us compare the

---

[33] The original paper is Werner Karl Heisenberg, 'Über quantentheoretische Umdeutung kinematischer und mechanischer Beziehungen', *Zeitschrift für Physik* 33 (1) 1925: 879–893.

procedure for generating descriptions of scientific theory with that of practice theory. A description tells us what to observe. On some accounts of scientific observation, such as Gilbert Harman's, there is a causal link between what happens (an event) in the natural world and *the fact* that a scientist observes the event, under some description – as a this or a that – in accordance with the terms of physical theory.[34] The existence of a subatomic particle makes the scientist observe a trail in a Wilson chamber – with the aid of physical theory, this trail is interpreted as a 'proton'. For Harman, physical theory is responsible for the description under which we observe something, as a proton, but not for the (causally) prior and more elementary fact that the occurrence of a natural event beyond the theory *causes* us to observe something, as a not-yet-identified something, in the first place. It is assumed that from the standpoint of theory, facts are *statements* of events, but that, from the standpoint of reality, facts are events. This premise is shared by logical positivism and scientific realism.

Harman's argument elucidates the ground for the distinction between scientific observation and practice observation.[35] In science, the relation between the occurrence of an event or action (actions being a special sort of events) and its subsequent observation is one of causation. In a practice, conversely, we always do something under some description of it, so the description is *constitutive* of the doing (the rules defining the practice are the source of the description). The relation between an action and its observation is one of mutual constitution and not of causation.

In effect, practice theory removes the wedge that separates theoretical language from facts. This wedge was introduced by the precursor of scientific realism, logical positivism. Positivism underpins the so-called 'received view' of scientific theory popularised by Rudolf Carnap that was influential between the 1930s and the mid-1970s.[36] For Carnap, the language of a theory, L(*T*), is a calculus categorically distinct from the language of observation, L(O), whose frame of reference is

---

[34] See note 13.

[35] Gilbert Harman contrasts 'observation in ethics' with 'observation in science'. See Harman (see *The Nature of Morality*, pp. 6–9). However, the point we are making here is similar.

[36] A classic discussion of the 'received view' of scientific theory is Frederick Suppe (ed.), *The Structure of Scientific Theories*, 2nd ed. (Chicago: University of Illinois Press, 1977).

empirical.[37] Theoretical terms have the status of uninterpreted logical symbols in an axiomatic system. They acquire meaning only after the axioms have been translated into theorems by virtue of 'correspondence rules' that connect a given theoretical term to a corresponding observational term. To take a provisional example, the symbol 't' in the calculus corresponds to the observational term 'time', which can be measured empirically by clocks. There is a rift between theory and reality, since on Carnap's premises, the language of theory is a self-referential, syntactic system. Observational terms alone refer to reality, and therefore 'observational protocols' must be used empirically to confirm or disconfirm the candidate theory. But on our practice account, observational terms are theory-laden. Here the distinction between theory and observation (fact) is a matter of degree. This is so because practice theory construes facts as linguistic *statements* (which may be statements about actions or events) and not simply as events in the so-called real world.

The claim that scientific theory gives us access to the real world is the central claim of scientific realism. It is important to outline it briefly, since the most sophisticated metatheory presently advanced in IR is wedded to scientific realist premises. Scientific realism in IR, in other words, is the main philosophical challenger to our practice theory.

Let us first sketch the premises of scientific realism as a philosophical programme before turning to its IR version.[38] Scientific realists reject Carnap's positivist assumption that observationally accessible facts alone can repudiate a theory. Despite this disagreement about the status of *theories*, positivists and scientific realists agree on the status of *facts* – facts are taken to be mind-independent events. The following three premises differentiate scientific realism from its positivist predecessor. The first posits the ontological priority of unobservable entities. Reality comprises observable and unobservable entities, but it is the latter that figure in scientific explanation. Second, the mode of explanation is assumed to be ampliative: it includes, 'inference to the best explanation' with the proviso that any valid explanation must invoke unobservables. Finally, the terms of mature scientific theories are taken to refer to the real world and thus to unobservable entities. Because

---

[37] Rudolf Carnap, 'Testability and Meaning', *Philosophy of Science* 3 (4) 1936: 419–471.

[38] Key essays from the heyday of scientific realism are collected in Edward A. MacKinnon, *The Problem of Scientific Realism* (New York: Appleton-Century Crofts, 1972).

theoretical terms refer directly to reality (externally) and not to other terms (internally), scientific realism is a semantic rather than a syntactic type of theory. Semantics implies that theoretical terms have truth values and that, ideally, scientific realist propositions are true.

The crux of the disagreement between scientific realism and our practice-based perspective can now be pinpointed – it concerns the nature of theory and truth. Should theory be construed as a theory of *science* or as a theory of *practice?* For scientific realists, the answer, obviously, is 'science'. According to the so-called miracle argument introduced by Hilary Putnam, 'the positive argument for realism is that it is the only philosophy that does not make the success of science a miracle.'[39] But Putnam assumes without proof that science is success-ful. (And we may wonder, successful in what respect?) Many ethicists and post-structuralist have deplored the abuse of scientific technology by totalitarian regimes in the death camps of the twentieth century. Since technology – or the *application* of science – is not the same as the propositions of scientific theory, the claim for the success of science on the turf of theory is still in need of justification.

It seems that the attraction of scientific realist theory stems from its capacity to track truth: it tells us how the world really is and not how we might imagine it to be. Here the real world is external to human consciousness. Our Hegelian objection to this line of reasoning is that the world, including the world postulated by science, is internal to self-consciousness. Even hefty concepts such as 'reality' and 'truth' are products of human understanding. This does not mean that 'anything goes' because understanding is not solipsist; its spring is intersubjec-tively constituted self-consciousness grounded in shared norms that govern community discourse. Nor is such an intersubjective under-standing arbitrary, as relativism is often taken to imply, since inter-subjectively accepted norms can impose requirements of rationality. Practice theory regards science as a social practice committed to norms of rational argumentation, evidence and impartiality. On this view, science does not have a privileged status in investigating reality. For 'reality', as Peter Winch once remarked, is not a category of science; rather, 'a form of the conception of reality must already be presupposed

---

[39] Hilary Putnam, 'What Is Mathematical Truth?', in Hilary Putnam, *Mathematics, Matter and Method: Philosophical Papers*, Vol. I (Cambridge: Cambridge University Press, 1975), pp. 60–78, p. 73.

before we can make any sense of the expression "what science reveals to be the case."'[40]

Once again, we encounter the epistemological clash between the external and the internal points of view. The realist asserts that an external world exists and that proper (i.e., scientific) theorising should account for it. This world is mind independent and would be 'out there' even if no human beings ever had thoughts or acted in it. In contrast, the claim of practice theory is that we, thinking and choosing human beings, make our shared social reality by participating in diverse, quasi-autonomous normative domains – practices – that are reproduced through our shared understandings.

And yet our practice theory is not directed against science *tout court*. It is hospitable to scientific theorising in the anti-realist, interpretive mode. To this class of scientific theories belong Thomas Kuhn's doctrine of historically shifting scientific paradigms that is familiar to IR students but also Bas van Fraassen's constructive empiricism.[41] Van Fraassen writes of a 'hermeneutic circle' involved in scientific observation: 'To find the limits of what is observable in the world described by a theory $T$ we must inquire into $T$ itself, and the theories used as auxiliaries in the testing and application of T.'[42] Here in accord with the hermeneutic tradition, interpreting a single observation requires interpreting the entire world of which it is a part, and this world is a whole constituted by theory. Where hermeneutic science and the hermeneutic of practice theory differ is over the object of observation – meaningful actions as opposed to inanimate events. Since the meaningful actions performed within a practice are *self-understandings* (that the observer seeks to understand more coherently), this indicates that interpretation plays a more central role in non-scientific practices than in the practice of science. But science is also an interpretive enterprise.

If practice theory has a general message, it is that what we do within the framework of a common institution ('a practice') is constituted by what we understand ourselves to be doing ('theory'). Here, theory

[40] Peter Winch, 'Understanding a Primitive Society', in Peter Winch, *Ethics and Action* (London: Routledge, 1972 [1964]), pp. 8–49, p. 27.

[41] Thomas Kuhn, *The Structure of Scientific Revolutions*, 3rd ed. (Chicago: Chicago University Press, 1996 [1962]); Bas C. van Fraassen, *The Scientific Image* (Oxford: Oxford University Press, 1980).

[42] Van Fraassen, *The Scientific Image*, p. 57.

comprises not a set of abstract postulates but a form of understanding. Specifically, it is an engagement in *critical understanding* by a theorist understood as a third-party observer who, in observing what participants in a practice are saying and doing, seeks to attain a more coherent understanding not just of their sayings and doings but also of their practice as a whole.

## Normative Theory and Practice Theory

The opposition between scientific realism and practice theory explicated thus far can be understood in terms of a more elementary incongruence between scientific theory and normative theory as rival metatheoretical standpoints. In North American academia, where IR is categorised as a sub-field of Political Science (the opposite is the case in Europe, where Political Science is one strand within IR), the usual advice to students is that since Political Science is a science, they must engage in a value-free mode of enquiry. But if the position presented in the previous section bears scrutiny, science is a social practice with its own internal norms and values. Does this suggest that we are advocating a return to normative theory in IR? The answer is affirmative, but certain qualifications apply.

The expression 'normative theory' is ambiguous. It can designate, broadly, the study of meaningful conduct. Our project did not exclusively focus on the difference between 'behaviour' and 'conduct', where conduct includes acting on the basis of meanings and reasons, and behaviour is whatever is left over once meanings and reasons have been excised from conduct. The problem of meaning is important, but it does not exhaust the logical architecture of a practice. Further, normative theory can designate, more narrowly, the study of norms. In Chapter 3, we laid down a philosophical template of practice theory which identified the five components that make up the analytical core of a practice – rule-following, internalism, constitutive rules, the understanding of meaning, and norms. Norms are just one piece in the jigsaw of practices. To substantiate this idea, let us go back to Searle's account of promising. It hinges on a key distinction between the constitutive *rule* of promising and the *institution* of promising. In Searle's oft-quoted example, when John utters the words 'I promise to pay you, Smith, five dollars' in the appropriate circumstances, then John has undertaken an obligation towards Smith to pay him five dollars.[43] The rule of promising specifies that the utterance of certain words in the appropriate circumstances counts as the performance of a specific type of action (promising, in this case). This rule is a constitutive rule of promising (or a rule with the form 'Doing X counts as action A in context C'). By defining what counts as a certain type of action (making a promise), this rule enables, makes possible or constitutes its performance (this type of action cannot be performed without the rule). However, the constitutive *rule* of promising is an element within a wider social whole, the *institution* of promising, which includes other elements besides the rule. For example, it includes the normative *principle* that promises ought to be kept. There is a difference between the rule and the principle – since although the constitutive rule of promising is a defining rule (it defines what a promise is), it need not be a prescriptive rule or principle (a norm which prompts agents to keep promises). Once again, this reveals the complexity of a practice as an analytical object and its holist character: practices are complex social wholes.

The corollary is that the practice theory we advanced includes, but also goes beyond, normative analysis. In the book, we did not examine *individual* norms – for example, the gradual recognition of the anti-Apartheid norm in international relations since the 1990s.[44] Rather, we set out to elucidate the basic features of practices as *systems* of rules and norms that determine the normative contours of international and global affairs. While our brand of practice theory shares affinities with the norm-based constructivisms of IR scholars Nicholas Onuf, Friedrich Kratochwil and Antje Wiener and with theories of international ethics more broadly, its distinctive feature is that it weds description to normativity.[45]

---

[43] Searle, 'How to Derive "Ought" from "Is"', in Foot (ed.), *Theories of Ethics*, p. 102.

[44] See Audie Klotz, 'Norms Reconstituting Interests: Global Racial Equality and U.S. Sanctions against South Africa', *International Organization* 49 (3) 1995: 451–478.

[45] Friedrich V. Kratochwil, *Rules, Norms, Decisions: On the Conditions of Practical and Legal Reasoning in International Relations and Domestic Affairs* (Cambridge: Cambridge University Press, 1989); Nicholas Onuf, *World of Our Making: Rules and Rule in Social Theory and International Relations* (Columbia: University of South Carolina Press, 1989); Antje Wiener, *The Invisible Constitution of Politics: Contested Norms and International Encounters* (Cambridge: Cambridge University Press, 2008).

But granting that the object of observation within practice theory includes the constitutive *norms* that integrate a given practice does not entail that the *procedure* of observation that third parties rely on must be prescriptive. This procedure remains descriptivist, resonating with Wittgenstein's and Oakeshott's insight that the task of a philosopher, as a philosopher, is to describe and not to prescribe or explain (see the Introduction). This descriptivist approach can be contrasted with the prescriptive procedures embraced by utilitarians or Kantians who insist that the principle of utility or, correspondingly, the moral law, *ought* to govern agents, regardless of what considerations in fact govern their conduct. The advantage of practice theory is that it explicates what actors in practices *actually* think and do and does not issue prescriptions to instruct them what they ought to be doing instead.

Concretely, practice theory seeks to understand, more fully and coherently, the understandings of the practice participants under study. In this, it adopts the internal point of view and breaks with the external point of view. A quintessential example of an externalist explanation is Marx's theory of capital, in which economic agents *do not* understand themselves to be labouring under oppressive economic structures (collectively known as capital) but whose actions are nonetheless *explained* by the social scientist by invoking these structures. Bourdieu's theory of practice has similar externalist, Marxist overtones, since in his study of the Kabyle, Bourdieu concluded that ultimately, all Kabyle practices are motivated by economic self-interest.[46] The difficulty with externalism is not just that it treats (wrongly, as we claim) all practices as if they were at bottom alike but that its observational procedure involves an illegitimate overextension. The externalist procedure stipulates, first, that the observer must seek to understand what participants are thinking and doing within their practice. But then, as if this were insufficient, the observer is required, in a second step, to *replace* the internalist understanding just acquired by generating an explanation *de novo*. But such a second step, which superimposes an 'explanation from the outside' over an 'understanding from the inside', is a distorting overextension. As observers, we must go no further than describing the self-understandings of the practice participants observed: our task properly construed is not to

---

[46] Bourdieu, *A Theory of Practice*, p. 177.

conjure up explanations *de novo* but to describe more coherently their actually existing self-understandings.

Nevertheless, our practice theory shares one crucial premise with Bourdieu's social theory and with scientific realism – namely, the premise that large-scale structures are significant. In the context of our argument, this reinstates the importance of macro practices. Scientific realists, in their turn, pay attention to ontological structures that are 'global' in scope (pertaining to reality as a whole), and Bourdieu theorises society in a macro frame, as social totality.

Within IR, a scientific realist literature has emerged, including figures such as Alexander Wendt, Jonathan Joseph, Colin Wight and Heikki Patomäki.[47] These scholars have modified the philosophical programme of scientific realism in two ways. First, they have adopted a structuralist form of scientific realism.[48] To the general assumption of scientific realism stating that unobservable entities make up the ultimate furniture of reality, they add the specific assumption that these entities are related via deep structures governed by generative mechanisms. Structures are 'structures' because they include *relations* between entities, and they are 'deep' because these relations are ontological (and unobservable). Second, they link this type of structuralist scientific realism to Roy Bhaskar's 'critical realism', which incorporates elements of Marx's theory of capital.[49] Bhaskar argues that economic

---

[47] There are two branches of scientific realism in IR – a US strand associated with Wendt and Dessler and a UK strand associated with Patomäki, Wight and Joseph. See David Dessler, 'What's at Stake in the Agent-Structure Debate?', *International Organization* 43 (3) 1989: 441–473; and Alexander Wendt, 'Scientific Realism and Social Kinds', in Alexander Wendt, *Social Theory of International Politics* (Cambridge: Cambridge University Press, 1999), pp. 47–91. See also Heikki Patomäki and Colin Wight, 'After Postpositivism? The Promises of Critical Realism', *International Studies Quarterly* 44 (2) 2000: 213–237; and Forum on Scientific Realism in *Millennium – Journal of International Studies* 35 (2) 2007: 343–416, with contributions by Jonathan Joseph, Milja Kurki, and Colin Wight and critical assessments by Chris Brown and Fred Chernoff.

[48] Structuralism in not a defining feature of scientific realism but of various forms of scientific theory – for example, van Fraassen's constructive empiricism. The key premises of a structuralist theory of science are outlined in Carlos Ulises Moulines, 'Structuralism: The Basic Ideas', in Wolfgang Balzer and Carlos Ulises Moulines (eds.), *Structuralist Theory of Science: Focal Issues, New Results* (Berlin: De Gruyter, 1996), pp. 1–14.

[49] See Roy Bhaskar, *Scientific Realism and Human Emancipation* (London: Verso, 1986); and Jonathan Joseph, 'In Defence of Critical Realism', *Capital & Class*

reproduction depends on oppressive structures of capital that operate apart from human consciousness. If their hidden presence would be exposed, it would pave the way towards human emancipation.

For its proponents, the appeal of IR scientific realism stems from its invocation of deep structures. Scientific realism, as a metatheory of unobservable ('deep') structures, is called on to explain the ontological underpinnings of observable social interactions.[50] The intended contrast is between 'interaction' and 'structure' and between 'social' and 'scientific'. In our everyday dealings with one another, we are limited to observing surface interactions, the argument goes, but these surface interactions are generated by unobservable structures. So what explains the observable transaction of selling and buying on the market is the deep structure of the capitalist economy. In short, scientific realist theory in IR claims to be in a privileged position to explain the workings of *structures* – in the natural and, by implication, in the social world.[51] Our view is that realist philosophy of science relies on a narrow, largely positivist notion of observation and that it recruits one possible notion of structure. As we shall see, practice theory is structuralist as well, albeit in a different, non-realist sense of structure.

To support this claim, let us briefly return to the annals of structuralist IR theory. In the late 1970s, Kenneth Waltz pioneered *structural realism* (his label for a theory of international politics and not for an

---

22 (2) 1998: 73–106. On critical realism in IR, see Heikki Patomäki, *After International Relations: Critical Realism and the (Re)Construction of World Politics* (London: Routledge, 2002); and Kathryn Dean, Jonathan Joseph, John Michael Roberts and Colin Wight, *Realism, Philosophy and Social Science* (Basingstoke: Palgrave, 2006).

[50] See Joseph's contribution in Forum on Scientific Realism. Jonathan Joseph, 'Philosophy in International Relations: A Scientific Realist Approach', *Millennium – Journal of International Studies* 35 (2) 2007: 345–359.

[51] Roy Bhaskar gestures towards 'internalism' (in our terms) by making a concession to the differentia of social structures from natural structures that obey *nomic* and causal principles. As he puts it, 'Social structures, unlike natural structures, do not exist independently of the agents' conceptions of what they are doing in their activity'. Roy Bhaskar, *The Possibility of Naturalism* (Brighton: Harvester Press, 1979), pp. 48–49. However, he takes this concession to internalism back, claiming that *science* is the vantage point for making sense of reality and that the social sciences too must respond to the basic ontological puzzle of what there is in the world. In effect, the claim is that the differentia of *social structures* does not entail a differentia of the *social sciences*. Because it points to ontology, foundations and invariance, Bhaskar's project is ultimately 'externalist' in our terms (see esp. pp. 50–60).

ontology of science). Waltz employed a laissez-faire market model to explain the interaction of self-interested units, states, in the international realm. His theory is structuralist because the market exerts constraints over the behaviour of individual units. Waltz defines structure as action constraint – the agents would have acted differently were it not for the presence of structure.[52] As in micro economics, the constraint is generated not by a social whole but by the emergent pattern (market equilibrium) of prior, essentially atomistic interactions. Scientific realists properly remark that Waltz's scheme is atomist.[53] However, it is not quite correct to say that Waltz's notion of structure is defective because it is interactionist.[54] If a theory seeks to explain *action*, then it is fully appropriate to define structure as action constraint. Whether this constraint is a result of prior interaction or, conversely, of a social whole marks a difference not between no structure and structure but between two kinds of structure: interactionist versus relational.

Our practice theory is centred on the notion of practices as complex social wholes sustained by normative structures. Here 'structure' comprises normative *relations* which constrain the conduct of agents. So scientific realism does not hold a monopoly over the *relational* view of structure – only over the ontological view of deep structure. The notion of normative structure projected by practice theory includes the set of rules and norms that are defining of a given practice. What distinguishes this practice-based conception of normative structure from deep structure is that inside the former, agents always interact knowingly and deliberately.[55] The Marxist idea that agents are puppets controlled by a hidden structure whose functioning they are not even aware of is ruled out. Inside a practice, the agents are assumed deliberately to take into account its rules and norms when interacting. In contradistinction to scientific realism, then, practice theory neither exorcises interaction from social structures nor regards it as a positivist vestige. Indeed, the participants in a practice use its rules *in the course* of their interactions. This illustrates why the so-called 'agent-structure' problem in social theory and IR theory, which invites us to choose

---

[52] Kenneth N. Waltz, *Theory of International Politics* (Boston, MA: McGraw Hill, 1979), pp. 73, 90, 122–123.
[53] Joseph, 'Philosophy in International Relations', p. 347.
[54] Joseph, 'Philosophy in International Relations', pp. 347–348.
[55] Once again, 'deliberate' is not the same as 'purposeful'. See note 32.

between agents and structures while bracketing interaction, is an over-simplification: within practices, all three components count.[56]

Practice theory connects agents to normative structures via the concept of understanding. It is only because agents understand themselves to be acting and interacting within the normative bounds set by their common practice that the practice gets reproduced over time. One familiar objection to this is that any approach that focusses on understanding is prone to ignore the material basis of reality. IR scientific realists like Wendt have alleged that this is where idealist approaches go wrong – ideas matter all right, but we still need an account of material reality.[57] It should be stressed that the logical infrastructure of practice theory, a rule-based hermeneutic, is not a form of idealism. The central categories of the theory – *actors, actions, rules* – are not dualist but unitary: they are *simultaneously* ideational (related to the understanding) and material (related to the properties of the physical world). An *agent* is an embodied thinker, and *action* implies the bringing about of change in the world. This world is composed of understandings, and these understandings, which may be *rules*, are often about material stuff – for instance, the rules of waging war that govern the use of tanks, arsenals, missiles and military bases. It seems that scientific realist arguments for materiality are kept hostage to an antiquarian mind/matter dualism, which is overcome within practice theory.

## Conclusion: Practice Theory and the Study of International Relations

In closing, we consider how practice theory might affect the existing spectrum of IR theorising as well as the practice of teaching the subject of International Relations. Practice theory, as already noted, cannot be reduced to constructivism or normative theory, even though it has a connection to both. Its ethos is anti-realist, but it is not a form of

---

[56] On the agent-structure problem in IR, see Dessler, 'What's at Stake in the Agent-Structure Debate?'; and Alexander Wendt, 'Bridging the Theory/Meta-theory Gap in International Relations', *Review of International Studies* 17 (4) 1991: 383–392. See also Joseph, 'Philosophy in International Relations', pp. 355–358.
[57] Wendt, '"Ideas All the Way Down": On the Constitution of Power and Interest' (ch. 3), in Wendt, *Social Theory of International Politics* (Cambridge: Cambridge University Press, 1999), pp. 92–138.

idealism, as it captures the material furniture of reality under the concept of understanding. Understanding can be an understanding of material objects, of ideas, of actions and of propositions. Rules, the building blocks of practices, represent propositions (linguistic statements such as 'No smoking') that must be understood by agents. Since in this study we dealt with the problem of how individuals act within practices constituted by rules, the propositions expressing these rules concern actors, *actions* and *interactions*. The emphasis was not on rules which prohibit certain actions ('*Do not* deploy nuclear missiles in the Balkans!'); rather, central to our analysis have been two distinct categories of rules – *constitutive rules*, which define who counts as an actor within a specific practice ('A diplomat is a state representative whose credentials have been accepted by the host state') or what counts as an action of a specific type ('Doing such and such *counts as* signing a treaty in context C'), as well as *prescriptive rules*, which prescribe action ('Underdeveloped nations *ought* to be helped'). In emphasising the notion of constitution, practice theory discloses its affinity with constitutive theory, and in taking prescriptions seriously, it exhibits its ties to normative theory.[58]

For all these affinities, practice theory has a face of its own. Let us recapitulate its six distinguishing components. First, it is a holist account. A practice is a social whole – a system of rules. The expression 'system of rules' is an abridgement because, as Oakeshott never tired of pointing out, a practice has a penumbra that cannot be compressed into some set of rules without remainder.[59] The know-how which enables us to follow the rules of the practice is not contained in the propositions expressing these rules. For the same reason, Wittgenstein talked not of rules *per se* but of rule-following.[60] Rule-following is an activity that presupposes meaning in use (Chapter 3). We learn the meaning of a rule *in* using it, so the rule cannot be learned apart from its use – it is not an abstract algorithm. But then, it would seem that we cannot understand a practice without becoming active participants in it. Does this imply that generals alone can understand the art of warfare and intelligence specialists the workings of terrorist organisations? There

---

[58] See Mervyn Frost, *Ethics in International Relations: A Constitutive Theory* (Cambridge: Cambridge University Press, 1996).

[59] Oakeshott, *On Human Conduct*, p. 91.

[60] Wittgenstein, *Philosophical Investigations*, §§143–155, 185–219.

are different types and degrees of understanding. In its plasticity, understanding differs from the rigid concept of knowledge.

We begin to understand some unknown kind of activity by grasping it to some extent rather than completely. The possibility that we might misunderstand some aspect of it, or that we understand it, but only superficially, is always present. Generally, we are taught by more competent players to discern mistakes from appropriate performances in relation to the observed activity, bearing in mind that the seasoned players themselves may commit mistakes. The point is that intersubjective communication enables self-correction within practices. Crucial here is language – the second element of practice theory. We can say, with Hegel, that reality is *understood reality* and that reality therefore presupposes mediation by language. Language here is not just an endless interplay of signifiers (words or utterances) and signified (objects) that have no stable meaning, as in Jacques Derrida's post-structuralism.[61] Indeed, it is an intersubjective world in which statements can be meaningfully interpreted. The starting premise of practice theory is that, in principle, agents are able to understand each other's statements. If this premise looks suspect, the retort is that every theory relies on starting premises. The theory of quantum mechanics, for example, postulates the existence of subatomic particles, though this picture might be revised by a future theory of physics. Practice theory assumes that relatively stable intersubjective standards of understanding are available and intelligible to us as reflective agents. Once again, this understanding can be defective in particular cases and with respect to particular agents, but all the agents cannot be the victims of misunderstanding at all times. Most of the participants in a practice understand its basic standards most of the time. In the absence of this, no practice would exist.

A third feature of practice theory is *actuality*. The theory studies actual practices – that is, practices which are aspects of social reality – and not hypothetical practices.[62] We need not resort to an esoteric metaphysical apparatus to make sense of what is going on around us – people

---

[61] Jacques Derrida, *Of Grammatology*, corr. ed., trans. Gayatri Chakravorty Spivak (Baltimore, MD: Johns Hopkins University Press, 1998). The original distinction is due to Saussure. Ferdinand de Saussure, *Course in General Linguistics*, ed. Roy Harris (London: Bloomsbury, 2013 [1916]).

[62] 'Actual' is Hegel's term for 'real', the idea being that the actual is part of *social* reality, construed as the subject's understood experience shared with other experiencing subjects.

signing checks, diplomats conducting peace talks or hunters trapping rabbits. We, men and women, inhabit a social world that is modulated by practices and which, for the most part, we have no difficulty understanding.

But the fact that we are able to make sense of practices without resorting to a metaphysical doctrine of one sort or another but simply by virtue of being reflective beings does not mean that participation within practices is a facile undertaking. Often, agents, as participants in different practices, are torn by the conflicting requirements that the standards internal to these practices impose on them. For example, the patriotic allegiance to one's state may clash with the understanding that this state acts on the international scene by violating principles of international justice. This is how many Americans felt during the Iraq War of 2003. The presence of internal conflict can affect not just individual players but the practice as a whole. Thus a fourth core feature of practice theory is the internal tension (the 'dialectic') that unfolds within practices and between them (Chapter 5).

A fifth feature is *differentiation amidst integration*. Part of the difficulty in making coherent sense of the social world is having to differentiate between the multiplicity of its constituent practices. The sirens of externalism that lull us into explaining what is going on by methods of reduction and abstraction may be hard to resist. Thus it may be tempting to search for historically 'primordial' practices which ground all other forms of practical activity or to posit some ideal practice as foundational. But such temptations must be resisted. In our view, the only way properly to make sense of practices is by treading the internalist path or by understating each practice on its own concrete, yet evolving, terms. This is particularly important for international and global practices. All too often, philosophers, social theorists and political scientists have portrayed these practices in reductionist terms, by treating them as epiphenomena of more fundamental domestic practices. But the practice of global rights is not just a summation of the regimes of rights inside domestic states, and international society is not just a summation of the foreign policies of separate states. As we have seen, both globally extended practices have a *sui generis* character: they are macro practices, each representing a distinctive system of norms.

*Non-instrumentality* is the sixth key feature of practice theory. A venerable tradition extending from Aristotle, on to Aquinas and up to present day utilitarians explains human action by appealing to purposes. In an Oakeshottian vein, our practice theory does not deny that some actions of agents have purposes; what it denies is that *practices* must necessarily be construed as purposeful activities. In this concluding part of the discussion, we have argued that the principle macro practices in which men and women around the world are actively participating at present – the state, international society, and the global rights practice – are non-instrumental. Practices of this sort are not tools for attaining common purposes such as security, prosperity, truth or harmony with nature; they are common frameworks of rules and norms that accord us valued ethical statuses and enable us to pursue self-chosen goals.

Having outlined the core features of practices as understood within practice theory, we have located the theory on the map of IR. But what concrete procedures of research should IR students and teachers interested in practice theory adopt? We offer, rather schematically, a quartet of considerations. Most importantly, international and global affairs would have to be investigated holistically. Such a holist logic of enquiry must be distinguished from piecemeal approaches designed to tackle isolated 'issue areas' of international politics such as proliferation, international trade or terrorism. These 'issue areas' would have to be seen as activities taking place within the wider social practices that we have sketched previously.

Second, the typical division between methods of Political Science research – qualitative as opposed to quantitative – is too crude to capture the holist problematic of international practices. Practice theory is clearly qualitative in its methodology. But the standard qualitative research techniques deployed in IR such as interviewing and participant observation are of little help if the objects to be studied are complex social wholes or macro practices with international and global extension. (Who are the representatives of these macro practices that need to be interviewed or followed in a procedure of participant observation?) Furthermore, the qualitative research methodology established within Political Science is modelled on the hard sciences. This model remains positivist at its core: the stage of hypothesis generation (which may be theoretical or even interpretive) is followed by empirical testing.[63] Thus whenever qualitative methods such as

---

[63] Here 'positivism' is the IR cousin of Carnap-style positivism. See Steve Smith, 'Positivism and Beyond', in Steve Smith, Ken Booth and Marysia Zalewski

interviewing or participant observation are used, their hypotheses still have to be validated empirically – such hypotheses reflect the requirements of positive science (quantification, testability, operationalisation). One problem with this is that it excludes normative theory by default, since norms cannot be verified empirically: they present *relations* and understandings of such relations, not physical processes. A defence of norms is a conceptual and, indeed, a theoretical task. In this connection, a more serious problem arises – namely, that a set of hypotheses, defined as quantifiable relationships between variables, is not the same as theory. Theory has a holist character: it is a framework which organises concepts, premises and hypotheses into a coherent conceptual whole and which, in lieu of being a whole, provides clues about the proper interpretation of its putative conclusions. Relying on isolated quantifiable hypotheses would not tell us how to interpret these hypotheses if their conclusions conflict; we would be stuck in the swamp of interpretive arbitrariness. This is why we need theory or philosophy of practices over and above some quantifiable hypotheses about practices.

Third, the theorising of practices, including international and global ones, demands a serious engagement with general social theory, philosophy and ethical theory. Philosophy enables us to draw conceptual distinctions with precision – for instance, to distinguish between different types of practices and to differentiate the subject of practices from enquiries with which it may easily be confused (e.g., the much broader problem of human action). A general social theory such as Bourdieu's and its anthropological insights can illuminate the general puzzle of practices by giving it a more palpable texture. Ethical theory is indispensable for clarifying the prescriptive and normative aspects of practices as well as the relations (instrumental or non-instrumental) that bind agents within practices.

Above all, practice theory promises to reopen the conversation between different strands of IR theory that seems to have reached an impasse. From its inception, the discipline of IR has been burdened by a neurotic urge to find a single overarching paradigm that best explains international politics. The dominant paradigm has ranged from the historical and legal studies of international organisations in the 1920s,

(eds.), *International Theory: Positivism and Beyond* (Cambridge: Cambridge University Press, 1996), pp. 11–46.

to behaviouralism supplemented with statistical methodology in the 1960s and, presently, to microeconomic theory buttressed by rational choice methodology. As a result, the mainstream disciplinary discourse of IR has been narrowed down and is currently limited to the specialists who command esoteric knowledge of its technical jargon. By becoming inaccessible, however, the conclusions of mainstream IR theory have become irrelevant, not just to ordinary men and women, but also to the larger community of IR theorists not versed in the mathematical apparatus of economic science. The contribution of the practice theory articulated in this book is that it acknowledges the differentia of the contemporary global realm and its core macro practices – the practice of states and the practice of global rights – while bringing into focus their continuity with general social practices. This ensures that non-specialists can understand the talk of practices and has the effect of re-opening and broadening the conversation among various IR theorists. It is our conviction that the most important issues on the agenda of IR theorising today – the tension between state rights and individual rights, the diffusion of authority in the global sphere, the privatisation of security, global inequality and the problem of failed states – will be more adequately understood by adopting the standpoint of global macro practices.

# Bibliography

Adler, Emanuel, and Vincent Pouliot (eds.), *International Practices* (Cambridge: Cambridge University Press, 2011).

Adler, Emanuel, and Vincent Pouliot, 'International Practices: Introduction and Framework', in Emanuel Adler and Vincent Pouliot (eds.), *International Practices* (New York: Cambridge University Press, 2011), pp. 1–35.

'International Practices', *International Theory* 3 (1) 2011: 1–36.

Adler, Emanuel, and Michael Barnett (eds.), *Security Communities* (Cambridge: Cambridge University Press, 1998).

Adler-Nissen, Rebecca (ed.), *Bourdieu in International Relations: Rethinking Key Concepts in IR* (London: Routledge, 2013).

'Introduction', in Rebecca Adler-Nissen (ed.), *Bourdieu in International Relations: Rethinking Key Concepts in IR* (London: Routledge, 2013), pp. 1–23.

Alderson, Kai, and Andrew Hurrell (eds.), *Hedley Bull on International Society* (Basingstoke: Macmillan, 2000).

Allison, Graham T., and R. P. Beschel, 'Can the United States Promote Democracy?', *Political Science Quarterly* 107 (1) 1992: 81–98.

Anderson, Elizabeth, *Value in Ethics and Economics* (Cambridge, MA: Harvard University Press, 1995).

Aristotle, *Ethica Nicomachea (Nicomachean Ethics)*, in *The Works of Aristotle*, Vol. IX, trans. and ed. W. D. Ross (Oxford: Clarendon Press, 1925).

Aristotle, *Metaphysica (Metaphysics)*, in *The Works of Aristotle*, Vol. VIII, 2nd ed., ed. W. D. Ross (Oxford: Clarendon Press, 1928).

Arrington, Robert L., 'A Defence of Ethical Relativism', *Metaphilosphy* 14 (3/4) 1983: 225–239.

Aumann, Robert J., 'Game Theory', in John Eatwell, Murray Milgate and Peter Newman (eds.), *The New Palgrave: Game Theory* (London: Macmillan, 1989), pp. 1–53.

Austin, J. L., 'A Plea for Excuses', *Proceedings of the Aristotelian Society* 57 1956–1957: 1–30.

*How to Do Things with Words*, 2nd ed., ed. J. O. Urmson and Marina Sbisà (Cambridge, MA: Harvard University Press, 1975 [1962]).

Axelrod, Robert, *The Evolution of Cooperation* (New York: Basic Books, 1984).

Baldwin, David A., 'Power and International Relations', in Walter Carlsnaes, Thomas Risse and Beth A. Simmons (eds.), *Handbook of International Relations* (London: Sage, 2013), pp. 273–297.

Baker, G. P., and P. M. S. Hacker, *Wittgenstein: Rules, Grammar, and Necessity* (Oxford: Blackwell, 1985).

Beitz, Charles R., 'What Human Rights Mean', *Daedalus* 132 (1) 2003: 36–46.

*The Idea of Human Rights* (Oxford: Oxford University Press, 2009).

'The Moral Standing of States Revisited', *Ethics & International Affairs* 23 (4) 2009: 325–347.

Bellamy, Alex J., *Responsibility to Protect: The Global Effort to End Mass Atrocities* (Cambridge: Polity Press, 2009).

*The Responsibility to Protect: A Defence* (Oxford: Clarendon Press, 2015).

Bentham, Jeremy, *A Fragment of Government*, ed. J. H. Burns and H. L. A. Hart (Cambridge: Cambridge University Press, 1998 [1776]).

Bhaskar, Roy, *The Possibility of Naturalism* (Brighton: Harvester Press, 1979).

*Scientific Realism and Human Emancipation* (London: Verso, 1986).

Boghossian, Paul A., 'Rules, Meaning and Intention: Discussion', *Philosophical Studies* 124 (2) 2005: 185–197.

Bourdieu, Pierre, *Outline of a Theory of Practice*, trans. Richard Nice (Cambridge: Cambridge University Press, 1977 [1972]).

*In Other Words: Essays towards a Reflexive Sociology*, trans. Matthew Adamson (Stanford, CA: Stanford University Press, 1987).

*The Logic of Practice*, trans. Richard Nice (Stanford, CA: Stanford University Press, 1990 [1980]).

*Practical Reason: On the Theory of Action* (Stanford, CA: Stanford University Press, 1998 [1994]).

*Pascalian Meditations* (Cambridge: Polity Press, 2000 [1997]).

*Distinction: A Social Critique of the Judgement of Taste*, trans. Richard Nice (London: Routledge, 2010 [1984]).

Brooks, Thom, *Hegel's Political Philosophy: A Systematic Reading of Hegel's Philosophy of Right* (Edinburgh: Edinburgh University Press, 2012).

Brown, Chris, 'Cosmopolitanism, World Citizenship and Global Civil Society', *Critical Review of International Social and Political Philosophy* 3 (1) 2000: 7–26.

'The "Practice Turn", Phronesis and Classical Realism: Towards a Phronetic International Political Theory?', *Millennium: Journal of International Studies* 40 (3) 2012: 439–456.

*International Society, Global Polity: An Introduction to International Political Theory* (London: Sage, 2015).

Brown, Garrett W. and David Held (eds.), *The Cosmopolitanism Reader* (Cambridge: Polity Press, 2010).

Buchwalter, Andrew, 'Hegel's Conception of an International "We"', in Philip T. Grier (ed.), *Identity and Difference: Studies in Hegel's Logic, Philosophy of Spirit, and Politics* (New York: State University of New York Press, 2007), pp. 155–176.

Bueger, Christian, and Frank Gadinger, *International Practice Theory: New Perspectives* (Basingstoke: Palgrave, 2014).

Bull, Hedley, 'Society and Anarchy in International Relations', in Herbert Butterfield and Martin Wight (eds.), *Diplomatic Investigations: Essays in the Theory of International Politics* (London: Allen and Unwin, 1966), pp. 35–50.

'The Emergence of a Universal International Society', in Hedley Bull and Adam Watson (eds.), *The Expansion of International Society* (Oxford: Clarendon Press, 1984), pp. 117–126.

*The Anarchical Society: A Study of Order in World Politics*, 3rd ed. (Houndmills: Palgrave, 2002 [1977]).

Buzan, Barry, *From International to World Society? English School Theory and the Social Structure of Globalisation* (Cambridge: Cambridge University Press, 2004).

Cameron, Lindsey, and Vincent Chetail, *Privatizing War: Private Military and Security Companies under Public International Law* (Cambridge: Cambridge University Press, 2013).

Carnap, Rudolf, 'Testability and Meaning', *Philosophy of Science* 3 (4) 1936: 419–471.

Carothers, Thomas, *Critical Mission: Essays on Democracy Promotion* (Washington, DC: Carnegie Endowment for International Peace, 2004).

Carothers, Thomas, and Marina Ottaway (eds.), *Uncharted Journey: Promoting Democracy in the Middle East* (Washington DC: Carnegie Endowment for International Peace, 2005).

Cohen, Jean L., 'Whose Sovereignty? Empire versus International Law', *Ethics & International Affairs* 18 (3) 2004: 1–24.

Davidson, Donald, *Essays on Actions and Events*, 2nd ed. (Oxford: Oxford University Press, 2001).

Davis, Morton D., *Game Theory: A Non-technical Introduction* (New York: Dover, 1997).

Dean, Kathryn, Jonathan Joseph, John Michael Roberts and Colin Wight, *Realism, Philosophy and Social Science* (Basingstoke: Palgrave, 2006).

Derrida, Jacques, *Of Grammatology*, corr. ed., trans. Gayatri Chakravorty Spivak (Baltimore, MD: Johns Hopkins University Press, 1998).

De Saussure, Ferdinand, *Course in General Linguistics*, ed. Roy Harris (London: Bloomsbury, 2013 [1916]).

Dessler, David, 'What's at Stake in the Agent-Structure Debate?', *International Organization* 43 (3) 1989: 441–473.

De Tocqueville, Alexis, *Democracy in America*, trans. Henry Reeve, ed. Isaac Kramnick (New York: Norton, 2007).

Deutsch, Karl W., et al., *Political Community and the North Atlantic Area: International Organization in the Light of Historical Experience* (Princeton, NJ: Princeton University Press, 1957).

De Vattel, Emer *The Laws of Nations*, ed. B. Kapossy and R. Wahtmore (Indianapolis, IN: Liberty Fund, 2008 [1758]).

Dilthey, Wilhelm, *Introduction to the Human Sciences, Selected Works*, Vol. I, ed. Rudolf A. Makkreel and Frithjof Rodi (Princeton, NJ: Princeton University Press, 1989).

Donnelly, Jack, 'The Discourse of Anarchy in IR', *International Theory* 7 (3) 2015: 393–425.

Dresher, Melvin, *Games of Strategy: Theories and Applications* (Englewood Cliffs, NJ: Prentice-Hall, 1961).

Droysen, Johann G., *Grundriss Der Historik* (*Outline of the Principles of History*), trans. E. Benjamin Andrews as *Droysen's Principles of History* (Boston, MA: Ginn, 1893 [1858]).

Dummett, Michael, *Origins of Analytical Philosophy*, reprint ed. (London: Bloomsbury, 2014 [1993]).

Dworkin, Ronald, *Taking Rights Seriously* (London: Duckworth, 1977).

Edkins, Jenny, *Poststructuralism & International Relations: Bringing the Political Back In* (London: Lynne Rienner, 1999).

Evans, Gareth, *The Responsibility to Protect: Ending Mass Atrocity Crimes Once and for All* (Washington, DC: Brookings Institution Press, 2008).

Falk, Richard, 'The Global Promise of Social Movements: Explorations at the Edge of Time', *Alternatives* 12 (2) 1987: 173–196.

Fierke, Karin M., 'Links across the Abyss: Language and Logic in International Relations', *International Studies Quarterly* 46 (3) 2002: 331–354.

'Wittgenstein and International Relations Theory', in Cerwyn Moore and Chris Farrands (eds.), *International Relations Theory and Philosophy* (New York: Routledge, 2010), pp. 83–94.

Finnis, John, *Natural Law and Natural Rights* (Oxford: Oxford University Press, 1980).

Forum on Scientific Realism. *Millennium – Journal of International Studies* 2007 35 (2): 343–416.

Foucault, Michel, 'Truth and Power', in Michel Foucault, *Power/ Knowledge: Selected Interviews & Other Writings 1972–1977*, trans. Colin Gordon, Leo Marshall, John Mepham and Kate Soper, ed. Colin Gordon (New York: Vintage Books, 1980), pp. 109–133.

  *Madness and Civilization: A History of Insanity in the Age of Reason*, trans. Richard Howard (New York: Vintage Books, 1988 [1961]).

  *The Birth of the Clinic: An Archaeology of Medical Perception*, trans. Alan M. Sheridan (London: Routledge, 1989 [1963]).

  *Discipline and Punish: The Birth of the Prison*, trans. Alan Sheridan (New York: Vintage Books, 1995 [1975]).

  'Governmentality', in Michel Foucault, *The Essential Works of Michel Foucault, 1954–1984*, ed. Paul Rabinow (London: Penguin, 2002), pp. 201–222.

  'Lecture from 14 January 1976', in Michel Foucault, *Society Must Be Defended: Lectures at the Collège de France, 1975–1976*, trans. David Macey, ed. Mauro Bertani and Alessandro Fontana (New York: Picador, 2003), pp. 23–42.

Frege, Gottlob, *Die Grundlagen der Arithmetik: Eine Logisch Mathematische Untersuchung über den Begriff der Zahl* (Breslau: Wilhelm Koebner, 1884).

Frey, R. G., and Christopher W. Morris, 'Value, Welfare, and Morality', in R. G. Frey and C. W. Morris (eds.), *Value, Welfare and Morality* (Cambridge: Cambridge University Press, 1993), pp. 1–12.

Frost, Mervyn, *Ethics in International Relations: A Constitutive Theory* (Cambridge: Cambridge University Press, 1996).

  *Constituting Global Rights: Global Civil Society and the Society of Democratic States* (London: Routledge, 2002).

  *Global Ethics: Anarchy, Freedom and International Relations* (London: Routledge, 2009).

Frost, Mervyn, and Silviya Lechner, 'Two Conceptions of International Practice: Aristotelian *Praxis* or Wittgensteinian *Language-Games*', *Review of International Studies* 42 (2) 2016: 334–350.

  'Understanding International Practices from the Internal Point of View', *Journal of International Political Theory* 12 (3) 2016: 299–319.

Fukuyama, Francis, *The End of History and the Last Man*, 20th anniversary ed. (New York: Penguin Books, 2012 [1992]).

Gadamer, Hans-Georg, *Philosophical Hermeneutics*, trans. and ed. David E. Linge (Berkeley: University of California Press, 1977).

Garfinkel, Harold, *Studies in Ethnomethodology* (Malden, MA: Polity Press, 1967).

Garner, Richard T., and Bernard Rosen, *Moral Philosophy* (New York: Macmillan, 1967).

Gauss, Gerald F., 'Hobbesian-Inspired Liberalism: Public Reason Out of Individual Reason', in Gerald F. Gauss, *Contemporary Theories of Liberalism* (London: Sage, 2003), pp. 56–82.

*On Philosophy, Politics and Economics* (Belmond, CA: Wadsworth, 2008).

Gettier, Edmund L., 'Is Justified True Belief Knowledge?'*Analysis* 23 (6) 1963: 121–123.

Gintis, Herbert, *Game Theory Evolving: A Problem-Centered Introduction to Modeling Strategic Interaction* (Princeton, NJ: Princeton University Press, 2000).

Grice, H. P., 'Meaning', *Philosophical Review* 66 (3) 1957: 377–388.

Grotius, Hugo, *The Rights of War and Peace*, 3 vols., ed. R. Tuck (Indianapolis, IN: Liberty Fund, 2005 [1631]).

Gunnell, John G., 'Can Social Science Be Just?', *Philosophy of the Social Sciences* 39 (4) 2009: 595–621.

'Social Scientific Inquiry and Meta-Theoretical Fantasy: The Case of International Relations', *Review of International Relations* 37 (4) 2011: 1447–1469.

Hare, R. M., *The Language of Morals* (Oxford: Clarendon Press, 1952).

Harman, Gilbert, *The Nature of Morality: An Introduction to Ethics* (New York: Oxford University Press, 1977).

Harman, Gilbert, and Judith Jarvis Thompson, *Moral Relativism and Moral Objectivity* (Oxford: Blackwell, 1996).

Hart, H. L. A., 'Positivism and the Separation of Law and Morals,' *Harvard Law Review* 71 (4) 1958: 593–629.

*The Concept of Law* (Oxford: Clarendon Press, 1961).

H-Diplo/ISSF Roundtable: Review of Vincent Pouliot. *International Security in Practice* 2 (5) 2011: 1–53. www.h-net.org/~diplo/ISSF.

Hegel, G. W. F., *Hegel's Philosophy of Right*, trans. T. M. Knox (Oxford: Oxford University Press, 1967 [1821]).

*Hegel's Phenomenology of Spirit*, trans. A. V. Miller (Oxford: Oxford University Press, 1977 [1807]).

*Hegel's Science of Logic*, trans. A. V. Miller (Atlantic Highlands, NJ: Humanities Press International, 1989 [1812–1816]).

Heidegger, Martin, *Being and Time*, trans. John Macquarrie and Edward Robinson (San Francisco, CA: Harper and Row, 1962).

Heisenberg, Werner Karl, 'Über quantentheoretische Umdeutung kinematischer und mechanischer Beziehungen', *Zeitschrift für Physik* 33 (1) 1925: 879–893.

Herz, John H., 'Idealist Internationalism and the Security Dilemma', *World Politics* 2 (2) 1950: 157–180.

Hindriks, Frank, 'Constitutive Rules, Language and Ontology', *Erkenntnis* 71 (2) 2009: 253–275.

Hjorth, Ronnie, 'Hedley Bull's Paradox of the Balance of Power: A Philosophical Inquiry', *Review of International Studies* 33 (4) 2007: 597–613.

Hobbes, Thomas, *Leviathan*, ed. C. B. Macpherson (London: Penguin, 1968 [1651]).

Hohfeld, W. N., *Fundamental Legal Conceptions as Applied in Judicial Reasoning* (New Haven, CT: Yale University Press, 1919).

Holzgrefe, J. L., and Robert O. Keohane (eds.), *Humanitarian Intervention: Ethical, Legal, and Political Dilemmas* (Cambridge: Cambridge University Press, 2003).

Human Rights Watch. 'World Report 2016: Saudi Arabia'. www.hrw.org/world-report/2016/country-chapters/saudi-arabia.

Hume, David, *A Treatise of Human Nature*, ed. L. A. Selby-Bigge (Oxford: Clarendon Press, 1888 [1739]).

Hutchinson, Phil, Rupert Read and Wes Sharrock, *There Is No Such Thing as a Social Science: In Defence of Peter Winch* (Aldershot: Ashgate, 2008).

Jackson, Peter, 'Pierre Bourdieu, the "Cultural Turn" and the Practice of International History', *Review of International Studies* 34 (1) 2008: 155–181.

Jackson, Robert H., *Quasi States: Sovereignty, International Relations and the Third World* (Cambridge: Cambridge University Press, 1993).
  *The Global Covenant: Human Conduct in a World of States* (Oxford: Oxford University Press, 2000).

Joseph, Jonathan, 'In Defence of Critical Realism', *Capital & Class* 22 (2) 1998: 73–106.
  'Philosophy in International Relations: A Scientific Realist Approach', *Millennium – Journal of International Studies* 35 (2) 2007: 345–359.

Kant, Immanuel, *Perpetual Peace: A Philosophical Sketch*, in Immanuel Kant, *Political Writings*, trans. H. B. Nisbet, ed. H. Reiss (Cambridge: Cambridge University Press, 1991 [1795]), pp. 93–130.
  *Critique of Pure Reason*, unified ed., trans. Werner S. Pluhar (Indianapolis, IN: Hackett, 1996 [1781–1787]).
  *The Metaphysics of Morals*, ed. Mary Gregor (Cambridge: Cambridge University Press, 1996 [1797]).
  *The Doctrine of Right*, in Immanuel Kant, *The Metaphysics of Morals*, ed. Mary Gregor (Cambridge: Cambridge University Press 1996 [1797]), pp. 3–138.
  *Groundwork of the Metaphysics of Morals*, ed. Mary Gregor (Cambridge: Cambridge University Press, 1997 [1785]).

Kaplan, Morton A., *System and Process in International Politics* (New York: Wiley, 1957).

Kasher, Naomi, 'Deontology and Kant', *Revue Internationale de Philosophie* 126 (4) 1978: 551–558.

Kenny, Anthony, *Wittgenstein* (London: Penguin, 1973).

Kessler, Oliver, and Xavier Guillaume, 'Everyday Practices of International Relations: People in Organizations', *Journal of International Relations & Development* 15 (1) 2012: 110–120.

Kiersey, Nicholas J., (ed.), *Foucault and International Relations* (London: Routledge, 2011).

Kinsey, Christopher, *Corporate Soldiers and International Security: The Rise of Private Military Companies* (London: Routledge, 2006).

Kleingeld, Pauline, 'Approaching Perpetual Peace: Kant's Defence of a League of States and His Ideal of a World Federation', *European Journal of Philosophy* 12 (3) 2004: 304–325.

Klotz, Audie, 'Norms Reconstituting Interests: Global Racial Equality and U.S. Sanctions against South Africa', *International Organization* 49 (3) 1995: 451–478.

Kolodny, Niko and R. Jay Wallace, 'Promises and Practices Revisited', *Philosophy & Public Affairs* 31 (2) 2003: 119–154.

Koskenniemi, Martti, 'Constitutionalism as Mindset: Reflections on Kantian Themes about International Law and Globalization', *Theoretical Inquiries in Law* 8 (1) 2007: 9–36.

Kratochwil, Friedrich V., *Rules, Norms, Decisions: On the Conditions of Practical and Legal Reasoning in International Relations and Domestic Affairs* (Cambridge: Cambridge University Press, 1989).

Krausz, Michael, and Jack W. Meiland (eds.), *Relativism: Cognitive and Moral* (Notre Dame, IN: University of Notre Dame Press, 1982).

Kuhn, Thomas, *The Structure of Scientific Revolutions*, 3rd ed. (Chicago: Chicago University Press, 1996 [1962]).

Lake, David A., *Hierarchy in International Relations* (Ithaca, NY: Cornell University Press, 2009).

Lapid, Yosef, 'The Third Debate: On the Prospects of International Theory in a Post-positivist Era', *International Studies Quarterly* 33 (3) 1989: 235–254.

Lawrenz, Jürgen, 'Hegel, Recognition and Rights: "Anerkennung" as a Gridline of the Philosophy of Rights', *Cosmos and History: The Journal of Natural and Social Philosophy* 3 (2) 2007: 153–169.

Lebow, Richard Ned, *The Politics and Ethics of Identity: In Search of Ourselves* (Cambridge: Cambridge University Press, 2012).

Lechner, Silviya, 'Basic Rights and Global Justice: The Problem of International Coercion', in Matthew Happold (ed.), *International Law in a Multipolar World* (London: Routledge, 2012), pp. 158–178.

Lewis, David, *Convention: A Philosophical Study* (Oxford: Blackwell, 2002 [1969]), pp. 52–57.

Locke, John, *Second Treatise of Government*, ed. C. B. Macpherson (Indianapolis, IN: Hackett, 1980 [1690]).

Luttwak, Edward N., *Turbo Capitalism: Winners and Losers in the Global Economy* (London: Weidenfeld and Nicolson, 1998).

Lyons, David, 'The Correlativity of Rights and Duties', *Noûs* 4 (1) 1970: 45–55.

MacIntyre, Alasdair, *Whose Justice? Which Rationality?* (Notre Dame, IN: University of Notre Dame Press, 1988).

   *After Virtue*, 3rd ed. (Notre Dame, IN: University of Notre Dame Press, 2007 [1981]).

MacKinnon, Edward A., *The Problem of Scientific Realism* (New York: Appleton-Century Crofts, 1972).

Malcolm, Norman, *Nothing Is Hidden* (Oxford: Blackwell, 1986).

   'Wittgenstein on Language and Rules', *Philosophy* 64 (247) 1989: 5–28.

Mandel, Robert, *Armies without States: The Privatization of Security* (Boulder, CO: Lynne Rienner, 2002).

Martin, Jane R., 'Basic Actions and Simple Actions', *American Philosophical Quarterly* 9 (1) 1972: 59–69.

Martin, Rex, 'Human Rights and the Social Recognition Thesis', *Journal of Social Philosophy* 44 (1) 2013: 1–21.

Martin-Mazé, Médéric, 'Returning Struggles to the Practice Turn: How Were Bourdieu and Boltanski Lost in (Some) Translations and What to Do about It?', *International Political Sociology* 11 (2) 2017: 203–220.

Marx, Karl, *Early Writings* (New York: Vintage Books, 1975).

Mattingly, Garrett, *Renaissance Diplomacy* (New York: Dover, 1988 [1955]).

Mauss, Marcel, *The Gift: The Form and Reason for Exchange in Archaic Societies*, trans. W. D. Halls (London: Routledge, 2008 [1950]).

McKinsey, J. C. C., *Introduction to the Theory of Games* (New York: McGraw-Hill, 1952).

Mearsheimer, John J., *The Tragedy of Great Power Politics* (New York: W. W. Norton, 2001).

Melden, A. I., *Rights and Persons* (Berkeley: University of California Press, 1980).

Miller, Alexander, and Crispin Wright (eds.), *Rule-Following and Meaning* (Chesham: Acumen, 2002).

Milner, Helen, 'The Assumption of Anarchy in International Relations Theory: A Critique', *Review of International Studies* 17 (1) 1991: 67–85.

Mungiu-Pippidi, Alina, *The Quest for Good Governance* (Cambridge: Cambridge University Press, 2015).

Monten, Jonathan 'The Roots of the Bush Doctrine: Power, Nationalism and Democracy Promotion in U.S. Strategy', *International Security* 29 (4) 2005: 112–156.

Morgan, Patrick M., 'The Practice of Deterrence', in Emanuel Adler and Vincent Pouliot (eds.), *International Practices* (New York: Cambridge University Press, 2011), pp. 139–173.

Moulines, Carlos Ulises, 'Structuralism: The Basic Ideas', in Wolfgang Balzer and Carlos Ulises Moulines (eds.), *Structuralist Theory of Science: Focal Issues, New Results* (Berlin: De Gruyter, 1996), pp. 1–14.

Nagel, Thomas, *The View from Nowhere* (Oxford: Oxford University Press, 1989).

'The Problem of Global Justice', *Philosophy & Public Affairs* 33 (2) 2005: 113–147.

Nardin, Terry, *Law, Morality, and the Relations of States* (Princeton, NJ: Princeton University Press, 1983).

'International Pluralism and the Rule of Law', *Review of International Studies* 26 (5) 2000: 95–110.

*The Philosophy of Michael Oakeshott* (University Park: Pennsylvania State University Press, 2001).

'The Moral Basis of Humanitarian Intervention', *Ethics & International Affairs* 16 (2) 2002: 57–70.

'Justice and Coercion', in Alex J. Bellamy (ed.), *International Society and Its Critics* (Oxford: Oxford University Press, 2005), pp. 247–264.

'Globalization and the Public Realm', *Critical Review of International Social and Political Philosophy* 12 (2) 2009: 297–312.

'The Diffusion of Sovereignty', *History of European Ideas* 41 (1) 2015: 89–102.

Nardin, Terry, and Melissa S. Williams (eds.), *Humanitarian Intervention: NOMOS XLVII* (New York: New York University Press, 2006).

Neal, Andrew W., 'Michel Foucault', in Jenny Edkins and Nick Vaughan-Williams (eds.), *Critical Theorists and International Relations* (London: Routledge, 2009), pp. 161–170.

Neumann, Iver B., 'Returning Practice to the Linguistic Turn: The Case of Diplomacy', *Millennium: Journal of International Studies* 31 (3) 2002: 627–651.

Nozick, Robert, 'Coercion', in Sidney Morgenbesser, Patrick Suppes and Morton White (eds.), *Philosophy, Science and Method: Essays in Honour of Ernest Nagel* (New York: St. Martin's Press, 1969), pp. 440–472.

*Anarchy, State, and Utopia* (New York: Basic Books, 1974).

Oakeshott, Michael, *Experience and Its Modes* (Cambridge: Cambridge University Press, 1933).

*On Human Conduct* (Oxford: Clarendon Press, 1975).

'The Rule of Law', in Michael Oakeshott, *On History and Other Essays* (Indianapolis, IN: Liberty Fund, 1983), pp. 129–178.

'The Tower of Babel' (1948), in Michael Oakeshott, *Rationalism in Politics and Other Essays*, new expanded ed. (Indianapolis, IN: Liberty Fund, 1991 [1962]), pp. 465–487.

'Rational Conduct' (1950), in Michael Oakeshott, *Rationalism in Politics and Other Essays*, new expanded ed. (Indianapolis, IN: Liberty Fund, 1991 [1962]), pp. 99–131.

*Rationalism in Politics and Other Essays*, new ed. (Indianapolis, IN: Liberty Press, 1991 [1962]).

'Education: The Engagement and Its Frustration' (1972), in Michael Oakeshott, *The Voice of Liberal Learning* (Indianapolis, IN: Liberty Fund, 2001), pp. 62–104.

O'Hear, Anthony, *Verstehen and Humane Understanding* (New York: Cambridge University Press, 1996).

Onuf, Nicholas, *World of Our Making: Rules and Rule in Social Theory and International Relations* (Columbia: University of South Carolina Press, 1989).

Parekh, Bhikhu, 'The Political Philosophy of Michael Oakeshott', *British Journal of Political Science* 9 (4) 1979: 481–506.

Patomäki, Heikki, *After International Relations: Critical Realism and the (Re)Construction of World Politics* (London: Routledge, 2002).

Patomäki, Heikki, and Colin Wight, 'After Postpositivism? The Promises of Critical Realism', *International Studies Quarterly* 44 (2) 2000: 213–237.

Patten, Alan, *Hegel's Idea of Freedom* (Oxford: Oxford University Press, 1999).

Pelczynski, Z. A., (ed.), *Hegel's Political Philosophy: Problems and Perspectives* (Cambridge: Cambridge University Press, 1971).

(ed.), *The State and Civil Society: Studies in Hegel's Political Philosophy* (Cambridge: Cambridge University Press, 1984).

Pettit, Philip, *Republicanism: A Theory of Freedom and Government* (Oxford: Clarendon Press, 1997).

Pin-Fat, Véronique, *Universality, Ethics and International Relations* (London: Routledge, 2009).

Plato, *The Republic of Plato*, trans. Francis MacDonald Cornford (Oxford: Oxford University Press, 1945).

Plato, *Theaetetus*, trans. M. J. Levett, ed. Bernard Williams (Indianapolis, IN: Hackett, 1992).

Pogge, Thomas, *World Poverty and Human Rights: Cosmopolitan Respon-sibilities and Reforms*, 2nd ed. (Cambridge: Polity Press, 2008).

Polanyi, Michael, *Personal Knowledge: Towards a Post-critical Philosophy*, rev. ed. (Chicago: Chicago University Press, 1962).

*The Tacit Dimension* (Chicago: Chicago University Press, 2009 [1966]).

Pouliot, Vincent, '"Sobjectivism": Towards a Constructivist Methodology', *International Studies Quarterly* 51 (2) 2007: 359–384.

'The Logic of Practicality: A Theory of Practice of Security Communities', *International Organization* 62 (2) 2008: 257–288.

*International Security in Practice: The Politics of NATO-Russia Diplo-macy* (New York: Cambridge University Press, 2010).

Pouliot, Vincent, and Frédéric Mérand, 'Bourdieu's Concepts', in Rebecca Adler-Nissen (ed.), *Bourdieu in International Relations: Rethinking Key Concepts in IR* (London: Routledge, 2013), pp. 24–44.

Pufendorf, Samuel, *Eight Books on the Laws of Nature and Nations*, trans. C. H. Oldfather and W. A. Oldfather (Washington, DC: Carnegie Institution, 1964 [1688]).

*On the Duty of Man and Citizen according to Natural Law*, trans. Michael Silverthorne, ed. James Tully (Cambridge: Cambridge Univer-sity Press, 2000 [1673]).

Putnam, Hilary, 'What Is Mathematical Truth?', in Hilary Putnam, *Mathematics, Matter and Method: Philosophical Papers*, Vol. I (Cambridge: Cambridge University Press, 1975), pp. 60–78.

Rapoport, Anatol, *Two-Person Game Theory: The Essential Ideas* (Ann Arbor: University of Michigan Press, 1966).

Rawls, John, 'Two Concepts of Rules', *Philosophical Review* 64 (1) 1955: 3–32.

*A Theory of Justice* (Cambridge, MA: Harvard University Press, 1971).

*Political Liberalism*, pbk. ed. (New York: Columbia University Press, 1996).

*The Law of Peoples* (Cambridge, MA: Harvard University Press, 1999).

Raz, Joseph, *The Concept of a Legal System: An Introduction to the Theory of Legal System*, 2nd ed. (Oxford: Clarendon Press, 1970).

*Practical Reason and Norms* (London: Hutchinson, 1975).

*The Practice of Value* (Oxford: Oxford University Press, 2003).

Report of the International Commission on Intervention and State Sovereignty, *The Responsibility to Protect* (Ottawa: International Development Research Centre, 2001).

Ringmar, Erik, 'The Search for Dialogue as a Hindrance to Understanding: Practices as Inter-paradigmatic Research Program', *International Theory* 6 (1) 2014: 1–27.

Ripstein, Arthur, 'Authority and Coercion', *Philosophy & Public Affairs* 32 (1) 2004: 2–35.

Rorty, Richard, *Philosophy and the Mirror of Nature* (Oxford: Basil Black-well, 1980).

(ed.), *The Linguistic Turn: Essays in Philosophical Method* (Chicago: Chicago University Press, 1992).

Roundtable: International Relations as a Social Science. *Millennium: Journal of International Studies* 43 (1) 2014: 328–368.

Rosenberg, Justin, *The Empire of Civil Society* (London: Verso, 1994).

Ryle, Gilbert, 'Are There Propositions?', *Proceedings of the Aristotelian Society* 1930, 30: 91–126.

*The Concept of Mind* (London: Hutchinson, 1949).

'Are There Propositions?', in Gilbert Ryle, *Collected Papers*, Vol. II (1929–1968) (London: Hutchinson, 1971), pp. 12–38.

Scanlon, T. M., 'Practices and Promises', *Philosophy and Public Affairs* 19 (3) 1990: 199–226.

*What We Owe to Each Other* (Cambridge, MA: Harvard University Press, 1998).

Schatzki, Theodore R., *Social Practices: A Wittgensteinian Approach to Human Activity and the Social* (Cambridge: Cambridge University Press, 1996).

Schatzki, Theodore R., Karin Knorr-Cetina and Eike von Savigny (eds.), *The Practice Turn in Contemporary Theory* (London: Routledge, 2001).

Scheffler, Samuel, (ed.), *Consequentialism and Its Critics* (Oxford: Oxford University Press, 1988).

Schelling, Thomas, *The Strategy of Conflict* (New York: Oxford University Press, 1963).

*Arms and Influence* (New Haven, CT: Yale University Press, 1966).

Schleiermacher, Friedrich, *Hermeneutics and Criticism*, trans. and ed. Andrew Bowie (Cambridge: Cambridge University Press, 1998 [1838]).

Schmidt, Brian C., *The Political Discourse of Anarchy: A Disciplinary History of International Relations* (Albany: SUNY Press, 1998).

Schmidtz, David, 'A Place for Cost-Benefit Analysis', *Noûs* 35 (suppl. s1) 2001: 148–171.

Scruton, Roger, *Kant* (Oxford: Oxford University Press, 1982).

Searle, John R., 'How to Derive "Ought" from "Is"', *Philosophical Review* 73 (1) 1964: 43–58.

'How to Derive "Ought" from "Is"', in Philippa Foot (ed.), *Theories of Ethics* (Oxford: Oxford University Press, 1967), pp. 101–114.

*Speech Acts: An Essay in the Philosophy of Language* (Cambridge: Cambridge University Press, 1969).

*The Construction of Social Reality* (New York: Free Press, 1995).

'Consciousness as a Biological Problem', in John R. Searle, *The Mystery of Consciousness* (New York: New York Review of Books, 1997), pp. 1–18.

'Social Ontology. Some Basic Principles', *Anthropological Theory* (6)1 2006: 12–29.

Sending, Ole Jacob, and Iver B. Neumann, 'Banking on Power: How Some Practices in an International Organization Anchor Others', in Emanuel Adler and Vincent Pouliot (eds.), *International Practices* (New York: Cambridge University Press, 2011), pp. 231–254.

Shue, Henry, *Basic Rights: Subsistence, Affluence, and U.S. Foreign Policy*, 2nd ed. (Princeton, NJ: Princeton University Press, 1996).

Slaughter, Anne-Marie, *A New World Order* (Princeton, NJ: Princeton University Press, 2004).

Smith, Steve, 'Positivism and Beyond', in Steve Smith, Ken Booth and Marysia Zalewski (eds.), *International Theory: Positivism and Beyond* (Cambridge: Cambridge University Press, 1996), pp. 11–46.

Smith, Steve, Ken Booth and Marysia Zalewski (eds.), *International Theory: Positivism and Beyond* (Cambridge: Cambridge University Press, 1996).

Stopford, John M., and Susan Strange with John S. Henley, *Rival States, Rival Firms: Competition for World Market Shares* (Cambridge: Cambridge University Press, 1991).

Strange, Susan, *States and Markets*, 2nd ed. (London: Bloomsbury, 2015 [1988]).

Sumner, L. W., *The Moral Foundation of Rights* (Oxford: Clarendon Press, 1989).

Suppe, Frederick, (ed.), *The Structure of Scientific Theories*, 2nd ed. (Chicago: University of Illinois Press, 1977).

Swartz, David L., *Culture and Power: The Sociology of Pierre Bourdieu* (Chicago: University of Chicago Press, 1997).

*Symbolic Power, Politics and Intellectuals: The Political Sociology of Pierre Bourdieu* (Chicago: University of Chicago Press, 2013).

Taylor, Charles, 'Interpretation and the Sciences of Man', *The Review of Metaphysics* 25 (1) 1971: 3–51.

Thompson, Judith Jarvis, *Acts and Other Events* (Ithaca, NY: Cornell University Press, 1977).

*Normativity* (Peru, IL: Open Court, 2008).

Tönnies, Ferdinand, *Community and Association (Gemeinschaft und Gesellschaft)* (London: Routledge, 1955 [1887]).

United Nations General Assembly 2005 A/60/L.1 (World Summit Outcome), available at www.un.org.

2009 A/63/677 (UN Secretary General's Report on the Responsibility to Protect), available at www.un.org.

US Department of State. 'Country Reports on Human Rights Practices for 2014'. www.state.gov/j/drl/rls/hrrpt/humanrightsreport/#wrapper.

Van Fraassen, Bas C., *The Scientific Image* (Oxford: Oxford University Press, 1980).

Von Neumann, John, and Oskar Morgenstern, *Theory of Games and Economic Behavoir*, 60th anniversary commemorative ed. (Princeton, NJ: Princeton University Press, 2007 [1944]).

Wæver, Ole, 'Still a Discipline after All These Debates?', in Tim Dunne, Milja Kurki and Steve Smith (eds.), *International Relations Theories: Discipline and Diversity*, 2nd ed. (Oxford: Oxford University Press 2010), pp. 297–318.

Walker, R. B. J., 'Social Movements/World Politics', *Millennium: Journal of International Studies* 23 (3) 1994: 669–700.

Waltz, Kenneth N., *Theory of International Politics* (Boston, MA: McGraw-Hill, 1979).

Walzer, Michael, *Spheres of Justice: A Defense of Pluralism and Equality* (New York: Basic Books, 1983).

'The Politics of Michel Foucault', in David Couzens Hoy (ed.), *Foucault: A Critical Reader* (London: Basil Blackwell, 1986), pp. 51–68.

*Interpretation and Social Criticism* (Cambridge, MA: Harvard University Press, 1987).

*Just and Unjust Wars: A Moral Argument with Historical Illustrations*, 2nd ed. (New York: Basic Books, 1992).

'Equality and Civil Society', in Simone Chambers and Will Kymlicka (eds.), *Alternative Conceptions of Civil Society* (Princeton, NJ: Princeton University Press, 2002), pp. 34–49.

Warrender, Howard, *The Political Philosophy of Hobbes: His Theory of Obligation* (Oxford: Clarendon Press, 1957).

Watson, Adam, 'The European International Society and Its Expansion', in Hedley Bull and Adam Watson (eds.), *The Expansion of International Society* (Oxford: Clarendon Press, 1984), pp. 13–32.

*The Evolution of International Society: A Comparative Historical Analysis* (London: Routledge, 1992).

Weber, Max, *Economy and Society: An Outline of Interpretive Sociology*, ed. G. Roth and C. Wittich (Berkley: University of California Press, 1978).

Wendt, Alexander, 'The Agent-Structure Problem in International Relations Theory', *International Organization* 41 (3) 1987: 335–370.

'Bridging the Theory/Meta-theory Gap in International Relations', *Review of International Studies* 17 (4) 1991: 383–392.

*Social Theory of International Politics* (Cambridge: Cambridge University Press, 1999).

'Scientific Realism and Social Kinds', in Alexander Wendt, *Social Theory of International Politics* (Cambridge: Cambridge University Press, 1999), pp. 47–91.

'"Ideas All the Way Down": On the Constitution of Power and Interest', in Alexander Wendt, *Social Theory of International Politics* (Cambridge: Cambridge University Press, 1999), pp. 92–138.

Wheeler, Nicholas J., *Saving Strangers: Humanitarian Intervention in International Society* (Oxford: Oxford University Press, 2002).

Wiener, Antje, *The Invisible Constitution of Politics: Contested Norms and International Encounters* (Cambridge: Cambridge University Press, 2008).

'Enacting Meaning-in-Use: Qualitative Research on Norms and International Relations', *Review of International Studies* 35 (1) 2009: 175–193.

Williams, Robert R., *Hegel's Ethics of Recognition* (Berkeley: University of California Press, 2000).

Winch, Peter, *The Idea of a Social Science and Its Relation to Philosophy* (London: Routledge, 1958).

'Understanding a Primitive Society', in Peter Winch, *Ethics and Action* (London: Routledge, 1972 [1964]), pp. 8–49.

'Facts and Superfacts', in Peter Winch, *Trying to Make Sense* (Oxford: Basil Blackwell, 1987), pp. 54–63.

Windelband, Wilhelm, 'Rectorial Address, Strasbourg, 1894' ('Windelband on History and Natural Science'), *History and Theory* 19 (2) 1980: 169–185.

Windelband, Wilhelm, and Guy Oakes, 'History and Natural Science', *History and Theory* 19 (2) 1980: 165–168.

Wittgenstein, Ludwig, *Tractatus Logico-Philosophicus*, trans. C. K. Ogden (London: Routledge 1922).

*Tractatus Logico-Philosophicus*, trans. D. F. Pears and B. F. McGuinness (London: Routledge, 1961 [1921]).

*Philosophical Investigations*, 3rd ed., trans. G. E. M. Anscombe (Oxford: Blackwell 1968 [1953]).

'Cause and Effect: Intuitive Awareness', trans. Peter Winch, *Philosophia* 6 (3) and (4) 1976: 409–425.

Wolff, Christian, *Jus Gentium Methodo Scientifica Pertractatum*, trans. Joseph H. Drake (Oxford: Clarendon Press, 1934 [1749]).

Wright, Crispin, 'Wittgenstein on Following a Rule: Five Themes', unpublished manuscript.

Zagare, Frank C., *Game Theory: Concepts and Applications* (Newbury Park, CA: SAGE, 1984).

# Index